Top Accounting Issues
FOR 2015 | CPE COURSE

CCH Editorial Staff Publication

. Wolters Kluwer

Contributors

Contributing Editors . . . . Steven C Fustolo, CPA;

Steven G. Frost;

Brian Ertmer;

Robert Sash

Technical Review . . . . Sharon R. Brooks, CPA;

Colleen Neuharth McClain, CPA

Production Coordinator . . . . Mariela de la Torre;

Jennifer Schencker

Production . . . . Lynn J. Brown

This publication is designed to provide accurate and authoritative information in regard to the subject matter covered. It is sold with the understanding that the publisher is not engaged in rendering legal, accounting, or other professional service. If legal advice or other expert assistance is required, the services of a competent professional person should be sought.

ISBN: 978-0-8080-3820-7

© 2014 CCH Incorporated. All Rights Reserved.
4025 W. Peterson Ave.
Chicago, IL 60646-6085
800 344 3734
CCHGroup.com

MIX
From responsible
sources
FSC® C099992
www.fsc.org

Introduction

CCH's *Top Accounting Issues for 2015 CPE Course* helps CPAs stay abreast of the most significant new accounting standards and important projects. It does so by identifying the events of the past year that have developed into hot issues and reviewing the opportunities and pitfalls presented by these changes. The topics reviewed in this course were selected because of their impact on financial reporting and because of the role they play in understanding the accounting landscape in the year ahead.

Module 1 of this course reviews ongoing issues.

Chapter 1 reviews accounting standards update (ASU) 2014-07, which permits a private company lessee to elect an accounting alternative not to apply the variable interest entity (VIE) guidance to a lessor entity if certain conditions are met.

Chapter 2 discusses ASU 2014-03, which provides private companies an additional hedge accounting alternative to be applied to certain types of swaps that are entered into in order to economically convert a variable-rate borrowing into a fixed-rate borrowing.

Chapter 3 reviews accounting for uncertainty in state income taxes, looking at some of the complex issues an enterprise may face when applying recognition standards of FASB ASC 740 to its state and local income tax positions.

Module 2 of this course reviews financial statement reporting.

Chapter 4 discusses Accounting Standards Update (ASU) 2013-07—*Presentation of Financial Statements (Topic 205): Liquidation Basis of Accounting* that was issued in April 2013. The objective of ASU 2013-07 is to clarify when an entity should apply the liquidation basis of accounting. This chapter reviews this ASU and discusses its guidance for the recognition and measurement of assets and liabilities and requirements for financial statements prepared using the liquidation basis of accounting.

Chapter 5 covers ASC 220, *Comprehensive Income (formerly FAS 130)*, which was issued to address the presentation of certain items (other comprehensive income items) that historically have bypassed the income statement and were recorded directly to equity.

Chapter 6 covers questions concerning Other Comprehensive Bases of Accounting and provides practical answers for these often-asked questions. It includes numerous examples and illustrations.

Chapter 7 discusses ASC 405-40—*Liabilities (Topic 405): Obligations Resulting from Joint and Several Liability Arrangements*. It examines requirements of the ASC including the scope, disclosures, and transition rules. Numerous examples are included.

Module 3 of this course reviews current developments.

Chapter 8 explains the new optional method to amortize goodwill that is available to private (nonpublic) entities.

Chapter 9 discusses the changes that would be made to accounting for leases based on the May 2013 exposure draft, and the effects those changes may have.

Chapter 10 discusses several Accounting Standards Updates (ASUs) issued in 2013 and 2014, including ASU 2014-05 regarding service concession arrangements, ASU 2014-04 regarding troubled debt restructurings, ASU 2013-12 regarding the definition of a public business entity, ASU 2013-11, dealing with the presentation of unrecognized tax benefits, and ASU 2013-05 concerning foreign currency matters.

Finally, Chapter 11 discusses the accounting standards and proposals designed to move the accounting community toward fair value accounting.

Study Questions. Throughout the course you will find Study Questions to help you test your knowledge, and comments that are vital to understanding a particular strategy or idea. Answers to the Study Questions with feedback on both correct and incorrect responses are provided in a special section beginning at ¶ 10,100.

Index. To assist you in your later reference and research, a detailed topical index has been included for this course.

Quizzer. This course is divided into three Modules. Take your time and review all course Modules. When you feel confident that you thoroughly understand the material, turn to the CPE Quizzer. Complete one, or all, Module Quizzers for continuing professional education credit.

Go to **CCHGroup.com/PrintCPE** to complete your Quizzer online. The CCH Testing Center website lets you complete your CPE Quizzers online for immediate results and no Express Grading Fee. Your Training History provides convenient storage for your CPE course Certificates. Further information is provided in the CPE Quizzer instructions at ¶ 10,200.

September 2014

CCH'S PLEDGE TO QUALITY

Thank you for choosing this CCH Continuing Education product. We will continue to produce high quality products that challenge your intellect and give you the best option for your Continuing Education requirements. Should you have a concern about this or any other CCH CPE product, please call our Customer Service Department at 1-800-248-3248.

COURSE OBJECTIVES

This course provides an overview of important accounting developments. At the completion of this course, the reader will be able to:

- Identify at least one of the criteria for determining whether a reporting entity has a controlling financial interest in a VIE
- Identify one of the criteria that must be met in order for a private company lessee to elect an accounting alternative not to apply the VIE guidance to a lessor entity
- Identify FIN 46R's basic rule for determining whether an entity has sufficient equity
- Identify the type of entity that can elect the accounting alternative in ASU 2014-07
- Recognize certain activities that are and are not leasing activities
- Identify the scope of a lease arrangement for which the accounting alternative under ASU 2014-07 may be elected
- Recall some of the criteria that qualify and do not qualify for cash flow hedge accounting
- Identify an eligible entity that can use the simplified hedge accounting approach
- Recall how GAAP addresses uncertainty in state income taxes in FASB Accounting Standards Codification (ASC) Subtopic 740-10
- Identify the GAAP recognition threshold for state tax positions
- Review the GAAP measurement guidance for state tax positions

- Recall GAAP's two-step process to state tax positions arising from intercompany transactions
- Recall how assets should be measured using the liquidation basis of accounting
- Identify a financial statement that is required when using the liquidation basis of accounting
- Recognize whether fair value disclosures are required when using the liquidation basis of accounting
- Identify what is included in other comprehensive income
- Define comprehensive income
- Recognize the allowed presentation formats for other comprehensive income in the financial statements and notes
- Identify the ASC 220 requirements regarding reclassification adjustments
- List and describe three bases of accounting that are considered Other Comprehensive Bases of Accounting
- Identify how certain transactions should be presented, recorded, and disclosed when an entity uses the income tax basis of accounting
- Identify how a reporting entity measures an obligation under ASC 405-40
- State the obligations to which ASC 405-40 applies
- Describe the obligations to which ASC 460 applies
- Recall the accounting treatment for an intangible asset with a finite life
- Identify the life over which a private company may elect to amortize goodwill under ASU 2014-02
- Identify a private company's new, single-step quantitative test for goodwill impairment loss authorized by ASU 2014-02
- Identify the changes that will be made under the proposed lease standard
- Recall how lessees would account for leases under the new standard
- Recall how the lessee calculates the liability for a lease under the new standard
- Recognize how existing leases will be handled when the new statement is adopted
- Recognize a situation in which an in-substance repossession or foreclosure occurs
- Recognize a public business entity
- Determine how to present an unrecognized tax benefit when a net operating loss carryforward, a similar tax loss, or a tax credit carryforward exists
- Recall the accounting rules concerning the sale of an investment in a foreign entity
- Recall the arguments for and against fair value measurement
- Identify the levels in the three-level hierarchy developed by ASC 820

Contents

MODULE 1: ONGOING ISSUES—Chapter 1: VIEs: Applying Guidance to Common Control Leasing Arrangements

¶ 101 WELCOME

This chapter reviews accounting standards update (ASU) 2014-07, which permits a private company lessee to elect an accounting alternative not to apply the variable interest entity (VIE) guidance to a lessor entity if certain conditions are met.

¶ 102 LEARNING OBJECTIVES

Upon completion of this chapter, the reader will be able to:

- Identify at least one of the criteria for determining whether a reporting entity has a controlling financial interest in a VIE
- Identify one of the criteria that must be met in order for a private company lessee to elect an accounting alternative not to apply the VIE guidance to a lessor entity
- Identify FIN 46R's basic rule for determining whether an entity has sufficient equity
- Recall an example of a variable interest
- Recognize the type of guarantee of a lessor's debt that is treated as a guarantee made by an operating company lessee
- Identify the type of entity that can elect the accounting alternative in ASU 2014-07
- Recognize certain activities that are and are not leasing activities
- Identify the scope of a lease arrangement for which the accounting alternative under ASU 2014-07 may be elected
- Determine the extent to which the accounting alternative in ASU 2014-07 is applied to lessor entities under common control

¶ 103 INTRODUCTION

ASU 2014-07—*Consolidation (Topic 810): Applying Variable Interest Entities Guidance to Common Control Leasing Arrangements (a consensus of the Private Company Council)* was issued in March 2014. The objective of the ASU is to permit a private company lessee (the reporting entity) to elect an accounting alternative not to apply the variable interest entity (VIE) guidance to a lessor entity if certain conditions are met.

¶ 104 BACKGROUND

Under current U.S. GAAP, a reporting entity is required to consolidate an entity in which it has a controlling financial interest. GAAP has two models for assessing whether there is a controlling financial interest:

- Under the *voting interest model,* a controlling financial interest exists if there is ownership of more than 50 percent of an entity's voting interests.

- Under the *VIE model*, a reporting entity has a controlling financial interest in a variable interest entity (VIE) when it has both:

  - The power to direct the VIE's activities that most significantly affect the economic performance of the VIE

  - The obligation to absorb the VIE's losses or the right to receive benefits of the VIE that could potentially be significant to the VIE

The VIE model was introduced to GAAP by FASB Interpretation No. 46R, *Consolidation of Variable Interest Entities* (FIN 46R), now part of ASC 810, *Consolidation*. Under the VIE model, a reporting entity must determine whether it has a variable interest in a VIE (e.g., form of support), and whether the entity being evaluated is a VIE. Thus, under the VIE model, a reporting entity may be required to consolidate a VIE even though it has no direct ownership in the VIE.

With respect to nonpublic (private) companies, a common situation in which the VIE model applies is where there is a related-party lease involving an operating company lessee and a real estate lessor. In such a situation, the VIE model rules require the operating company lessee to consolidate the real estate lessor if three criteria are met:

- The real estate lessor must be a VIE.

- The operating company lessee must have a variable interest in the VIE, which is a form of support.

- The operating company lessee must be considered the primary beneficiary (de facto parent) of the VIE.

Issuance of FIN 46

Prior to 2003, for years, companies had been using off-balance-sheet entities for numerous reasons including shifting debt and certain assets off the balance sheet. Awareness of this practice culminated with the demise of Enron and 2001 Congressional hearings that addressed the reasons why Enron had folded. During those hearings and in the subsequently issued *Powers Report*, information was disclosed about Enron's use of hundreds of off-balance-sheet special purpose entities (SPEs), few of which were carried on Enron's balance sheet. The result was that millions of dollars of debt and assets were held off Enron's balance sheet. At that time, the GAAP rules as to whether a transaction could be carried off balance sheet were quite liberal, generally requiring only about three percent of outside investment equity to keep the SPE off balance sheet.

In 2003, Sarbanes-Oxley Act was passed by Congress. Part of Sarbanes included instructions for the SEC to study the off-balance-sheet transactions issue. In January 2003, the FASB issued FASB Interpretation No. 46, *Consolidation of Variable Interest Entities* as its first effort to tighten the off-balance-sheet rules. In originally issued FIN 46, the FASB introduced the concept of a VIE, variable interests, and primary beneficiary, among other terms.

The FASB has gone through several iterations of the consolidation of VIE rules. In December 2003, the FASB replaced FIN 46 with a revised FASB Interpretation No. 46R (FIN 46R) (now part of ASC 810) that was supposed to provide greater clarity as to how to apply the FIN 46 rules in practice. FIN 46R is still in effect and has been folded into ASC 810, *Consolidation*.

Since the issuance of FIN 46R, the FASB has issued a series of interpretations and modifications, including those found in the 2009 issuance of FAS 167, *Amendments to FASB Interpretation No. 46R*, which had as its primary goal to improve the application of certain provisions found in FIN 46R, including changes made to the Qualified Special Purpose Entity (QSPE) rules.

One particular FASB interpretation, FIN 46(R)-5, has had a critical impact on related-party lease arrangements which is now the focal point of ASU 2014-07. When it was originally issued in 2003, FASB Staff Position No. FIN 46(R)-5, *Implicit Variable Interests under FASB Interpretation No. 46* addressed the controversial concept of the implicit guarantee. The concept of the implicit guarantee is a theoretical exercise that calls for assigning the obligation of an explicit guarantee that is provided by an individual owner on a lessor entity's debt, to a related-party lessee. Few elements of the FIN 46R rules have had as significant an impact on related-party lease transactions than the implicit guarantee rules found in FIN 46(R)-5. Further on in this chapter, the author brings the concept of the implicit guarantee to light.

Since the issuance of FIN 46R and its interpretations, practitioners have had difficulty implementing the FIN 46R rules. In particular, there have been questions as to whether a related-party leasing arrangement with a common owner should require the lessor real estate entity to be consolidated into the financial statements of the operating company lessee. In practice, some private companies consolidate the lessee and lessor, while others do not.

PCC's Private Company Exemption

ASU 2014-07 represents the third accounting standards update (ASU) issued by the FASB's Private Company Council (PCC).

The PCC was established in 2012 to provide exemptions and modifications to existing GAAP for nonpublic (private) entities. The PCC added ASU 2014-07's VIE project to its agenda in response to feedback from private company stakeholders that indicated that the benefits of consolidating a lessee and lessor under common control using the FIN 46R VIE guidance did not justify the related costs. In general, private company respondents stated that:

- Unlike a public company, a common owner establishes a lessor entity separate from the private company lessee for tax, estate-planning, and legal-liability purposes—not to structure off-balance-sheet debt arrangements.

- In instances in which a lessor entity is consolidated by a private company lessee, most users of the private company lessee's financial statements find that the consolidation is not relevant because the users focus on the financial statements of the private lessee on a standalone basis, rather than on a consolidated basis.

- Consolidation of the lessor entity under common control distorts financial statements of the private company lessee entity because:

  - The assets held by the lessor entity would not be available to satisfy the obligations of the lessee entity. Such assets are beyond the reach of the lessee's creditors, even in bankruptcy or other receivership.

  - When users receive consolidated financial statements of a private company lessee and lessor, they often request a consolidating schedule to enable them to reverse the effects of consolidating the lessor entity.

Based on the concerns cited by private company users, the PCC approved an elective accounting alternative for private companies in applying the VIE rules to lessor entities under common control. In early 2014, the FASB endorsed the PCC's proposal which resulted in the issuance of ASU 2014-07.

The general provisions of ASU 2014-07 are summarized below:

- A private company lessee (the reporting entity) may elect an accounting alternative not to apply the FIN 46R VIE guidance to a lessor entity (not consolidate a real estate lessor) if four criteria are met:

    - The private company lessee and the lessor entity are under common control.

    - The private company lessee has a lease arrangement with the lessor entity.

    - Substantially all of the activities between the private company lessee and the lessor entity are related to leasing activities (including supporting leasing activities) between those two entities.

    - If the private company lessee explicitly guarantees or provides collateral for any obligation of the lessor entity related to the asset leased by the private company, the principal amount of the obligation at inception of the guarantee or collateral arrangement does not exceed the value of the asset leased by the private company from the lessor entity.

- A private company lessee that elects the accounting alternative not to consolidate the real estate lessor would expand disclosures to include:

    - The amount and key terms of liabilities recognized by the lessor entity that expose the private company lessee to providing financial support to the lessor entity

    - A qualitative description of circumstances not recognized in the financial statements of the lessor entity that expose the private company lessee to providing financial support to the lessor entity

- The accounting alternative is an accounting policy election that, when elected, should be applied by a private company lessee to all current and future lessor entities under common control that meet the criteria for applying this approach.

- The accounting alternative would be applied retrospectively by restating all periods presented.

As part of the amendments, the Board also removed implementation guidance codified from FASB Staff Position No. FIN 46(R)-5, *Implicit Variable Interests under FASB Interpretation No. 46* (revised December 2003), and identified as Example 4 within ASC 810, paragraphs 810-10-55-87 through 55-89.

Other related-party transactions not involving leasing arrangements are still subject to the FIN 46R rules and may result in the consolidation of a VIE. Moreover, ASU 2014-07 does not change existing practice involving the voting-interest model under which consolidation is required if one entity owns more than 50 percent of the voting interest in another entity.

¶ 105 EXAMPLE OF CURRENT PRACTICE

The scope of ASU 2014-07's election is generally limited to a lessor-lessee lease arrangement involving entities under common control.

In this section, the author presents an example that demonstrates the current practice of dealing with a related-party leasing arrangement that led to the issuance of ASU 2014-07.

In this section, the author presents the typical structure that exists to which ASU 2014-07 provides an exemption for a private (nonpublic) lessee.

The general rules found in FIN 46R follow:

An operating company lessee is required to consolidate a real estate lessor if certain conditions are met:

- The real estate lessor must be a VIE: an entity that cannot support itself without support from other entities.
- The operating company lessee must have a variable interest in the VIE (e.g., must provide some form of support to the VIE in the form of a guarantee, loan, above market lease, etc.).
- The operating company lessee must be considered the primary beneficiary of the VIE.

The three requirements above must be determined by the operating company lessee, which is the entity that is issuing the financial statements. If all three of the above conditions are met, the operating company lessee (reporting entity) consolidates the real estate lessee even though there is no direct ownership among the two entities.

FASB Staff Position No. FIN 46(R)-5, *Implicit Variable Interests under FASB Interpretation No. 46* (revised December 2003) provides the key element that has motivated the PCC and FASB to provide the special election for nonpublic (private) entities to avoid the VIE rules for related-party leasing arrangements. What FIN 46(R)-5 addresses is the concept of the implicit guarantee and the fact that an operating company lessee that has a common owner who guarantees the loan of a related-party real estate lessor is deemed to provide an implicit guarantee of the lessor's debt.

Let's look at the three requirements in the context of a lessee-lessor real estate leasing arrangement where the entities are under common control.

The players involved are:

- Operating company lessee
- Real estate entity lessor
- Common individual owner (owner owns both entities 100 percent)

Requirement 1: The Real Estate Lessor Must Be a VIE.

The simplest way to explain a VIE is that it is an entity that is not self-sufficient and relies on others for financial support. Under the current FIN 46R rules, a real estate lessor is considered a VIE if:

The total equity investment at risk is *not sufficient to permit it to finance its activities* without obtaining *additional subordinated financial support* provided by any parties (e.g., individual or entity), including equity holders.

That means if a real estate lessor requires outside financial support (such as loans, guarantees, equity) from others to survive, that real estate company is a VIE.

One method that can be used to demonstrate that the real estate lessor's equity is sufficient and that it is *not* a VIE is the following:

FIN 46R states that an entity's equity is sufficient if the entity:

"Has demonstrated that it can obtain non-recourse, investment-grade financing from an unrelated party without additional subordinated financial support (loan guarantees, etc.) from other entities or individuals, including equity holders."

What the above paragraph means is that a real estate lessor is not a VIE (and is not consolidated) if it has demonstrated that it can obtain financing on its own, without the help of other entities or individuals that provide a guarantee, additional collateral, loans, etc.

Although FIN 46R does not define how the real estate lessor "has demonstrated that it can obtain non-recourse, investment-grade financing," an informal, general rule has evolved in practice that suggests that if the real estate lessor has an existing loan-to-value of 60-65 percent of the fair value of the underlying real estate, the entity has demonstrated its ability to obtain non-recourse financing.

The theory behind the 60-65 percent threshold is that a real-estate lessor should be able to refinance its existing debt with new non-recourse financing (without a personal guarantee or collateral from others), if the loan-to-value is not more than 65 percent. The 65-percent threshold is a benchmark at which many lenders are willing to grant non-recourse financing.

EXAMPLE:

Company X is a real estate lessor:

Fair value of real estate	$1,000,000
Mortgage balance	$500,000
Loan to value	50 percent

Because X's loan to value is less than 60-65 percent, X probably could obtain non-recourse financing (e.g., without additional support from others such as guarantees, additional collateral, etc.). Thus, X is probably not a VIE and will not be consolidated by a related-party lessee under the VIE rules.

Change the facts: Assume the loan to value is 80 percent.

X is probably a VIE as X cannot obtain non-recourse financing (e.g., without additional support from others such as guarantees, additional collateral, loans, etc.).

FIN 46R provides other qualitative and quantitative methods that can be used to test whether a real estate lessor is a VIE. However, those methods are tedious thereby leaving the non-recourse financing method as the quickest and most effective method to use in most instances.

If a real estate lessor has a loan-to-value that is less than 60-65 percent, the entity is probably not a VIE and there is no further work required as there is no consolidation. That is, there is no need to determine whether the lessee has a variable interest (Requirement 2) or whether the lessee is the primary beneficiary (Requirement 3).

But, assuming the entity *is* a VIE (e.g., its loan to value is greater than 65 percent), the VIE rules are applicable in determining whether the related-party lessee (operating company) should consolidate the VIE lessor into its financial statements. That means that Requirement 2 (identifying variable interests held by the lessee) and Requirement 3 (determining if the lessee is the primary beneficiary) must be tested.

Requirement 2: The Operating Company Lessee Must Have a Variable Interest in the VIE.

Assuming the real estate lessor is a VIE (Requirement 1), the second requirement for consolidation is that the operating company lessee must have a variable interest in the VIE in terms of giving some financial support to the VIE. A variable interest is nothing more than a form of support given by the lessee to a VIE lessor that exposes the lessee to the risks and rewards as if the lessee were an owner.

The common forms of variable interests that an operating company lessee might have in a real estate lessor (VIE) are:

- A guarantee of the lessor's debt
- Collateral for the lessor's bank loan
- A direct loan from the lessee to the lessor

- An above-market lease, residual value guarantee, purchase option, or lease renewal option
- Equity ownership in the VIE

If the lessee provides any of the above support to the real estate lessee (VIE), the operating company lessee has a variable interest in the real estate VIE.

The Implicit Guarantee

One form of a variable interest is where an operating company lessee guarantees the real estate lessor's mortgage. Such a guarantee is an explicit guarantee and clearly a form of financial support.

But what happens when the guarantee is indirect, or an implicit guarantee?

FIN 46R-5 (now part of ASC 810) provides rules that, in certain cases, treat a guarantee of the lessor's debt by the owner as being a guarantee also made by the operating company lessee. Thus, FIN 46R-5 introduces the concept of an implicit guarantee.

ASC 810-10-25-54 (formerly found in FSP FIN 46(R)-5) states that the determination of whether an implicit guarantee exists shall be based on whether an entity giving the implicit guarantee (lessee) may absorb variability of the VIE. In other words, is it possible that the lessee may have to absorb the losses or receive the residual benefits of a VIE due to the lessee's relationship with the common owner? If so, the fact that the common owner has guaranteed the debt of the lessor means that the lessee may have to implicitly stand behind that owner's guarantee if it is called. Thus, there is the concept of the implicit (or indirect) guarantee.

An implicit guarantee acts the same as an explicit guarantee except that the lessee's risk of having to absorb losses is indirect instead of direct.

In a related-party leasing arrangement, if a lessee has an implicit guarantee and is a related party with the lessor through common ownership, there is a possibility that the lessee may have to consolidate a VIE lessor even though there is no explicit variable interest (e.g., there is no explicit guarantee of the VIE's debt).

EXAMPLE: Company X is a real estate lessor and VIE. Company Y is an operating company lessee. John is the common owner who guarantee's X's real estate loan. Y is a prime asset of John's.

John has provided an explicit guarantee of X's debt. Y has probably provided an implicit guarantee of X's debt through John. If John's explicit guarantee is called by the lender, John may have to call upon Y to pay for that guarantee.

In looking at the previous example, an operating company lessee can have a variable interest in a real estate lessor VIE through having an implicit guarantee of the VIE's debt through the common owner's explicit guarantee. This implicit guarantee exists even though the lessee has not explicitly guaranteed any of the VIE's debt.

Requirement 3: The Operating Company Lessee Must Be the Primary Beneficiary of the VIE.

If the real estate lessor is a VIE (Requirement 1), and the operating company lessee has a variable interest in the VIE (Requirement 2), the third and final requirement for consolidation is that the operating company lessee must be considered the primary beneficiary of the real estate lessor VIE.

A primary beneficiary is defined as the entity or individual that has a variable interest in the VIE and has a *controlling financial interest* in the VIE in that the entity or individual both:

- Has the power to direct the VIE's most significant activities
- Has the obligation to absorb the VIE's losses, or right to receive the VIE's benefits that could be significant

In the traditional real estate leasing situation, there are three parties:

- Real estate lessor (VIE)
- Related party operating company lessee
- Common owner (typically an individual)

The following is an example that addresses the common problem practitioners have with related party leases under current practice.

EXAMPLE 1: Lease with loan guarantee by owner

John is a 100 percent shareholder of Company X (real estate lessor) and Company Y (operating company lessee). X owns real estate that it leases to Company Y. The loan-to-value of X's debt is 80 percent as follows:

Fair value of real estate	$1,250,000
Mortgage balance	$1,000,000
Loan to value	80 percent

X is a VIE because its loan-to-value is greater than 65 percent and it cannot demonstrate that it can obtain non-recourse financing.

The lease is at a market rate with no residual value guarantee, no option to purchase at a fixed price, and no renewal options. There are no variable interests between the parties such as loans, guarantees, etc. (e.g., no financial support is coming from the lessee).

X has a $1 million bank loan and John has personally guaranteed that loan. Y has not guaranteed X's loan although there are no restrictions to Y if it had chosen to guarantee X's loan. Y has not guaranteed the loans of any entities in the past. John's primary assets are his 100 percent equity holding in Y and X.

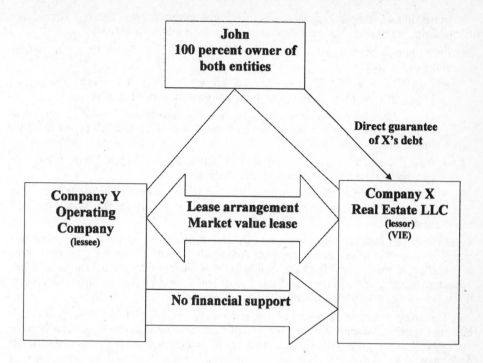

Should Y consolidate X? Let's look at the three requirements:

Requirement 1: X must be a VIE.

It is given that X is a VIE because (with a loan-to-value of 80 percent), it does not has sufficient equity to obtain non-recourse financing without additional support from other entities or individuals.

Requirement 2: Y must have a variable interest in X.

Remember that the list of variable interests includes:

- Guarantee of lessor's debt
- Providing collateral for the lessor's bank loan
- A direct loan from the lessee to the lessor
- An above-market lease
- Equity ownership in the VIE

Because the lease is at a market rate, with no residual value guarantee, no purchase option, and no lease renewal option, the lease is not a variable interest. There is also no guarantee of X's debt, no collateral put up by Y for X's debt, no direct loans, and no equity. Thus, on the surface, it would appear that Y has no variable interests in X. If Y has no variable interests in X, Y fails Requirement 2 and there is no consolidation.

Without any additional information, Y would have no variable interests and would not consolidate X. However, there is one additional piece of information that changes this conclusion. John is the guarantor of X's bank loan. A primary asset of John that would be used to satisfy that guarantee if it were to be called would be Y's net assets. Thus, Y may have an *implicit guarantee* of X's loan even though there is no "explicit" guarantee. In other words, John's guarantee is assigned to Y (implicit guarantee) based on the theory that John may have to call upon Y to pay for its guarantee.

In making a determination as to whether Y has an implicit guarantee, Y should ask the following questions that are included in originally issued FIN 46(R)-5.

Even though there is no contractual obligation for Y to do so (e.g., no explicit guarantee of X's debt):

- *Does Y have the obligation to protect X against loss?* Yes. Y is a primary asset of John that would be used to fulfill John's obligation under the guarantee.
- *Does Y have the economic incentive to protect X against loss?* Yes. Y's incentive is through its relationship with John, and as a lessee that needs X's property for its operations.
- *Has Y acted as a protector in similar situations in the past?* No. Y has not guaranteed the loans of other entities in the past.
- *Would Y acting as a protector of X be a conflict of interest or be illegal?* No. The facts state that Y would not be precluded from guaranteeing X's loan if it chose to do so.

Y indirectly has *both the obligation and incentive* to protect X against a loss (first two questions above) if John's guarantee were to be called. That is, if John's guarantee were to be called, Y would have both the obligation and incentive to pay for the loss. Y has not acted as a guarantor in the past (question 3) and Y would have no conflict of interest if Y acted as a guarantor of X's loan (question 4).

The answers to the questions above, particularly questions 1 and 2, support that Y has an implicit guarantee of X's loan which is a variable interest in X. The implicit guarantee exists even though there is no explicit (contractual) variable interest through its lease with X.

Once it is determined that Y has an implicit guarantee of X's debt, the chart now looks like this:

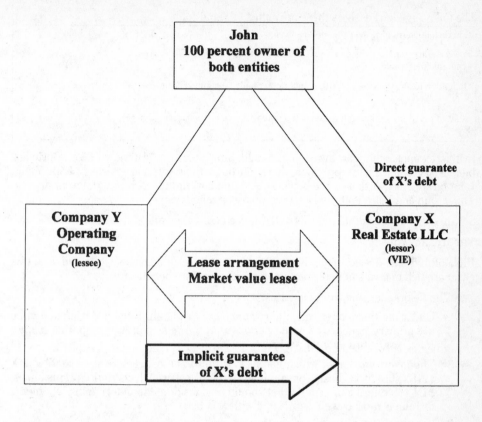

With an implicit guarantee of X's debt, Y now has a variable interest in X (a form of support) and thus, the second requirement for consolidation is satisfied.

Who holds the variable interests in X?

The variable interests in X are held as follows:

- Equity ownership in X: John holds 100 percent of the equity ownership in X.
- Guarantee of X's debt- John holds an explicit guarantee and Y holds an implicit guarantee of X's debt.

John holds variable interests in X through John's (explicit) guarantee and his equity ownership in X.

Y holds a variable interest in X through its implicit guarantee of X's bank loan.

Requirement 3: Y must be the primary beneficiary.

The last requirement for Y to consolidate X is that Y must be considered the primary beneficiary (de facto parent) of X.

In looking at the rules to determine whether Y is the primary beneficiary, one can conclude that the rules are nonsensical and the conclusions reached are not always clear. The primary beneficiary of X (VIE) is the party that has the:

- *Power to direct the activities of X* that most significantly impact X's economic performance, and
- *obligation to absorb losses of X* or the *right to receive benefits from X* that could potentially be significant to X.

The following chart assigns these attributes to Y and John.

Criteria for determining the Primary Beneficiary	Y	John
Power to direct the activities of X that most significantly impact X's economic performance	Yes	Yes
Obligation to absorb losses of X that could potentially be significant to X, or	Yes	Yes
Right to receive benefits from X that could potentially be significant to X	Yes	Yes

In this example, one can argue that Y and John meet the criteria to be the primary beneficiary noted in the previous chart. Through their variable interests, both Y and John have some portion of the power, obligation and rights, each to a different degree. Thus, John and Y are both tied as the primary beneficiary.

In order to break that tie, FIN 46R offers a tie-breaker rule.

Tie-breaker rule

FIN 46R has a tie-breaker rule that applies when two related parties (John and Y, in this case) are tied in terms of determining who is the primary beneficiary.

The tie-breaker rule works like this:

- Under the tie-breaker rule, the related party (Y or John) that is designated to be the primary beneficiary is the party within the related-party group, that is *most closely associated with the X (VIE)*.

- The determination of which party (Y or John) is most closely associated with X (VIE) should be based on an analysis of all relevant facts and circumstances. FIN 46R offers four criteria that should be considered in determining whether Y or John is most closely associated with X (VIE):

  1. The existence of a principal-agency relationship between parties within the related party group

  2. The relationship and significance of the activities of X (VIE) to Y and John.

  3. Y and John's exposure to the variability associated with the anticipated economic performance of X (VIE) (i.e., who (Y or John) absorbs the most losses or receives the most benefits from X)

  4. The design of X (VIE), such as the purpose for which X was created

When one performs an analysis of the four criteria above, it is easy to see that the conclusions are not clear. An argument can be made that any one of the four criteria noted above could support Y or John being the primary beneficiary.

Let's look at the analysis:

SCENARIO 1: Argument that Y is the Primary Beneficiary that Consolidates X

Factor	Factor supports	Analysis
The existence of a principal-agency relationship between parties within the related party group	NA	Not applicable as none of the related parties has a principal-agency relationship with X
The relationship and significance of the activities of the VIE to the various parties within the related party group	Y	Favors Y being the primary beneficiary: Because X and Y have a lessor-lessee relationship, X's activities are more significant to Y than any other party.

Factor	Factor supports	Analysis
A related party's exposure to the variability associated with the anticipated economic performance of the VIE	John	Favors John because John is the explicit guarantor and the sole holder of equity
The design of the VIE, such as the purpose for which the entity was created	Y	Favors Y being the primary beneficiary as X was purchased or created for the purpose of leasing to Y
CONCLUSION	**Y is the PB**	

Based on the tie-breaker rules, Scenario 1 provides a stronger argument that Y is the primary beneficiary as it satisfies Criteria 2 and 4, while John satisfies Criteria 3. Using the Scenario 1 argument, Y consolidates X.

SCENARIO 2: Argument that John is the Primary Beneficiary-No Consolidation

Factor	Factor supports	Analysis
The existence of a principal-agency relationship between parties within the related party group	NA	Not applicable as none of the related parties has a principal-agency relationship with X
The relationship and significance of the activities of X to the various parties within the related party group	Y and John	Both John and Y: The primary activity of X is significant to Y (due to the lessor-lessee relationship) and to John as an equity owner.
A related party's exposure to the variability associated with the anticipated economic performance of the VIE	John	Favors John because John is the explicit guarantor and the sole holder of equity: As equity holder, John is exposed to the greatest losses and greatest return on the real estate.
The design of the VIE, such as the purpose for which the entity was created	John	Favors John: X was designed to assist John in *asset protection and estate planning.* Otherwise, the real estate could have been held individually without the need for a separate entity.
CONCLUSION	**John is the PB**	**Because John is an individual, no consolidation.**

As the reader can see, one can make a legitimate argument supporting either Y or John as the primary beneficiary. If one wants to consolidate X into Y, the facts supporting Y being the primary beneficiary are found in Scenario 1. If, instead, one wants to avoid consolidation, Scenario 2 supports a conclusion that John is the primary beneficiary. If John is the primary beneficiary, there is no consolidation of X.

The FIN 46R rules can be used to manipulate a result supporting consolidation or no consolidation of a VIE. Either way, it takes extensive time and effort to go through a series of steps to support consolidating or not consolidating a VIE. For private (nonpublic entities), the rules require extensive work and expertise that may not be available for the nonpublic entity, thereby requiring the outside CPA to decipher.

ASU 2014-07 has as its primary goal to alleviate the requirement for the operating company lessee to consolidate the real estate lessor when the two entities are under common control.

¶ 106 DEFINITIONS USED IN ASU 2014-07

Financial Statements Are Available to Be Issued

Financial statements are considered available to be issued when they are complete in a form and format that complies with GAAP and all approvals necessary for issuance have been obtained, for example, from management, the board of directors, and/or significant shareholders. The process involved in creating and distributing the financial statements will vary depending on an entity's management and corporate governance structure as well as statutory and regulatory requirements.

Legal Entity

A legal entity includes any legal structure used to conduct activities or to hold assets. Some examples of such structures are corporations, partnerships, limited liability companies, grantor trusts, and other trusts.

Private Company

A private company is an entity, other than a public business entity, a not-for-profit entity, or an employee benefit plan on plan accounting. (Such benefit plans are covered by ASC 960 and 965.)

Public Business Entity

A public business entity is a business entity meeting any one of the criteria below. (Neither a not-for-profit entity nor an employee benefit plan is a business entity.):

- It is required by the U.S. Securities and Exchange Commission (SEC) to file or furnish financial statements, or does file or furnish financial statements (including voluntary filers), with the SEC (including other entities whose financial statements or financial information are required to be or are included in a filing).

- It is required by the Securities Exchange Act of 1934 (the Act), as amended, or rules or regulations promulgated under the Act, to file or furnish financial statements with a regulatory agency other than the SEC.

- It is required to file or furnish financial statements with a foreign or domestic regulatory agency in preparation for the sale of, or for purposes of, issuing securities that are not subject to contractual restrictions on transfer.

- It has issued, or is a conduit bond obligor for, securities that are traded, listed, or quoted on an exchange or an over-the-counter market.

- It has one or more securities that are not subject to contractual restrictions on transfer, and it is required by law, contract, or regulation to prepare U.S. GAAP financial statements (including footnotes) and make them publicly available on a periodic basis (e.g., interim or annual periods). An entity must meet both of these conditions to meet this criterion.

An entity may meet the definition of a public business entity solely because its financial statements or financial information is included in another entity's filing with the SEC. In that case, the entity is only a public business entity for purposes of financial statements that are filed with or furnished to the SEC.

STUDY QUESTIONS

1. With respect to consolidations, general GAAP states that a reporting entity must consolidate an entity in which it has a (an):

    a. Investment

    b. Controlling financial interest

    c. Loan receivable

    d. Minority interest

2. Which of the following is a comment made by private company respondents as noted by the PCC in issuing ASU 2014-07?

    a. A common owner private company typically establishes a lessor entity separate from a private company in order to structure off-balance-sheet debt arrangements.

    b. Establishing a lessor entity separate from a private company does not allow for effective tax planning.

    c. Most users of private company lessee's financial statements state that consolidation in the lessor entity is relevant to them.

    d. A common owner may establish a lessor entity separate from the private company lessee for legal-liability purposes.

3. Company Y is a lessee and wants to test to determine whether it is a primary beneficiary of a lessor that is a VIE. A primary beneficiary is defined as the entity or individual that has a variable interest in the VIE and has a controlling financial interest in the VIE. Which of the following is *not* a factor that Y should consider in determining whether it is the primary beneficiary?

    a. Does Y have the power to direct the VIE's most significant activities?

    b. Does Y have the obligation to absorb the VIE's losses?

    c. Does Y have the right to receive the VIE's benefits that could be significant?

    d. Does Y have at least a 50 percent investment in the VIE?

4. Which of the following would FIN 46R's tie-breaker rule apply to?

    a. Two related parties that are tied in terms of determining which is the primary beneficiary

    b. Two lessors each of which is tied for determining which one is a VIE

    c. One related party and one unrelated party determining which is the primary beneficiary

    d. Two entities, each of which has a variable interest and is determining which has the most significant variable interest in a VIE

¶ 107 RULES IN ASU 2014-07

ASU 2014-07 offers rules to apply if a private company wants to elect the ASU's accounting alternative and not apply the VIE consolidation rules to a lessor related by common ownership.

A private company (nonpublic entity) may elect an accounting alternative in applying the variable interest entity rules to a lessor under common ownership.

Under the accounting alternative, a private company (nonpublic entity) lessee is not required to evaluate a lessor legal entity under the guidance in the variable interest entity (VIE) rules if all of the following four criteria are met:

- **Criterion 1:** The private company lessee (the reporting entity) and the lessor legal entity are under common control.
- **Criterion 2:** The private company lessee has a lease arrangement with the lessor legal entity.
- **Criterion 3:** Substantially all activities between the private company lessee and the lessor legal entity are related to leasing activities (including supporting leasing activities) between those two entities.
- **Criterion 4:** If the private company lessee explicitly guarantees or provides collateral for any obligation of the lessor legal entity related to the asset leased by the private company, then the principal amount of the obligation at inception of such guarantee or collateral arrangement does not exceed the value of the asset leased by the private company from the lessor legal entity.

Application of this accounting alternative is an *accounting policy election* that shall be applied by a private company lessee to all lessor legal entities, provided that all of the four criteria for applying this accounting alternative are met.

For lessor legal entities that as a result of this accounting alternative are excluded from applying the VIE rules (e.g., are exempt from being consolidated), a private company lessee shall continue to apply other GAAP guidance as applicable.

A private company that elects the accounting alternative shall make two specific disclosures identified in this ASU, unless the lessor legal entity is consolidated through other GAAP rules other than VIE guidance (e.g., there is more than 50 percent ownership in the voting shares of the lessor).

If, after making the election, any of the first three conditions (Criterion (1), (2) or (3)) for applying the accounting alternative cease to be met, a private company shall apply the guidance for consolidation of a VIE at the date of change on a prospective basis.

> **NOTE:** An entity must satisfy the first three criteria continuously after the election is made.

¶ 108 DISCUSSION OF THE FOUR CRITERIA FOR ELECTION OF THE ACCOUNTING ALTERNATIVE

CRITERION 1: The Private Company Lessee (The Reporting Entity) and the Lessor Legal Entity are Under Common Control.

In order for Criterion 1 to be met, both the lessee and lessor must be under *common control.*

The PCC decided not to formally define the term "common control." In Paragraph BC14 of ASU 2014-07, the PCC states:

> "The PCC acknowledged the concerns raised by stakeholders, but decided not to define common control. The PCC noted that the term common control currently exists in other areas of U.S. GAAP (for example, Topic 805, *Business Combinations*). Establishing a definition for common control would be a change that could affect all entities including public business entities and, therefore, was outside the scope of this PCC Issue. Furthermore, establishing a definition of common control would require further analysis, which could have delayed significantly the issuance of this Update."

The definition of "common control" is limited within U.S. GAAP.

EITF Issue No. 02-5, *Definition of "Common Control" in Relation to FASB Statement No. 141,* provides a proposed definition of "common control," but there was never a final consensus reached in the EITF Issue. Nevertheless, within EITF Issue No. 02-5, the FASB references a definition of "common control" that the SEC staff uses. In EITF

Issue No. 02-5, the FASB staff states that the SEC staff has indicated that common control exists between (or among) separate entities only in the following situations:

- An individual or enterprise holds more than 50 percent of the voting ownership interest of each entity.
- Immediate family members hold more than 50 percent of the voting ownership interest of each entity (with no evidence that those family members will vote their shares in any way other than in concert).

  - Immediate family members include a married couple and their children, but not the married couple's grandchildren.

  - Entities might be owned in varying combinations among living siblings and their children. Those situations would require careful consideration regarding the substance of the ownership and voting relationships.

- A group of shareholders (or other equity owners) holds more than 50 percent of the voting ownership interest of each entity, and contemporaneous written evidence of an agreement to vote a majority of the entities' shares in concert exists.

Although the definition of "common control" found in EITF Issue No. 02-5 provides guidance as to how to use the term within ASU 2014-07, the PCC made the following comments:

> "For the purposes of applying this accounting alternative, the Board and the PCC concluded that common control is *broader than* the notion provided by the SEC observations on EITF Issue 02-5. For example, an entity owned by a grandparent and an entity owned by a grandchild could, on the basis of facts and circumstances, be considered as entities under common control for the purposes of applying this accounting alternative. Because common control is not an entirely new concept within U.S. GAAP, stakeholders in current practice should be able to assess whether common control exists."

> **OBSERVATION:** A private company wants a broader definition of "common control" in order to qualify a related-party lease for the ASU 2014-07 election. Obviously, the election qualifies when there is one single owner of both the lessor and lessee entities. But what about a situation in which the lessor real estate entity is owned by a son and the lessee operating company is owned by a father?

Although not authoritative, the following appears to be a list of related party relationships that should qualify for common ownership. Assume there is one lessor real estate entity, and one lessee operating company:

Qualifies as common control (consistent with examples found in EITF 02-5):

- The same individual or enterprise holds more than 50 percent of the voting ownership interest of both the lessor and lessee entities.
- Immediate family members own more than 50 percent of the lessee and lessor and there is no evidence that they would not vote their interests as a block:

  - One spouse owns more than 50 percent of voting ownership interest in the lessor entity and the other spouse owns more than 50 percent in the voting ownership interest lessee entity.

  - A father owns more than 50 percent of the voting ownership interest in the lessor entity and the son owns more than 50 percent of the voting ownership interest in the lessee entity (or, in reverse).

- A group owns more than 50 percent of the voting ownership interest in both the lessor and lessee entities and there is no evidence they would not vote their interests as a block.

¶108

May qualify as common control:

- A grandfather owns more than 50 percent of the voting ownership interest in the lessor entity and the grandchild owns more than 50 percent of the voting ownership interest in the lessee entity.
- Two family members each own more than 50 percent of the voting ownership interest in each entity.

Probably does not qualify as common control:

- Lessee entity is owned by parent and lessor entity is owned by a trust with the children as beneficiaries of the trust and an independent trustee other than the parents.

   OBSERVATION: A private company wants to make sure there is a common ownership between the private company lessee and the lessor. If there is no common ownership, the ASU 2014-07 election is not available to the private company lessee. Although the PCC did not formally adopt the definition found in EITF 02-5, that EITF's definition of common control gives guidance as to the minimum family relationships that companies should be able to use in applying the ASU 2014-07.

Examples of Common Control

Relationship	Example[1]	Meets the definition of "common control"	May meet the definition of "common control"
Husband and wife	Husband owns > 50 percent of lessee and wife owns > 50 percent of lessor	X	
Parent and child	Father owns > 50 percent of lessee and son owns > 50 percent of lessor	X	
Siblings	One brother owns > 50 percent of lessee and one brother owns > 50 percent of lessor	X	
A group has common control of both entities	The same group of entities or individuals owns > 50 percent of lessee and lessor[2]	X	
Grandparent and grandchild	Grandmother owns > 50 percent of lessee and granddaughter owns > 50 percent of lessor[2]		X
Other relatives: Uncles, cousins, etc.	One relative owns > 50 percent of the lessee and another relative owns > 50 percent of the lessor[2]		X

[1] As used in the examples, ownership is deemed to be voting equity so that there is control of the entity.

[2] When the relationship is other than immediate family members (parents and children), there should be no evidence that the parties would not vote as a block.

Although the SEC definition of common control found in EITF 02-5 is rather restrictive, in ASU 2014-07, the PCC made it clear that it expects the definition of common control referenced in ASU 2014-07 is *broader than* the one found in EITF 02-5.

   Certainly, where there is a lessee and lessor with more than 50 percent owners as immediate family members (such as parents and children), there is common ownership. Similarly, where there are the same parties that own more than 50 percent of both the lessee and lessor and no evidence exists that they will not vote as a block, there is common ownership.

Ambiguity exists in instances in which other family members own more than 50 percent of the lessee and lessor. For example, an uncle may own one entity and that uncle's niece or nephew owns the other entity. Or, a grandfather owns the lessee and the grandson owns the lessor. In these instances EITF 02-5 gives no guidance. However, in ASU 2014-07, the PCC noted the following:

> "For the purposes of applying this accounting alternative, the Board and the PCC concluded that common control is *broader than* the notion provided by the SEC observations on EITF Issue 02-5."

CRITERION 2: The Private Company Lessee has a Lease Arrangement with the Lessor Legal Entity.

ASU 2014-05 limits the election to avoid the VIE rules to a lease arrangement. Yet, the ASU does not define the term "lease arrangement." If a transaction is not a lease arrangement, the election is not available.

For example, a transaction between a lessor and lessee under common ownership might be a service contract, and not a lease arrangement. A service contract does not qualify for the election so that the VIE rules must continue to be applied to the two related parties.

GAAP provides some guidance as to the definition of a lease. Existing ASC 840, *Leases*, defines a lease as:

> "An agreement conveying the right to use property, plant or equipment (land and/or depreciable assets), usually for a stated period of time."

The FASB has issued an exposure draft in which the FASB proposes changes to the rules for lease accounting. In that exposure draft is a proposed revision to the definition of a lease as follows:

> "A contract that conveys the right to *use an asset* (the underlying asset) for a period of time in exchange for consideration."

The exposure draft would expand on the existing definition of a lease in that it must have two elements:

- Fulfillment of the contract depends on the use of an identified asset.
- The contract conveys the right to control the use of the identified asset for a period of time in exchange for consideration.

Although the exposure draft has not been issued as a final document, the proposed definition of a lease found in the exposure draft, coupled with the existing definition of a lease in ASU 840, *Leases*, means that a lease arrangement has certain common components and involves:

- Use and control of an underlying asset
- Use for a period of time
- Exchange of consideration

In situations in which a contract between two entities involves providing services, and not use of an underlying asset, the contract is most likely not a lease arrangement and instead is a service contract. If it is a service contract, the election to use ASU 2014-07's accounting alternative and avoid the VIE rules is not available.

Does Criterion 2 require there to be a lease involving real estate?

No. There has to be a lease but it is not limited to real estate. Therefore, a lease involving personal property would qualify as a lease arrangement under Criterion 2.

¶108

CRITERION 3: Substantially All Activities Between the Private Company Lessee and the Lessor Legal Entity are Related to Leasing Activities Between Those Two Entities.

The third criterion for a lessee to elect the accounting alternative is that substantially all of the activities between the lessee and lessor must involve leasing activities, including supporting leasing activities, between the two entities. The "substantially all activities" criterion does not mean that either entity cannot engage in other activities with unrelated third parties. What it does mean is that substantially all of the activities between the lessor and lessee under common control must be limited to leasing activities between the two entities, including supporting leasing activities.

The ASU also states that the concept of "leasing activities" includes any support provided to the leasing activities between the two entities.

The following are examples included in the ASU, as modified by the author, of activities that are considered to be leasing activities (including supporting leasing activities) between the private company lessee and the lessor legal entity:

Leasing activities, including supporting leasing activities include:

- A lease between a private company lessee and lessor under common control
- An *explicit guarantee or collateral* provided by the private company lessee to the lender of a lessor entity under common control for debt that is *secured by the asset(s) leased by the private company lessee.*

    NOTE: An implicit guarantee is not considered to be a supporting leasing activity.

- A joint and several liability arrangement for debt of the lessor legal entity, for which the private company lessee is one of the obligors, that is *secured by the asset(s) leased* by the private company lessee
- Paying property taxes, negotiating the financing, and maintaining the *asset(s) leased by the private company lessee*
- Paying income taxes of the lessor legal entity when the only asset owned by the lessor legal entity is being leased either by only the private company or by both the private company lessee and an unrelated party
- A purchase commitment or option, for the acquisition of or the support of the asset(s) leased by the private company lessee
- A lease option related to the asset(s) leased by the private company lessee

Activities that are *not* leasing activities, including supporting leasing activities:

- An agreement that is not a lease, such as a service contract between a private company lessee and lessor under common control
- An explicit guarantee or collateral provided by the private company lessee to the lender of a lessor entity under common control for indebtedness that is secured by asset(s) *other than* the asset(s) leased by the private company lessee
- An implicit guarantee of debt of the lessor entity, regardless of whether the debt is secured by asset(s) leased by the private company lessee or other parties
- A joint and several liability arrangement for debt of the lessor, for which the private company lessee is one of the obligors, that is secured by asset(s) *other than* the asset(s) leased by the private company lessee
- Paying property taxes, negotiating the financing, and maintaining asset(s) of the lessor entity, *other than* the asset(s) leased by the private company lessee

- Paying income taxes of the lessor entity on income generated by *an asset that is not being leased by the private company lessee*
- A purchase commitment for assets of the lessor entity that are assets other than the asset(s) leased by the lessee.
- A lease option related to an asset(s) not leased by the private company lessee

What is the definition of "substantially all?"

The ASU does not define the term "substantially all." Therefore, one must look elsewhere within U.S. GAAP for guidance.

ASC 840, *Leases*, defines "substantially all" in the context of whether a lease is classified as a capital lease and uses a *90 percent threshold* in determining whether there is an effective transfer of an asset.

Using 90 percent as a guide, it would seem that the *substantially all threshold* is satisfied as long as 90 percent or more of the private company lessee's activities relate to leasing activities (including supporting leasing activities) involving the asset that is leased by the lessee from the lessor. Determining the 90 percent threshold can most effectively be measuring based on the amount of debt guaranteed or collateral provided by the lessee as follows:

Debt guaranteed by lessee secured by leased asset leased to lessee	= **≥90 percent**	Satisfies the substantially all threshold in Criterion 3
Debt guaranteed by lessee secured by assets leased to lessee and other parties	= **< 90 percent**	May not satisfy the substantially all threshold in Criterion 3

EXAMPLE: Company Y, a private company lessee leases Property B from Company X, a lessor with common ownership. Y has guaranteed X's $1 million debt that is secured by Property B. Y has also guaranteed another loan of X's for $100,000 that is secured by Property C, a property that is leased to an unrelated party.

Y's guarantee of the $1 million debt secured by Property B is clearly a leasing activity (including supporting a leasing activity involving the underlying leased asset). The guarantee of the $100,000 debt is not a leasing activity (including supporting leasing activity) because the debt to which this guarantee pertains is secured by real estate other than the asset that is leased to Y.

The question is, despite the $100,000 guarantee, whether substantially all (90 percent or more) of Y's activities with X relate to leasing (and supporting leasing activities) of Property B.

The fact is that more than 90 percent of the debt guaranteed by Y relates to debt secured by Property B ($1,000,000 divided by $1,100,000 = 91 percent), which is leased by Y. Using the amount of debt guaranteed by Y and the fact that 91 percent relates to the debt on the leased asset, Y can most likely conclude that substantially all of its activities with lessor relate to leasing activities (including supporting leasing activities) involving Property B.

Support of non-leased property

In order for an activity performed by the lessee to qualify as a supporting leasing activity, the activity provided by the lessee must pertain to the underlying leased asset.

¶108

To the extent that such activities relate to another asset of the lessor that is not leased by the lessee, that activity is outside the scope of a leasing activity. Consequently, in many cases, that outside activity disqualifies the lessee from using the election to avoid the VIE rules. The reason is because "substantially all" of the activities between the lessee and lessor are no longer related to leasing activities involving the asset leased by the lessee. Instead, they involve activities related to other non-leased assets.

Assume the following facts:

- Company X is a real estate lessor.
- Company Y is an operating company lessee (private company) that leases property from X.
- X and Y has one common owner, Ralph.

EXAMPLE 1:

- Y leases Warehouse 1 from X.
- Y guarantees the debt of X secured by Warehouse 1.
- Y maintains Warehouse 1 and pays the real estate taxes for Warehouse 1.

Substantially all of the activities between X and Y relate to leasing activities (including supporting leasing activities) between X and Y.

The guarantee of the debt on Warehouse 1, the maintenance of Warehouse 1, and payment of real estate taxes for Warehouse 1 are all supporting leasing activities provided by Company Y (lessee) related to the underlying asset (Warehouse 1) leased by Company Y.

Y satisfies Criterion 3 in that substantially all of the activities between Y (private company lessee) and X (lessor) relate to leasing activities (including supporting leasing activities) involving Warehouse 1.

EXAMPLE 2:

- Y leases Warehouse 1 from X.
- Y guarantees the debt of X secured by Warehouse 1.
- Y maintains Warehouse 1 and pays the real estate taxes for Warehouse 1.
- Y also has provided a guarantee and collateral for additional debt of X secured by Warehouse 2, which is leased to an unrelated party. The additional debt secured by Warehouse 2 is significant.

Y does not satisfy Criterion 3 and cannot elect the alternative accounting to avoid using the VIE rules with respect to X. The reason is because substantially all of the activities between Y and X do *not* relate to leasing activities (including supporting leasing activities) involving Warehouse 1 (the asset leased by Y).

Y's guarantee and collateral provided to X for Warehouse 2 is considered an additional activity outside the leasing of Warehouse 1. That means that Y's activities involve not only the lease of Warehouse 1 from X (including the guarantee of the debt on Warehouse 1, and maintenance of Warehouse 1), but also Y's guarantee and collateral provided on an unrelated asset (Warehouse 2). Moreover, the additional debt for which Y provided a guarantee is significant.

CRITERION 4: The Private Company Lessee Explicitly Guarantees or Provides Collateral for the Lessor (Additional Requirement)

Criterion 4 applies only if the private company lessee explicitly guarantees or provides collateral for any obligation of the lessor legal entity related to the asset leased by the private company. If there is no explicit guarantee or collateral provided, Criterion 4 does not apply and the determination of whether a private company lessee qualifies for the election to use the accounting alternative is based on Criteria 1, 2, and 3 only.

If the private company lessee explicitly guarantees or provides collateral for any obligation of the lessor legal entity related to the asset leased by the private company, then the principal amount of the obligation at inception of such guarantee or collateral arrangement *does not exceed the value* (The PCC decided to use the term "value" instead of "fair value" so that the user would not get involved in valuation issues. The PCC's intent is for the term "value" to be similar to the term "fair value" or "appraisal value.") *of the asset* leased by the private company from the lessor legal entity.

At the time at which the guarantee or collateral is provided (at inception), the debt to which the guarantee or collateral applies cannot exceed the value of the leased asset.

At inception:

Principal balance	≤	Value of leased asset =	CRITERION 4 SATISFIED
Principal Balance	>	Value of leased asset =	CRITERION 4 FAILED

Criterion 4 is assessed at the *inception* of the lessee providing the guarantee or collateral for the debt secured by the leased property. If there is no guarantee or collateral provided by the lessee, Criterion 4 does not apply.

> **EXAMPLE 1:** On December 1, 20X1, Lessee provides a guarantee of Lessor's mortgage that has a balance of $800,000. The mortgage is secured by real estate that is leased by Lessor to Lessee. The real estate has a value of $1 million on December 1, 20X1.

Conclusion: On December 1, 20X1 (inception date), Criterion 4 is assessed because the lessee has provided a guarantee or collateral on debt secured by the leased asset. On December 1, 20X1, the principal balance of $800,000 is compared with the $1 million value of the leased asset. The fact that the principal balance of $800,000 is less than the value of the asset ($1 million) at inception, means that Criterion 4 is satisfied.

The Criterion 4 assessment is *not* updated subsequently unless the lessor entity refinances or enters into a new obligation that requires a new guarantee or collateral by the private company lessee.

> **EXAMPLE 2:** Same facts as Example 1. At December 31, 20X2, the mortgage balance is $750,000 and the real estate value has plummeted to $700,000. There has been no refinancing of the original mortgage.

Conclusion: There is no reassessment made under Criterion 4. The fact that in 20X2, the principal balance of $750,000 now is greater than the value of the real estate ($700,000) is not considered because a reassessment is not permitted unless the debt is refinanced and a new guarantee or collateral is required from Lessee.

The Criterion 4 is reassessed *only if* the lessor entity subsequently refinances or enters into any new obligation or obligations that require collateralization and/or a guarantee by the private company lessee.

> **EXAMPLE 3:** On July 1, 20X3, Lessor refinances the debt and requires Lessee to provide a new guarantee on the new debt secured by the leased asset. At July 1, 20X3, the new debt balance is $1,200,000 and the value of the leased asset is $1,100,000.

Conclusion: Because the debt is refinanced and requires Lessee to provide collateral and/or a guarantee on the new debt, Lessee is required to perform a new assessment of Criterion 4 at the inception date of providing the new guarantee, July 1, 20X3. On the new inception date (July 1, 20X3), the principal balance of $1,200,000 is compared with the value of the leased asset ($1,100,000). Because the principal balance is greater than the value of the leased asset at the new inception date, Criterion 4 fails and Lessor cannot elect to accounting alternative.

If the debt represents a blanket mortgage on several properties, including the property leased by the lessee, the entire debt balance is used to compare with the value of the leased asset. If the lessee leases a portion of a facility owned by the lessor, the value of the entire facility is included in the comparison with the entire debt balance.

> **EXAMPLE:** Company X, lessor, owned Property A. 50 percent of Property A is leased to Company Y (private company lessee). X and Y are related by common ownership. Y has guaranteed the entire mortgage on Property A.

Conclusion: In determining whether the principal balance does not exceed the value of the leased asset, the entire mortgage balance and value of the entire Property A are used.

> **OBSERVATION:** Criterion 4 was added to mitigate off-balance-sheet structuring opportunities through the use of highly leveraged lessor entities that would have a nominal leasing arrangement with a private company lessee from being excluded from a consolidation assessment under the VIE model.

> The purpose of the *at inception* language is to prevent a private company lessee from continually reassessing whether a value of a leased asset continues to exceed the principal amount of obligations that are guaranteed or collateralized by a private company lessee when the only change is due to the change in value of the leased asset. For example, a subsequent decline in the value of a leased asset below the principal amount of a corresponding mortgage held by a lessor entity would not cause a private company to fail Criterion 4-as long as criterion 4 was met *at inception* of the arrangement. However, if the lessor entity subsequently refinances or enters into any new obligation or obligations that require collateralization and/or guarantee by the private company lessee, then the private company lessee would be required to reassess whether Criterion 4 is met at the inception of the new arrangement(s).

STUDY QUESTIONS *

---

5. Which of the following relationships would qualify as "common control" under ASU 2014-07?

    a. Husband owns 25 percent of lessee's voting equity and wife owns 100 percent of lessor's voting equity.

    b. Father owns 60 percent of lessee's voting equity and son owns 75 percent of lessor's voting interest.

    c. The same group of individuals owns 40 percent of lessee's voting interest and 100 percent of lessor's voting interest.

    d. Brother owns 30 percent of lessee's voting interest and his sister owns 51 percent of lessor's voting interest.

6. Which of the following is a leasing activity, including supporting leasing activity that is included within the scope of ASU 2014-07's election?

    a. A lease between a public company lessee and a private company lessor

    b. Lessee paying property taxes on the asset leased to an unrelated entity

    c. A lease option related to an asset(s) not leased by the private company lessee

    d. A purchase commitment for the acquisition of the asset leased by the private company lessee

---

¶ 109 CAN A PRIVATE COMPANY LESSEE STILL CONSOLIDATE A LESSOR EVEN IF THE LESSEE ELECTS THE ACCOUNTING ALTERNATIVE?

Remember, under current U.S. GAAP, a reporting entity is required to consolidate an entity in which it has a controlling financial interest. GAAP has *two models* for assessing whether there is a controlling financial interest: the voting interest model and the VIE model.

- Under the *voting interest model*, a controlling financial interest exists if there is ownership of more than 50 percent of an entity's voting interests.

- Under the *VIE model*, a reporting entity has a controlling financial interest in a VIE when it has both (1) the power to direct the VIE's activities that most significantly affect the economic performance of the VIE and (2) the obligation to absorb the VIE's losses or the right to receive benefits of the VIE that could potentially be significant to the VIE.

An operating entity lessee may not have to consolidate a lessee entity under the VIE model because either of the following is true:

- The operating entity lessee, as a private entity, elects the accounting alternative under ASU 2014-07.

- The operating entity lessee that does not elect the accounting alternative tests the lessee entity under the VIE rules and concludes that it is not the primary beneficiary that should consolidate the lessee entity.

However, that does not mean that the lessee entity is not consolidated into the operating entity using the voting interest model. That is, if the operating entity lessee owns more than 50 percent of the voting interests in the lessee entity, the operating entity would be required to consolidate the lessee entity under the voting interest model, even though not required to consolidate under the VIE model.

¶ 110 IF THE LESSEE ELECTS TO USE THE ACCOUNTING ALTERNATIVE, IS A SUBSEQUENT ASSESSMENT REQUIRED?

The ASU states:

> "If any of the conditions for applying the accounting alternative *cease to be met*, a private company shall apply the guidance in the Variable Interest Entities Subsections at the date of change on a prospective basis."

What this means is that satisfying the criteria to make the election must be done on a continuous basis. This continuous assessment applies to the first three criteria (Criteria 1 through 3) and does not apply to Criterion 4.

Criterion 4 states that a reassessment of whether the debt balance does not exceed the value of the underlying leased asset is not done unless the debt is refinanced and a new guarantee and/or collateral is required from the lessee.

EXAMPLE 1: Subsequent Change in One of the Criteria (1 to 3)

Effective January 1, 2014, Company Y (a private company lessee) tests the four criteria to elect to use the accounting alternative with respect to Company X, a lessor under common ownership. Y leases its facility from X. Since 20X1, Y has guaranteed X's bank loan secured by the facility leased to Y. On January 1, 2014, Y satisfies the four criteria and does not consolidate X into its 2014 financial statements.

Details on the four criteria follow:

- Company Y and X are under common control.

- Company Y has a *lease arrangement* with X.

- *Substantially all activities* between Y and X are related to leasing activities (*including supporting leasing activities*) between those two entities.

- Because Y guarantees X's debt, the principal balance on the debt did not exceed the value of the leased asset at the 20X1 inception date.

Throughout 2014, all four of the criteria remain intact. On January 1, 2015, events change for Y.

- X purchases an additional building that it leases to an unrelated third party.

- Y guarantees the new debt secured by the additional building.

Conclusion: As of January 1, 2015, one of the criteria (Criterion 3) has changed in that Y has guaranteed debt not related to the asset leased by Y from X. This guarantee represents an activity that is outside the lease arrangement between Y and X, including supporting leasing activities. Now, substantially all activities between Y and X do not relate to leasing activities (including supporting leasing activities), involving the asset leased to Y.

The result is that Y may no longer make the election to use the accounting alternative. Effective January 1, 2015, Y must apply FIN 46R VIE rules and test X to determine whether it should be consolidated into Y's financial statements. If X must be consolidated using the VIE rules, the consolidation is done prospectively starting on January 1, 2015.

EXAMPLE 2: Subsequent Change in Criterion 4

Same facts as Example 1, except the only change on January 1, 2015 is that the principal balance *exceeded* the value of the lease asset because the value of that leased asset plummeted. There are no changes to Criteria 1-3.

Conclusion: The rules of the ASU require that an entity continuously assess whether the ASU 2014-07 criteria are met. However, those rules apply to Criteria 1-3 and do not require a continuous assessment of Criterion 4. The exception is that Criterion 4 is reassessed only if the debt is refinanced and a new mortgage and/or collateral is required from the lessee. In this case, the debt has not been refinanced so that Criterion 4 is not reassessed since inception. Given the fact that Criteria 1-3 have not changed, those criteria remain satisfied. The conclusion is that Y may continue to elect to use the accounting alternative.

NOTE: Other examples illustrating the application of ASU 2014-07's accounting alternative are included in Appendix A.

¶ 111 OTHER MATTERS

The ASU states that the accounting alternative is an accounting policy election that, when elected, should be applied by a private company lessee to all current and future lessor entities under common control that meet the criteria for applying this approach.

EXAMPLE: Lessee Y, a private company, has leases with several lessor real estate entities, all under common ownership as follows:

- Lessor X
- Lessor Z
- Lessor C

Harry owns 100 percent of all entities and guarantees all of the bank loans for each of the Lessor X, Z, and C mortgages. Lessee Y has consolidated Lessors X, Z and C into Y's financial statements in prior years based on the FIN 46R VIE consolidation rules. At January 1, 20X1, Y wants to make the election to apply the accounting alternative and avoid consolidation under the VIE rules.

Conclusion: Because Y is a private company, Y can elect the accounting alternative provided, at the January 1, 20X1 election date, Y can satisfy the four criteria to use the accounting alternative. If Y seeks to use the accounting alternative, Y must test the four criteria to all current and future lessor entities under common control. That means that Y must assess X, Z and C, individually, to determine whether the four criteria are satisfied for each of these lessors.

To the extent that the four criteria are satisfied for any particular lessor, the lessee may elect the accounting alternative for that lessor. For any lessor for which the four criteria are not satisfied, Y will continue to test for consolidation of that lessor under the VIE rules.

The key point is that once Y decides to make the election for the accounting alternative, Y must do so for all lessors under common control with Y. Y is not permitted to cherry pick lessors.

OBSERVATION: The above analysis is not authoritative because the ASU does not provide a "unit of measure" to qualify for the ASU election when there is one private-company lessee with more than one lessor under common ownership, and even a lessee-lessor relationship involving more than one lease.

¶ 112 ASU 2014-07'S DISCLOSURES

A private company lessee that elects the accounting alternative to one or more lessor legal entities because it meets the four criteria, shall disclose the following *if the lessor legal entity is not consolidated:*

- The amount and key terms of liabilities (e.g., debt, environmental liabilities, and asset retirement obligations) recognized by the lessor legal entity that expose the private company lessee to providing financial support to the legal entity.

  EXAMPLE: A private company lessee exposed to debt of the lessor should disclose information such as the amount of debt, interest rate, maturity, pledged collateral, and guarantees associated with the debt.

- A qualitative description of circumstances (e.g., certain commitments and contingencies) not recognized in the financial statements of the lessor legal entity that expose the private company lessee to providing financial support to the legal entity.

In applying the disclosure guidance, a private-company lessee shall consider the lessee's *exposure through implicit guarantees.* The determination as to whether an implicit guarantee exists is based on facts and circumstances. Those facts and circumstances include, but are not limited to, whether:

- There is an economic incentive for the private company lessee to act as a guarantor or to make funds available.

- Such actions have happened in similar situations in the past.
- The private company lessee acting as a guarantor or making funds available would be considered a conflict of interest or illegal.

In disclosing information about the lessor legal entity, a private company lessee should present the disclosures in combination with the disclosures required by other guidance such as:

- ASC 460, *Guarantees*, disclosures related to guarantees
- ASC 850, *Related Party Disclosures*, disclosures about related party transactions
- ASC 840, *Leases*, disclosures about leases

The disclosures can be made by combining all disclosures in a single note or by including cross-references within the notes to the financial statements.

In applying the alternative accounting, a private company lessee is not required to provide VIE disclosures about the lessor entity.

Is a Private Company Lessee That Elects the Accounting Alternative Required to Include the Disclosures Found in FIN 46R Related to a Variable Interest Holder or Primary Beneficiary?

FIN 46R has a series of disclosures that are required to be made by a primary beneficiary that consolidates a VIE. There are also other disclosures that are required in situations in which:

- An entity does not consolidate a VIE but holds a significant variable interest in a VIE. For example, an entity that holds a significant variable interest in a VIE, but does not consolidate that VIE as the primary beneficiary, must disclose under ASC 810:
  - The nature of its involvement with the VIE and the date on which it began
  - The nature, purpose, size and activities of the VIE
  - The reporting entity's maximum exposure to loss as a result of its involvement with the VIE
- An entity that holds a variable interest in a VIE, but does not consolidate the VIE.

So the question is whether a private company lessee who makes the ASU 2014-07 election not to apply the VIE rules to a lessor under common control, has to include the numerous disclosures found in ASC 810 related to entities that hold variable interests in a VIE but do not consolidate the VIE. Or, is that private company only required to include the two disclosures found in ASU 2014-07?

The answer is found in the amendments to ASC 810 that are made by ASC 2014-07. ASC 810-10-15-17A states that a private company lessee does not have to evaluate a lessor under the "guidance in the Variable Interest Entities Subsections" to determine whether that lessor should be consolidated, if the four criteria are met. Those "variable interest entities subsections" include the various disclosures required by ASC 810. Moreover, if a private company lessee does not evaluate a lessor under the VIE rules, how could it determine whether it has a variable interest in the VIE, which, in turn, would require VIE disclosures?

Thus, if a private company lessee elects the accounting alternative, it does not follow any of the "variable interest entity" subsections of ASC 810 (including the related disclosures). Instead, its disclosures are limited to the two disclosures found in ASU 2014-07 as follows:

- The amount and key terms of liabilities (e.g., debt, environmental liabilities, and asset retirement obligations) recognized by the lessor legal entity that expose the private company lessee to providing financial support to the legal entity
- A qualitative description of circumstances (e.g., certain commitments and contingencies) not recognized in the financial statements of the lessor legal entity that expose the private company lessee to providing financial support to the legal entity.

Examples: Sample Disclosures

EXAMPLE 1: Lessee Has an Explicit Guarantee of Lessor's Debt

- Company X is a real estate lessor that leases its plant to Company Y, a lessee.
- Both entities are owned 100 percent by Frank.
- Company Y and Frank are guarantors of X's bank loan which is secured by the plant leased to Y.
- For year ended December 31, 2013, Y consolidated X into Y's financial statements under the VIE rules.
- Effective January 1, 2014, Y elects the accounting alternative under which Y will not consolidate X. Y satisfies the four criteria and is permitted to apply the accounting alternative.

Conclusion: For 2014, Y will not consolidate X but will be required to include certain disclosures as follows:

NOTE 1: Summary of Significant Accounting Policies:

Consolidation of Variable Interest Entity:

Effective January 1, 2014, the Company made an accounting policy election authorized for private companies by Accounting Standards Update (ASU) 2014-07, *Consolidation (Topic 810): Applying Variable Interest Entities Guidance to Common Control Leasing Arrangements*. Under this new accounting policy, the Company elects not to apply the accounting principles for the consolidation of variable interest entities (VIEs) to a real estate leasing company that is related to the Company through common ownership. Consequently, the 2014 financial statements do not reflect the effect, if any, of having consolidated the real estate leasing company.

For the year ended December 31, 2013, the Company had previously consolidated the real estate leasing company. Those financial statements have been *adjusted retrospectively* (When there is a change in accounting principle (policy), ASC 250 requires that the previous financial statements presented by adjusted retrospectively. The term "restated" is set aside in ASC 250 to reflect adjustments for corrections of errors and should not be used to describe a change in accounting principle (policy) such as ASU 2014-07 provides.) to deconsolidate the real estate leasing company as of January 1, 2013. The deconsolidation of the real estate leasing company resulted in an adjustment of the January 1, 2013 noncontrolling interest in the amount of $_____, which is reflected in the statement of stockholders' equity.

NOTE 2: Contingencies and Guarantees:

The Company is the guarantor of a $3,000,000 note due to a local bank by an entity related to the Company through common ownership. Under the terms of the guarantee, the Company and its common owner, have both guaranteed the note which is secured by commercial real estate located in Boston, Massachusetts. The

Company is the primary lessee of the real estate that acts as collateral for the note and which is further discussed in Note XX, *Leases*. The terms of the $3,000,000 note require the real estate leasing company to make monthly principal and interest payments of $60,000, including interest at five percent per annum, through December 2024. In accordance with the guarantee, upon the real estate leasing company having an uncured default of the $3,000,000 loan, the Company is jointly and severely liable with the common owner, for repayment of the entire $3,000,000 loan balance.

EXAMPLE 2: Lessee Has an Implicit Guarantee of Lessor's Debt

Same facts as Example 1 except that Y has not guaranteed X's mortgage. Y does have an implicit guarantee of X's debt through Frank's guarantee. Y represents a primary asset of Frank and Y would have a significant incentive to fulfill Frank's guarantee if it were called.

Conclusion: Even though Y is not an explicit guarantor of X's note, Y does have an implicit guarantee of the note through the common owner, Frank's guarantee.

NOTE 1: Summary of Significant Accounting Policies:

Consolidation of variable interest entity:

Same as example 1.

NOTE 2: Contingencies and Guarantees:

As further discussed in Note XX, *Leases,* the Company leases its primary plant in Boston, Massachusetts, from a real estate leasing entity, related to the Company through common ownership.

The real estate leasing company has a $3,000,000 note due to a local bank which is guaranteed by the common owner. Although the Company has not directly guaranteed the $3,000,000 note, the Company may have an implicit guarantee of the note through its owner's direct guarantee. For example, the Company may be expected to make funds available to the leasing entity to prevent the owner's guarantee from being called on. Additionally, the Company may be expected to make funds available to the owner to fund all or a portion of the call on the debt guarantee.

Because of the importance of the plant and related lease to the Company's business, the Company would be incentivized to use its assets to fund the owner's guarantee as a means to ensure that its plant and related lease, remain intact, and that there is no disruption of its operations.

Under the terms of the common owner's guarantee, the common owner has guaranteed the $3,000,000 note, which is secured by commercial real estate located in Boston, Massachusetts.

The terms of the $3,000,000 note require the real estate leasing company to make monthly principal and interest payments of $60,000, including interest at 5 percent per annum through December 2024. In accordance with the common owner's guarantee, upon the real estate leasing company having an uncured default of the $3,000,000 loan, the common owner is jointly and severely liable with the real estate leasing company, for repayment of the entire $3,000,000 loan balance.

OBSERVATION: In applying the alternative accounting, the PCC decided that a private company lessee would not be required to provide VIE disclosures about the lessor entity.

Rather, the private company lessee would disclose (a) the amount and key terms of liabilities recognized by the lessor entity that expose the private company lessee to providing financial support to the lessor entity and (b) a qualitative description of circumstances not recognized in the financial statements of the lessor entity that expose the private company lessee to providing financial support to the lessor entity. In applying the disclosure guidance, a private-company lessee shall also consider the lessee's *exposure through implicit guarantees.*

The disclosures under this alternative are required in combination with the disclosures required by other Topics (e.g., ASC 460, *Guarantees*, ASC 840, *Leases*, and ASC 850, *Related Party Disclosures*) about the lessor entity.

The disclosures could be made by aggregating all disclosures in a single note or by including cross-references within the notes to financial statements. In addition, entities that elect this alternative should continue to apply consolidation guidance other than VIE guidance in Topic 810 as well as other applicable guidance, including Topics 460 and 840.

¶ 113 EFFECTIVE DATE AND TRANSITION

The following represents the effective date and transition information related to ASU 2014-07—*Consolidation (Topic 810): Applying Variable Interest Entities Guidance to Common Control Leasing Arrangements.*

Effective Date

The election to apply the accounting alternative shall be effective for the first annual period beginning after December 15, 2014, and interim periods within annual periods beginning after December 15, 2015. Early application is permitted for any annual or interim period before which an entity's financial statements are available to be issued.

That means that many private companies can elect the ASU for calendar year 2014 as long as the financial statements for 2014 are not yet available to be issued. Financial statements are considered available to be issued when:

- They are complete in a form and format that complies with GAAP.
- All approvals necessary for issuance have been obtained.

For most private companies, that date is likely to be somewhere around March or April 2015.

If the entity chooses to present comparative financial statements for 2013 along with 2014, the four-criteria test must be met on January 1, 2013, the beginning of the first year presented.

Moreover, if applied to the beginning of the prior year (e.g., January 1, 2013) and assuming the four criteria are met, those same criteria must be satisfied from January 1, 2013 forward through December 31, 2014.

Retrospective Application

Application of the accounting alternative is an *accounting policy election.* The election shall be applied *retrospectively* to all periods presented. Retrospective application is defined in ASC 250, *Accounting Changes and Error Corrections*, and requires application of the accounting policy election to all previously issued financial statements, or to the statement of financial position at the beginning of the current period if comparative financial statements for prior periods are not presented. The test of the four criteria is done as of the beginning of the first year presented.

If a reporting entity deconsolidates a VIE as a result of the application of the ASU, the reporting entity shall initially measure any retained interest in the deconsolidated VIE at its carrying amount at the date the ASU first applies. In this context, *carrying amount* refers to the amount at which any retained interest would have been carried in the reporting entity's financial statements if the ASU had been effective when the reporting entity became involved with the VIE. Any difference between the net amount removed from the statement of financial position of the reporting entity and the amount of any retained interest in the deconsolidated VIE shall be recognized as a cumulative-effect adjustment to retained earnings. The amount of any cumulative-effect adjustment related to deconsolidation shall be disclosed separately.

Transition Disclosures

An entity shall provide the disclosures in ASC 250, *Accounting Changes and Error Corrections,* paragraphs 250-10-50-1 through 50-3 except for paragraph 250-10-50-1(b)(2) in the period the entity adopts the election found in the ASU.

An entity shall disclose all of the following in the fiscal period in which a change in accounting principle is made:

- The nature of and reason for the change in accounting principle, including an explanation of why the newly adopted accounting principle is preferable.
- The method of applying the change, including all of the following:

  - A description of the prior-period information that has been retrospectively adjusted, if any

  - The cumulative effect of the change on retained earnings or other components of equity or net assets in the statement of financial position as of the beginning of the earliest period presented

  - If retrospective application to all prior periods is impracticable, disclosure of the reasons why and a description of the alternative method used to report the change

- If indirect effects of a change in accounting principle are recognized, both of the following shall be disclosed:

  - A description of the indirect effects of a change in accounting principle, including the amounts that have been recognized in the current period, and the related per-share amounts, if applicable

  - Unless impracticable, the amount of the total recognized indirect effects of the accounting change and the related per-share amounts, if applicable, that are attributable to each prior period presented (Compliance with this disclosure requirement is practicable unless an entity cannot comply with it after making every reasonable effort to do so.)

An entity that issues interim financial statements shall provide the required disclosures in the financial statements of both the interim period of the change and the annual period of the change.

In the fiscal year in which a new accounting principle is adopted, financial information reported for interim periods after the date of adoption shall disclose the effect of the change on income from continued operations, net income (or other appropriate captions of changes in the applicable net assets or performance indicators), and related per-share amounts, if applicable, for those post-change interim periods.

Examples

> **EXAMPLE 1:** Company Y is a lessee with a calendar year end. For year ended December 31, 2013, Y consolidated a real estate lessee under common ownership, as required under the VIE rules.

Y wishes to elect the accounting alternative under ASU 2014-07 to a lessor entity as soon as possible. Lessee's accountant performs a review engagement on an annual basis. The engagement is completed and the financial statements are generally "available to be issued" by March 31 of each year. Y wants to continue to present comparative financial statements for 2013.

Conclusion: Y can implement the election and avoid consolidating the real estate leasing entity effective January 1, 2014 as long as the election is reflected in the financial statements on or before the 2014 year-end financial statements are available to be issued. That date is March 31, 2015.

Because Y wants to present comparative financial statements for 2013, Y must perform the four-criteria test *retrospectively to January 1, 2013*. Assuming the four criteria are satisfied as of January 1, 2013 and continue to be satisfied through 2014, Y is permitted to use the election for 2014 and also restate 2013 financial statements to reflect the retrospective application of the ASU.

What that means is that for December 31, 2014:

- Y will not consolidate the lessor entity into Y's financial statements.
- Y will restate the 2013 financial statements to exclude X from Y's financial statements and Y's opening balance sheet on January 1, 2013, the beginning of the earliest year presented.
- In the restated 2013 financial statements, the January 1, 2013 noncontrolling interest should be reversed off in the statement of equity.

When done, the 2013 and 2014 comparative financial statements will have no consolidation of the lessor entity, as if consolidation had never occurred.

> **EXAMPLE 2:** Same facts as Example 1, except that Y decides to elect the accounting alternative for 2014, but does not want to present comparative financial statements for 2013.

Conclusion: Y elects the accounting alternative as of January 1, 2014 and should issue Y's 2014 financial statements without any consolidation of X. The opening balance sheet at January 1, 2014 (the beginning of the earliest year presented), shall be restated to exclude the previous year's consolidation of X. The noncontrolling interest balance at January 1, 2014 should be reversed in the statement of stockholders' equity.

> **NOTE:** Examples illustrating the application of ASU 2014-07 in the financial statements are included in Appendix B.

STUDY QUESTIONS

---

7. A private manufacturing company lessee has guaranteed the mortgage for a lessor under common control, secured by real estate leased to the private company lessee. Subsequently, the lessee guarantees an additional mortgage of the lessor, secured by real estate not leased by the lessee. Which of the following is correct?

- **a.** The lessee satisfies Criterion 3 of ASU 2014-07.
- **b.** The lessee probably fails Criterion 3 of ASU 2014-07.
- **c.** The fact that the lessee guarantees the additional mortgage has no bearing on whether the lessee satisfies Criterion 3 of ASU 2014-07.
- **d.** The lessee satisfies Criterion 3 as long as the additional mortgage is not greater than 50 percent of the first mortgage's balance.

8. Company Y, a private company lessee, elects not to consolidate X, a lessor, using ASU 2014-07's election to use the accounting alternative. Which of the following is correct?

    a. Y will not consolidate X under any circumstances.

    b. Y could still consolidate X.

    c. Y is not permitted to consolidate X once the election is made.

    d. GAAP does not address what to do outside of the ASU 2014-07 election.

9. In accordance with ASU 2014-07, how should the election to apply the accounting alternative be applied?

    a. Prospectively by applying it only for future periods

    b. Retrospectively to all periods presented

    c. Retroactively with a cumulative effect of the change presented as a line item in the income statement

    d. As a change in accounting estimate

MODULE 1: ONGOING ISSUES—Chapter 2: ASU 2014-03: Derivatives and Hedging—Certain Interest-Rate Swaps

¶ 201 WELCOME

This chapter discusses Accounting Standards Update (ASU) 2014-03, which provides private companies an additional hedge accounting alternative to be applied to certain types of swaps that are entered into to economically convert a variable-rate borrowing into a fixed-rate borrowing.

¶ 202 LEARNING OBJECTIVES

Upon completion of this chapter, the reader will be able to:

- Review some of the criteria that qualify and do not qualify for cash flow hedge accounting
- Identify an eligible entity that can use the simplified hedge accounting approach
- Recall the effective date and transition rules for ASU 2014-03

¶ 203 INTRODUCTION

ASU 2014-03—*Derivatives and Hedging (Topic 815): Accounting for Certain Receive-Variable, Pay-Fixed Interest-Rate Swaps—Simplified Hedge Accounting Approach (a consensus of the Private Company Council)*, was issued in January 2014. The objective of the ASU is to provide to nonpublic (private) entities an additional hedge accounting alternative within ASC 815, *Derivatives and Hedging*, for certain "plain-vanilla" swaps that are entered into by a private company for the purpose of economically converting a variable-rate borrowing into a fixed-rate borrowing.

¶ 204 BACKGROUND

Accounting Standards Update (ASU) 2014-03 represents the second ASU issued by the FASB's Private Company Council (PCC). The PCC, which was established in 2012, placed several projects on its docket to provide exemptions and modifications to existing GAAP for nonpublic (private) entities.

Based on its outreach, the PCC received input that private companies often find it difficult to obtain fixed-rate borrowing. Therefore, some private companies enter into a receive-variable, pay-fixed interest-rate swap to economically convert their variable-rate borrowing into a fixed-rate borrowing.

Under existing U.S. GAAP, an interest-rate swap is a derivative instrument. ASC 815, *Derivatives and Hedging*, requires that an entity recognize all interest-rate swaps on its balance sheet as either assets or liabilities and measure them at fair value. To mitigate the income statement volatility of recording a swap's change in fair value, ASC 815 permits an entity to elect hedge accounting if certain requirements under ASC 815 are met, including formal designation and concurrent documentation at hedge inception and periodic evaluations of hedge effectiveness. For perfectly matching swap and borrowing, cash flow hedge accounting means displaying interest expense in the income statement as if the entity had issued a fixed-rate borrowing.

Some private company stakeholders contend that because of limited resources and the fact that hedge accounting is difficult to understand and apply, many private companies lack the expertise to comply with the requirements to qualify for hedge accounting. Therefore, they do not elect to apply hedge accounting, which results in income statement volatility. This is due to changes in the fair value of the receive-variable, pay-fixed interest-rate swap being recognized in earnings without any other accounting entries to show that the private company has economically converted its variable-rate borrowing into a fixed-rate borrowing by entering into that swap. In addition, some stakeholders have questioned the relevance and cost associated with determining and presenting the fair value of a swap that is entered into for the purpose of economically converting a variable-rate borrowing to a fixed-rate borrowing.

ASU 2014-03 provides private companies an additional hedge accounting alternative to be applied to certain types of swaps that are entered into in order to economically convert a variable-rate borrowing into a fixed-rate borrowing.

¶ 205 EXPLANATION OF CURRENT INTEREST-RATE SWAP RULES FOR PRIVATE COMPANIES

Private companies enter into receive-variable, pay-fixed interest-rate swaps to economically convert their variable-rate debt to fixed-rate debt. Under existing GAAP, an interest-rate swap is a derivative. Using a receive-variable, pay-fixed interest-rate swap, an entity receives a variable rate and pays the swap counterparty a fixed rate (the swap rate) on the notional amount of the swap. The variable rate paid on the debt is offset by the variable rate received from the swap counterparty; however, the company still has to pay the agreed fixed rate on the swap (and any credit spread on the debt). In essence, the interest-rate swap fixes the interest rate associated with the debt and mitigates the exposure to the risk of changes in cash flows due to changes in interest rates.

ASC 815, *Derivatives and Hedging*, requires that an entity recognize all of its derivative instruments on its balance sheet as either assets or liabilities and measure them at fair value.

To mitigate the income statement effect of recording an interest-rate swap on the balance sheet at fair value, ASC 815 permits an entity to elect "cash flow hedge" accounting. A cash flow hedge is a hedge of the exposure to variability in the cash flows of a recognized asset or liability, or of a forecasted transaction, that is attributable to a particular risk, such as interest rate risk.

In applying cash flow hedge accounting, ASC 815, *Derivatives and Hedging*, paragraph 815-20-35-1 provides that:

- The effective portion of the gain or loss on a derivative instrument designated in a cash flow hedge should be initially reported in *other comprehensive income*.
- The ineffective portion should be reported in earnings.

The amounts in accumulated other comprehensive income (see above) are reclassified into earnings in the same period or periods during which the hedged forecasted transaction affects earnings.

The result is that in a plain-vanilla interest-rate swap with variable-rate debt, the accounting should result in presenting interest expense in the income statement as if the entity had issued fixed-rate debt. That is, interest expense should equal the amount of interest had a fixed-rate loan been obtained.

In order to qualify for cash flow hedge accounting, ASC 815-20-25 states that the following criteria must be met. There must be:

- Formal designation and documentation at hedge inception
- Eligibility of hedged items and transactions
- Eligibility of hedging instruments
- Hedging effectiveness

GAAP also requires timely documentation and formal designation of a hedging relationship to qualify for hedge accounting at the inception of the hedge.

Yet, many nonpublic (private) companies lack the expertise to comply with the requirements to qualify for cash-flow hedge accounting and do not have the resources necessary to prepare the documentation. Therefore, many private companies do not elect to apply hedge accounting.

¶ 206 DEFINITIONS USED WITHIN ASU 2014-03

The ASU adds the following definitions to the glossary of ASU 815, *Derivatives and Hedging:*

Nonperformance Risk

Nonperformance risk is the risk that an entity will not fulfill an obligation. Nonperformance risk includes, but may not be limited to, the reporting entity's own credit risk.

Financial Statements Are Available to Be Issued

Financial statements are considered available to be issued when they are complete in a form and format that complies with GAAP and all approvals necessary for issuance have been obtained, for example, from management, the board of directors, and/or significant shareholders. The process involved in creating and distributing the financial statements will vary depending on an entity's management and corporate governance structure as well as statutory and regulatory requirements.

Not-for-Profit Entity

A not-for-profit entity is an entity that possesses the following characteristics, in varying degrees, that distinguish it from a business entity:

- Contributions of significant amounts of resources from resource providers who do not expect commensurate or proportionate pecuniary return
- Operating purposes other than to provide goods or services at a profit
- Absence of ownership interests like those of business entities

Entities that clearly fall outside this definition include the following:

- All investor-owned entities
- Entities that provide dividends, lower costs, or other economic benefits directly and proportionately to their owners, members, or participants, such as mutual insurance entities, credit unions, farm and rural electric cooperatives, and employee benefit plans.

Private Company

A private company is an entity, other than a public business entity, a not-for-profit entity, or an employee benefit plan on plan accounting. (Such benefit plans are covered by ASC 960 and ASC 965.)

Public Business Entity

A public business entity is a public business entity meeting any one of the criteria below. Neither a not-for-profit entity nor an employee benefit plan is a business entity.

- It is required by the U.S. Securities and Exchange Commission (SEC) to file or furnish financial statements, or does file or furnish financial statements (including voluntary filers), with the SEC (including other entities whose financial statements or financial information are required to be or are included in a filing).

- It is required by the Securities Exchange Act of 1934 (the Act), as amended, or rules or regulations promulgated under the Act, to file or furnish financial statements with a regulatory agency other than the SEC.

- It is required to file or furnish financial statements with a foreign or domestic regulatory agency in preparation for the sale of, or for purposes of, issuing securities that are not subject to contractual restrictions on transfer.

- It has issued, or is a conduit bond obligor for, securities that are traded, listed, or quoted on an exchange or an over-the-counter market.

- It has one or more securities that are not subject to contractual restrictions on transfer, and it is required by law, contract, or regulation to prepare U.S. GAAP financial statements (including footnotes) and make them publicly available on a periodic basis (e.g., interim or annual periods). An entity must meet both of these conditions to meet this criterion.

An entity may meet the definition of a public business entity solely because its financial statements or financial information is included in another entity's filing with the SEC. In that case, the entity is only a public business entity for purposes of financial statements that are filed or furnished with the SEC.

¶ 207 SCOPE

The simplified hedge accounting approach may be used only for an eligible entity. An eligible entity is one that is a private company. It is *not* available for any of the following entities:

- A public business entity
- Not-for-profit entity
- Employee benefit plan
- Financial institutions, including banks, savings and loan associations, savings banks, credit unions, finance companies, and insurance entities

The PCC decided not to include financial institutions because those entities usually use many derivative instruments recorded at fair value. Therefore, introducing the concept of settlement value for certain types of swaps could be confusing to users. Also, financial institutions generally have sufficient resources to comply with the current ASC 815 GAAP requirements. Additionally, the PCC noted that application of the scope exception to swaps accounted for under the simplified accounting approach may not be appropriate for financial institutions, considering their greater exposure to financial instruments and the relevance of fair value accounting for those instruments. The FASB and the PCC recognize that decisions about whether an entity may apply alternatives within U.S. GAAP for private companies may ultimately be decided by regulators, lenders, and other creditors or other financial statement users that require U.S. GAAP financial statements.

STUDY QUESTIONS

1. Which of the following is defined as a private company under ASU 2014-03?

    a. Nonpublic entity

    b. Not-for-profit entity

    c. Public business entity

    d. Employee benefit plan

2. Under ASU 2014-03, financial statements are considered _____ when they are complete in a form and format that complies with GAAP and all approvals for issuance have been obtained.

    a. Ready to distribute

    b. Issued

    c. Available to be issued

    d. Finalized

¶ 208 RULES

The general rule is that all derivative instruments shall be measured at fair value.

The simplified hedge accounting approach may be applied by an eligible entity (private company) to a cash-flow hedge of a variable-rate borrowing with a receive-variable, pay-fixed interest-rate swap.

A receive-variable, pay-fixed interest-rate swap for which the simplified hedge accounting approach is applied may be measured subsequently at *settlement value* instead of fair value. The primary difference between settlement value and fair value is that nonperformance risk is not considered in determining settlement value. One approach for estimating the receive-variable, pay-fixed interest-rate swap's settlement value is to perform a present value calculation of the swap's remaining estimated cash flows using a valuation technique that is not adjusted for nonperformance risk.

Interest expense is recorded as though the entity had fixed-rate borrowing as opposed to a variable-interest rate borrowing.

In order to use the simplified hedge accounting approach, a private entity must satisfy all of the following additional conditions:

- Both the variable rate on the swap and the borrowing must be based on the same index and reset period. In complying with this condition, an entity is not limited to benchmark interest rates described in ASC 815, *Derivatives and Hedging*, Subtopic 815-20-25-6A.

  NOTE: ASC 815-20-25-6A defines benchmark interest rates to include rates on direct U.S. Treasury obligations and the London Interbank Offered Rate (LIBOR) swap rate.

  EXAMPLE: Both the swap and borrowing are based on one-month LIBOR, or both the swap and borrowing are based on the three-month LIBOR.

- The swap must be a typical, "plain-vanilla" swap, and there must be no floor or cap on the variable interest rate of the swap unless the borrowing has a *comparable* floor or cap.

  NOTE: In complying with this condition, the term "comparable" does not necessarily mean equal.

  EXAMPLE: If the swap's variable rate is the LIBOR and the borrowing's variable rate is LIBOR plus two percent, a 10 percent cap on the swap would be comparable to a 12 percent cap on the borrowing.

- The re-pricing and settlement dates for the swap and the borrowing must match or differ by no more than a few days.

- The swap's fair value at inception (i.e., at the time the derivative was executed to hedge the interest rate risk of the borrowing) must be at or near zero.

- The notional amount of the swap must match the principal amount of the borrowing being hedged. In complying with this condition, the amount of the borrowing being hedged may be less than the total principal amount of the borrowing.

> **NOTE:** For a forward-starting swap, only the effective term of the receive-variable, pay-fixed interest-rate swap (i.e., from its effective date through its expiration date) shall be considered in complying with this condition. The period from the swap's inception to the date the swap is effective shall not be considered in complying with this condition because the effective date of a forward-starting swap occurs after the swap's inception.

> **EXAMPLE:** A forward-starting receive-variable, pay-fixed, interest-rate swap with a five-year effective term and an effective date commencing one year after the swap's inception would meet this condition if designated as a hedge of a five-year, variable-rate borrowing forecasted to be entered into one year after the swap's inception.

- All interest payments occurring on the borrowing during the term of the swap (or the effective term of the swap underlying the forward starting swap) must be designated as hedged whether in total or in proportion to the principal amount of the borrowing being hedged.

> **NOTE:** A cash-flow hedge established through the use of a forward-starting receive-variable, pay-fixed interest-rate swap may be permitted in applying the simplified hedge accounting approach only if the occurrence of forecasted interest payments to be swapped is probable. When forecasted interest payments are no longer probable of occurring, a cash-flow hedging relationship will no longer qualify for the simplified hedge accounting approach and the General Subsections of ASC 815, *Derivatives and Hedging*, shall apply at the date of change and on a prospective basis.

Assumption That There is No Ineffectiveness in the Cash Flow Hedging Relationship

If all of the conditions to use a simplified hedging accounting approach are met, an entity may assume that there is no ineffectiveness in a cash-flow hedging relationship involving a variable-rate borrowing and a receive-variable, pay-fixed interest-rate swap.

Subsequent Change in Required Conditions

If any of the conditions for applying the simplified hedge accounting approach subsequently cease to be met or the relationship otherwise ceases to qualify for hedge accounting, the General Subsections of ASC 815, *Derivatives and Hedging,* shall apply at the date of change and on a prospective basis.

> **EXAMPLES:** If the related variable-rate borrowing is prepaid without terminating the receive-variable, pay-fixed interest-rate swap, the gain or loss on the swap in accumulated other comprehensive income shall be reclassified to earnings with the swap measured at fair value on the date of change and subsequent changes in fair value reported in earnings.

> If the receive-variable, pay-fixed interest-rate swap is terminated early without the related variable-rate borrowing being prepaid, the gain or loss on the swap in accumulated other comprehensive income shall be reclassified to earnings.

Documentation Requirements

In applying the simplified hedge accounting approach, the documentation required by ASC 815, *Derivatives and Hedging*, paragraph 815-20-25-3 to qualify for hedge accounting must be completed *by the date on which the first annual financial statements are available to be issued* after hedge inception rather than concurrently at hedge inception.

> **NOTE:** ASC 815-20-25-3 requires an entity to document certain items to qualify for hedge accounting including the hedging relationship, and the entity's risk management objective and strategy for undertaking the hedge, among others.

Disclosures

If the simplified hedge accounting approach is applied in accounting for a qualifying receive-variable, pay-fixed interest-rate swap, the settlement value of that swap may be used in place of fair value when disclosing the information required by this ASU or in providing other fair value disclosures, such as those required under ASC 820, *Fair Value Measurements and Disclosures*, on fair value. For the purposes of complying with these disclosure requirements, amounts disclosed at settlement value will be subject to all of the same disclosure requirements as amounts disclosed at fair value. Any amounts disclosed at settlement value shall be clearly stated as such and disclosed separately from amounts disclosed at fair value.

Private Company Exemption

Private companies that elect to use the simplified hedge accounting approach are exempt from most of the fair disclosures. Private companies electing to use the simplified hedge accounting approach are exempt from the fair value disclosures found in ASC 825, *Financial Instruments*, paragraphs 825-10-50-10 through 50-16.

The ASU clarifies that for purposes of determining whether an entity is exempt from fair value disclosures under ASC 825, *Financial Instruments*, an interest-rate swap recorded using the simplified hedge accounting approach is not considered a derivative instrument under ASC 815.

> **NOTE:** ASC paragraph 825-10-50-3 states that certain entities are exempt from fair value disclosures only if all of the following conditions are met:
>
> - The entity is a nonpublic entity.
> - The entity's total assets are less than $100 million on the date of the financial statements.
> - The entity has no instrument that, in whole or in part, is accounted for as a derivative instrument under ASC 815 other than commitments related to the origination of mortgage loans to be held for sale during the reporting period.

ASU 2014-03 confirms that an interest-rate swap is not considered a derivative if the simplified method is elected.

¶ 209 EFFECTIVE DATE AND TRANSITION

The provisions of ASU 2014-03 shall be effective for annual periods beginning after December 15, 2014, and interim periods within annual periods beginning after December 15, 2015. Early application of the ASU is permitted for any annual or interim period for which the entity's financial statements have not yet been made available for issuance.

The rules found in ASU 2014-03 related to the simplified hedge accounting approach shall be applied in either of the following ways:

- Using a modified retrospective approach in which corresponding adjustments shall be made to the assets, liabilities, and opening balance of accumulated other comprehensive income and retained earnings (or other appropriate components of equity) of the current period presented to reflect application of hedge accounting under the ASU from the date the receive-variable, pay-fixed interest-rate swap was entered into (or acquired) by the entity

- Using a full retrospective approach in which the financial statements for each individual prior period presented shall be adjusted to reflect the period-specific effects of applying hedge accounting under ASU 2014-03 from the date the receive-variable, pay-fixed interest-rate swap was entered into (or acquired) by the entity. Corresponding adjustments shall be made to the assets, liabilities, and opening balance of accumulated other comprehensive income and retained earnings (or other appropriate components of equity) of the earliest period presented to reflect application of hedge accounting under this ASU from the date the receive-variable, pay-fixed interest-rate swap was entered into (or acquired) by the entity.

The simplified hedge accounting approach may be elected for any qualifying receive-variable, pay-fixed interest-rate swap, whether existing at the date of adoption of the ASU or entered into after that date. The election to apply the simplified hedge accounting approach to an existing swap shall be made upon adoption of the ASU.

In determining whether an existing swap meets all of the conditions to qualify for applying the simplified hedge accounting approach, the condition that the swap's fair value at the time of application of this approach is at or near zero need not be considered. Instead, as long as the swap's fair value was at or near zero at the time the swap was entered into (or acquired) by the entity, the entity may apply the simplified hedge accounting approach. For an existing swap, the documentation required by ASC 815, *Derivatives and Hedging*, paragraph 815-20-25-3 to qualify for hedge accounting must be completed in the period of adoption by the date on which the first annual financial statements are available to be issued, rather than concurrently at hedge inception.

An entity shall provide the disclosures in ASC 250, *Accounting Changes and Error Corrections*, paragraphs 250-10-50-1 through 50-3 in the period that the entity adopts ASU 2014-03.

STUDY QUESTION

---

3. Under ASU 2014-03, the simplified hedge accounting approach may be used for which of the following?

    a. Foreign exchange hedge

    b. Cash flow hedge

    c. Materials purchase commitments

    d. Inflation rate hedge

MODULE 1: ONGOING ISSUES — CHAPTER 3: Accounting for Uncertain State Tax Positions

¶ 301 WELCOME

This chapter reviews accounting for uncertainty in state income taxes, looking at some of the complex issues an enterprise may face when applying recognition standards of FASB ASC 740 to its state and local income tax positions.

¶ 302 LEARNING OBJECTIVES

Upon completion of this chapter, the reader will be able to:

- Recall how GAAP addresses uncertainty in state income taxes in FASB Accounting Standards Codification (ASC) Subtopic 740-10
- Identify the GAAP recognition threshold for state tax positions
- Review the GAAP measurement guidance for state tax positions
- Recall GAAP's two-step process to state tax positions arising from intercompany transactions
- Recognize the incremental disclosures required for unrecognized tax benefits

¶ 303 BACKGROUND

GAAP states that the two objectives of accounting for income taxes are to recognize current tax consequences, whether payable or refundable, and future tax consequences of events that have been recognized, again, whether these taxes will be payable or refundable. (FASB ASC 740-10-10-1.)

Often, there are temporary differences (FASB ASC Master Glossary) because of inconsistencies between tax laws and the GAAP requirements. A deferred tax liability is recognized for temporary differences that will result in taxes payable in future years, while a deferred tax asset is a temporary difference that will result in tax savings in future years. GAAP addresses related issues, such as measurement and consequences of changes in tax laws and rates. (FASB ASC 740)

Compliance with state and local income tax laws for entities with complex legal structures and operations in numerous jurisdictions can be a daunting undertaking. One matter that arises is whether and how uncertainty in income taxes, including state and local income taxes, should affect the related accounting.

Therefore, it should come as no surprise that complex issues will arise when accounting for uncertainty in state and local income tax positions. GAAP addresses these issues by setting forth a recognition threshold for all tax positions and a measurement attribute to be applied to tax positions that meet the threshold. Through the use of an example, this chapter will highlight a few of the complex issues an entity may face when applying this guidance to its state and local income tax positions.

(As a result of Codification, the guidance formerly found in FIN 48 and FAS 109 is now incorporated in FASB ASC 740, *Income Taxes*.)

STUDY QUESTION

1. How does GAAP address state income tax positions that involve uncertainty?
    a. Recognize those meeting a basic threshold and apply the stated measurement attribute
    b. Recognize all and measure at fair value
    c. Combines recognition and measurement based on the expected outcome
    d. Merely disclose uncertainty in income taxes

¶ 304 TAX POSITIONS

Introduction

GAAP defines a tax position (FASB ASC Master Glossary) to include a filing position on a previously filed return and an expected filing position in a future tax return reflected in measuring current or deferred income tax assets and liabilities for interim or annual periods.

Significantly, the GAAP definition of a tax position includes:

- A decision not to file a tax return
- An allocation or a shift of income between jurisdictions
- The characterization of income or a decision to exclude reporting taxable income in a tax return
- A decision to classify a transaction, entity, or other position in a tax return as tax exempt
- An entity's status, including its status as a pass-through entity or a tax-exempt not-for-profit entity

The Two-Step Process

GAAP uses a two-step process for evaluating an entity's tax position taken or expected to be taken in a tax return (FASB ASC 740-10-55-3). Before a tax position can be evaluated through this two-step process, the appropriate unit of account must be determined.

GAAP requires that the determination of the unit of account to be used consider the manner in which the entity prepares and supports its income tax return and the approach the entity anticipates the taxing authority will take during an examination. (FASB ASC 740-10-25-13)

After the unit of account for determining what constitutes an individual tax position has been identified, the tax position must then be analyzed under the two-step process involving a basic recognition threshold (step one) and a measurement attribute (step two). For purposes of the first step (recognition), an entity must determine whether it is more-likely-than-not that a tax position, based on the technical merits, will be sustained upon ultimate resolution in the court of last resort. (FASB ASC 740-10-55-3) In considering the technical merits, GAAP requires that the entity take into account widely understood past administrative practices and precedents. (FASB ASC 740-10-25-7(b))

A tax position that isn't recognized (step one) isn't measured (step two). If a tax position meets the more-likely-than-not recognition threshold and is recognized (step one), then it is measured (step two). (FASB ASC 740-10-30-7)

The Recognition Standard

GAAP provides that an entity recognize the effects of a tax position "when it is more-likely-than-not, based on the technical merits, that the position will be sustained upon examination." (FASB ASC 740-10-25-6)

Because GAAP requires the entity to presume that the tax position will be examined, the likelihood of a tax audit is irrelevant. As one might imagine, the key issue is definition of the phrase "more-likely-than-not." GAAP assumes all of the following criteria when assessing whether the more-likely-than-not recognition threshold is met:

- The tax position will be examined by the relevant taxing authority and the tax authority has full knowledge of all relevant information.
- Technical merits of the tax position derive from sources of tax law authority and facts and circumstances are applicable to the tax position, including consideration of certain administrative practices and precedents of the taxing authority.
- Tax position is evaluated without considering the possibility of offset or aggregation with other positions. (FASB ASC 740-10-25-7)

While a legal tax opinion is not needed to demonstrate that the more-likely-than-not recognition threshold has been met, paragraph B34 of FASB Staff Interpretation (FIN) No. 48 states that "a tax opinion can be external evidence supporting a management assertion and that management should decide whether to obtain a tax opinion after evaluating the weight of all available evidence and the uncertainties of the applicability of the relevant statutory or case law." That paragraph also states that:

> [o]ther evidence, in addition to or instead of a tax opinion, supporting the assertion also could be obtained; the level of evidence that is necessary and appropriate is a matter of judgment that depends on all available information." Thus, the tax opinion of a qualified expert is only one item of evidence that management may consider in reaching its reporting conclusions. (Paragraph B34 of FIN 48 is historical information about the basis for FASB's conclusions about accounting for uncertainty in income taxes and was not codified in the FASB ASC.)

Derecognition

GAAP also addresses the consequences when a tax position no longer meets the more-likely-than-not recognition threshold. In this event, the position is derecognized (removed from the financial statements) by increasing or decreasing the deferred tax liability or deferred tax asset. (FASB ASC 740-10-40-2)

STUDY QUESTIONS

2. What must a taxpayer do before applying the two-step process?

- **a.** Determine a more-likely-than-not tax position
- **b.** Measure the tax position
- **c.** Decide whether to file a tax return
- **d.** Determine an appropriate unit of account

3. All of the following are true statements about the more-likely-than-not recognition threshold, *except:*

   a. It is assumed that the tax position will be examined by the relevant tax authority.

   b. As required, the entity has obtained a legal tax opinion with regard to its tax position.

   c. The tax position is evaluated without considering offset with other tax positions.

   d. The technical merits of the tax position derive from sources of tax law authority.

¶ 305 APPLICATION

Introduction

The following example highlights some of the key issues that an entity may face when applying GAAP on uncertainty in income taxes to its state income tax positions.

Company A is a retailer that has income tax nexus with all states and files income tax returns in the appropriate jurisdictions. Company A has a subsidiary, Company B, that manages Company A's intangibles. Company A and Company B also have various intercompany transactions related to management services that Company B provides to Company A. Company B was incorporated in a state without an income tax, and does not file state income tax returns in any state. Both Company A and Company B have been operating at a profit for the last 20 years.

The GAAP definition of "tax position" encompasses a decision by an entity not to file a tax return. Therefore, Company B's decision in the above example not to file state income tax returns in any state is a tax position in each state in which a tax return was not filed.

The unit of account for analyzing each tax position will vary from state to state based, in part, on the approach the entity anticipates the taxing authority will take during an examination. (FASB ASC 740-10-25-13) In other words, the states may use various approaches to attempt to tax Company B's income. We will now focus on four possible approaches a state taxing authority might take and how the unit of account related to Company B's non-filing position may vary.

Nexus Approach

A state taxing authority may assert that Company B has nexus (e.g., an economic nexus) with their state based on a statute, regulation, case or other applicable authority.

If an economic nexus approach is expected to be taken by the state, is it possible for Company B to meet the more-likely-than-not recognition threshold The more-likely-than-not recognition threshold is met if the reporting entity (the taxpayer) concludes it is more-likely-than-not that it will sustain its tax position in a dispute with the state taxing authority if the taxpayer takes the dispute to the court of last resort. (FASB ASC 740-10-55-3)

In the case of a nexus determination, as with other constitutional issues, the court of last resort is the U.S. Supreme Court. Is there more than a 50 percent likelihood that the U.S. Supreme Court would sustain Company B's tax position on its technical merits? If not, Company B would account for the direct taxation of its income in all economic nexus states without being able to recognize the benefit of the tax position.

Remember that, in assessing the likelihood, Company B would consider widely understood past administrative practices or precedents. (FASB ASC 740-10-25-7(b)). Company B's assessment would not include other tax positions, such as those related to apportionment factor determinations. (FASB ASC 740-10-25-7(c))

Forced Combination Approach

A state taxing authority may attempt to force combination of Company A and Company B. If Company B cannot reach the more-likely-than-not recognition threshold that it can preclude forced combination, then the entities would not be permitted to recognize the benefit of the tax position as part of accounting for any tax liability.

However, for purposes of determining any tax liability, additional analysis would be required, as the tax liability under a forced combination may be different than it would be if Company B's income were taxed directly by the state.

Expense Adjustment Approach

A state taxing authority may attack the transactions between the two companies in an attempt to reduce the expense in Company A. The intercompany transactions between Company A and Company B may give rise to uncertainty in the tax positions if they are not supported by a valuation or a current transfer-pricing study.

What if a transfer-pricing study is in place, but it is based on 10-year-old comparables and there has been a significant change in facts and circumstances? In both circumstances, this introduces uncertainty about the tax position due to potential state income tax exposure for the entity whose taxable income is understated.

Income Reallocation Approach

Finally, a state taxing authority may look to a more general statutory or regulatory authority to reallocate income between the two related entities to properly reflect the income related to each entity's activity in the state.

For example, if it is believed that a state will take this approach, and Company B does not believe it is more-likely-than-not that its tax position will be sustained, then Company B must account for income taxes based upon the manner in which it believes the state will reallocate income.

The Look-Back Issue

What if, after determining the unit of account to address the potential attack on Company B's income (or Company A's expenses), it is not more-likely-than-not that the entity's non-filing position will be sustained upon examination in a particular state? In some states, the decision not to file a state tax return may never start the statute of limitations. Under these circumstances, is Company B required to look back 20 years?

In determining a state income tax provision, GAAP requires that an entity consider widely understood past practices and precedents of a particular state to determine the look-back period. (FASB ASC 740-10-25-7(b)) What if the practice or precedent in State X is to analyze each taxpayer's facts and circumstances on a case-by-case basis to determine the appropriate look-back periods? What is the best way to document this practice or precedent?

These questions need to be addressed to determine whether the more-likely-than-not recognition threshold has been met. A 20-year liability plus growing interest and penalties can quickly become a large amount, even though it is sometimes the case that a state will limit its look-back period to significantly less than 20 years.

STUDY QUESTIONS

---

4. All of the following are approaches a taxing authority may use when attempting to tax Company B's income, ***except:***

    a. Income Reallocation Approach

    b. Forced Combination Approach

    c. Look-Back Approach

    d. Nexus Approach

5. Which approach used by a state taxing authority to attempt to tax Company B's income would require Company A and Company B to support their tax position with a current transfer pricing study?

    a. Expense Adjustment Approach

    b. Forced Combination Approach

    c. Nexus Approach

    d. Income Reallocation Approach

¶ 306 THE MEASUREMENT STANDARD

Regarding any tax position discussed in the example above, what if the entities (Company A and Company B) determine that it is more-likely-than-not that the tax position will be sustained upon examination in a particular state? The entities would then measure the tax position under the second step of the process.

For purposes of measurement, the entities must consider the amounts and probabilities of the outcomes that could be realized upon ultimate settlement to determine the tax benefit to be recognized. (FASB ASC 740-10-30-7)

Therefore, it is possible that an entity can determine that the tax position meets the more-likely-than-not recognition threshold on the same state income tax position covering several states, but the relative "measured" tax benefit may vary in each of those states because the states may approach an ultimate plan of settlement differently.

¶ 307 INCREMENTAL DISCLOSURES

Every entity is required to disclose all of the following about its unrecognized tax benefits: (ASC 740-10-50-15)

- The total amounts of interest and penalties recognized in the statement of operations
- The total amounts of interest and penalties recognized in the statement of financial position
- For each tax position for which it is reasonably possible that the total amount of unrecognized tax benefits will significantly increase or decrease within 12 months of the reporting date, all of the following:

    - The nature of the uncertainty

    - The nature of the event that could occur in the next 12 months that would cause the change

    - An estimate of the range of the reasonably possible change or a statement that an estimate of the range cannot be made

Originally, the Financial Accounting Standards Board (FASB) undertook the liquidation basis of accounting as part of a going concern project whereby the FASB was attempting to incorporate going concern guidance into GAAP. In October 2008, the FASB issued an exposure draft entitled *Going Concern*. Based on the responses in letters of comment, the FASB chose to separate the liquidation basis of accounting from the going concern project, which, in July 2012, resulted in the FASB issuing an exposure draft entitled, *Presentation of Financial Statements (Topic 205): The Liquidation Basis of Accounting*. The exposure draft was passed as a final statement ASU 2013-07 in April 2013.

The ASU applies to all entities that issue financial statements presented in conformity with U.S. GAAP, except investment companies that are regulated under the Investment Company Act of 1940 (the 1940 Act).

¶ 405 DEFINITIONS USED IN ASU 2013-07

The ASU uses certain terms that are defined as follows:

- *Fair Value:* The price that would be received to sell an asset or paid to transfer a liability in an orderly transaction between market participants at the measurement date
- *Liquidation:* The process by which an entity converts its assets to cash or other assets and settles its obligations with creditors in anticipation of the entity ceasing all activities. Upon cessation of the entity's activities, any remaining cash or other assets are distributed to the entity's investors or other claimants (albeit sometimes indirectly). Liquidation may be compulsory or voluntary. Dissolution of an entity as a result of that entity being acquired by another entity or merged into another entity in its entirety and with the expectation of continuing its business does not qualify as liquidation.
- *Statement of Changes in Net Assets in Liquidation:* A statement that presents the changes during the period in net assets available for distribution to investors and other claimants during liquidation
- *Statement of Net Assets in Liquidation:* A statement that presents a liquidating entity's net assets available for distribution to investors and other claimants as of the end of the reporting period

¶ 406 SCOPE OF ASU 2013-07

ASU 2013-07 applies to all entities except for investment companies regulated under the Investment Company Act of 1940.

¶ 407 RULES OF ASU 2013-07

An entity should prepare financial statements under the assumption that the entity will continue to operate as a going concern.

> **EXAMPLE:** As a going concern, GAAP records assets and liabilities at cost, lower of cost or market, fair value, replacement cost, etc.

Liquidation Basis of Accounting

An entity shall prepare financial statements using the liquidation basis of accounting when liquidation is imminent. If liquidation is imminent, there is no longer an assumption that the entity will continue to operate as a going concern. The liquidation basis of accounting should not be used if the liquidation follows a plan for liquidation that was specified in the entity's governing documents at the entity's inception (limited-life entity).

- A description of tax years that remain subject to examination by major tax jurisdictions.

Every public entity must further disclose both of the following at the end of each annual reporting period presented: (ASC 740-10-50-15A)

- A tabular reconciliation of the total amounts of unrecognized tax benefits at the beginning and end of the period which has to include, at a minimum, all of the following:
  - The gross amounts of the increases and decreases in unrecognized tax benefits as a result of tax positions taken during a prior period
  - The gross amounts of increases and decreases in unrecognized tax benefits as a result of tax positions taken during the current period
  - The amounts of decreases in the unrecognized tax benefits relating to settlements with the taxing authorities
  - Reductions to unrecognized tax benefits as a result of a lapse of the applicable statute of limitations
- The total amount of unrecognized tax benefits that, if recognized, would affect the effective tax rate

STUDY QUESTION

6. Which of the following is **not** a disclosure required with respect to uncertainty in income taxes?

- **a.** The total amounts of interest and penalties recognized in the income statement
- **b.** The nature of any event that could occur in the next 12 months that would cause a significant increase or decrease in the total amount of unrecognized tax benefits for a tax position
- **c.** The amounts of unrecognized tax benefits attributable specifically to each tax position with a detailed description of the nature and assessment of each tax position.
- **d.** The entity's accounting policy for interest on unrecognized tax benefits

¶ 308 CONCLUSION

There is no doubt that an entity looks to tax practitioners for opinions to support management assertions regarding tax positions in financial statements.

Through the foregoing example, we have only scratched the surface of the complex issues that a business might face when applying GAAP to uncertainty in its state and local income tax positions. This course highlights the need for an entity to consider whether it has the resources in place to identify and analyze state income tax positions for purposes of GAAP.

CPE NOTE: When you have completed your study and review of chapters 1-3, which comprise Module 1, you may wish to take the Quizzer for this Module. Go to **CCHGroup.com/PrintCPE** to take this Quizzer online.

MODULE 2: FINANCIAL STATEMENT REPORTING — CHAPTER 4: Presentation of Financial Statements - Liquidation Basis

¶ 401 WELCOME

Accounting Standards Update (ASU) 2013-07—*Presentation of Financial Statements (Topic 205): Liquidation Basis of Accounting* was issued in April 2013. The objective of ASU 2013-07 is to clarify when an entity should apply the liquidation basis of accounting. This chapter reviews this ASU and discusses its guidance for the recognition and measurement of assets and liabilities and requirements for financial statements prepared using the liquidation basis of accounting.

¶ 402 LEARNING OBJECTIVES

Upon completion of this chapter, the reader will be able to:

- Recognize the definition of liquidation
- Recall how assets should be measured using the liquidation basis of accounting
- Identify a financial statement that is required when using the liquidation basis of accounting
- Recognize whether fair value disclosures are required when using the liquidation basis of accounting

¶ 403 OBJECTIVE

Accounting Standards Update (ASU) 2013-07—*Presentation of Financial Statements (Topic 205): Liquidation Basis of Accounting* was issued in April 2013. The objective of ASU 2013-07 is to clarify when an entity should apply the liquidation basis of accounting. In addition, the ASU's guidance provides principles for the recognition and measurement of assets and liabilities and requirements for financial statements prepared using the liquidation basis of accounting.

¶ 404 BACKGROUND

Currently, GAAP assumes that an entity will continue as a going concern, which is the reason why financial statements are recorded at a mixture of cost, lower of cost or market, fair value, and other measurements.

If an entity is not going to continue as a going concern, the entity's balance sheet should be recorded at liquidation value. In fact, the reason why an auditor modifies his or her audit report when there is "substantial doubt" of an entity's ability to continue as a going concern is because that entity's balance sheet is incorrectly presented. That is, if there is substantial doubt of going concern, the balance sheet should be adjusted to liquidation value.

To date, there has been little authoritative guidance as to when liquidation accounting should be used and how to apply it as well as required disclosures. International standards currently do not provide explicit guidance on when and how to apply the liquidation basis of accounting.

NOTE: The ASU states that an entity shall presume that its plan of liquidation does not follow a plan that was specified in the entity's governing documents at its inception if the entity is forced to dispose of its assets in exchange for consideration that is not commensurate with the fair value of those assets (such as a forced sale).

Other aspects of the entity's plan of liquidation also might differ from a plan that was specified in the entity's governing documents at its inception (e.g., the date at which liquidation shall commence). However, those factors should be considered in determining whether to apply the liquidation basis of accounting only to the extent that they affect whether the entity expects to receive consideration in exchange for its assets that is not commensurate with fair value.

Definition of Imminent

Liquidation is imminent when either of the following occurs:

- A plan for liquidation has been approved by the person or persons with the authority to make such a plan effective, and the likelihood is remote that any of the following will occur:

  - Execution of the plan will be blocked by other parties (e.g., those with shareholder rights).

  - The entity will return from liquidation.

- A plan for liquidation is imposed by other forces (e.g., involuntary bankruptcy), and the likelihood is remote that the entity will return from liquidation.

STUDY QUESTION

---

1. In accordance with ASU 2013-07, an entity should use the liquidation basis of accounting when liquidation is _____.

  a. Reasonably possible

  b. Probable

  c. More likely than not

  d. Imminent

Measurement of Assets and Liabilities

Assets shall be measured to reflect the estimated amount of cash or other consideration that the entity expects to collect in settling or disposing of those assets in carrying out its plan for liquidation.

NOTE: The ASU notes that in some cases, fair value may approximate the amount that an entity expects to collect. However, an entity shall not presume this to be true for all assets.

Liabilities shall be measured based on other GAAP that otherwise would apply to those liabilities.

EXCEPTION: With respect to the accrual of estimated disposal costs and expected income and expenses, an entity shall adjust its liabilities to reflect changes in assumptions that are a result of the entity's decision to liquidate (e.g., timing of payments). However, an entity shall not anticipate being legally released from being the primary obligor under a liability, either judicially or by the creditor.

An entity shall not apply discounting provisions in measuring the accruals for estimated disposal costs and expected income and expenses.

An entity shall accrue estimated costs to dispose of assets or other items that it expects to sell in liquidation and present those costs in the aggregate separately from those assets or items. An entity shall accrue costs and income that it expects to incur or earn (e.g., payroll costs or income from preexisting orders that the entity expects to fulfill during liquidation) through the end of its liquidation if and when it has a reasonable basis for estimation.

> **OBSERVATION:** A liquidation period could continue for several years. Because the goal is to present end users with information to help them determine the amount of net assets that will be available for distribution, an entity using the liquidation basis of accounting should accrue as a liability any and all expenses it can reasonably estimate to the end of the liquidation period. Such expenses would include costs related to occupancy, employment, and all other costs that are expected to be incurred until the liquidation is completed.

When using the liquidation basis of accounting, an entity shall recognize other items that it previously had not recognized, such as trademarks or patents, but that it expects to sell in liquidation or use to settle liabilities.

> **EXAMPLE:** Company X adopts the liquidation basis of accounting effective June 1, 20X1. The company has several patents and trademarks that are not recorded. In adopting the liquidation basis of accounting, X should bring those assets onto the statement of net assets in liquidation, recording the patents and trademarks at liquidation value.

At each reporting date, an entity shall remeasure its assets and other items it expects to sell that it had not previously recognized (e.g., trademarks), liabilities, and the accruals of disposal or other costs or income to reflect the actual or estimated change in carrying value since the previous reporting date.

STUDY QUESTION

2. Company X has some old equipment in the warehouse that is fully depreciated. X is using the liquidation basis of accounting and plans to sell the old equipment as part of its plan of liquidation. Facts related to the equipment follow:

Original cost	$100,000
Recorded book value	0
Liquidation value	20,000
Fair value	30,000

Using the liquidation basis of accounting, X should record the equipment at _____.

a. $100,000

b. Zero

c. $20,000

d. $30,000

Presentation Rules

The ASU requires that at a minimum, an entity that applies the liquidation basis of accounting shall prepare two statements:

- A statement of net assets in liquidation
- A statement of changes in net assets in liquidation

The liquidation basis of accounting shall be applied prospectively from the day that liquidation becomes imminent. The initial statement of changes in net assets in liquidation shall present only changes in net assets that occurred during the period since liquidation became imminent.

Disclosures

An entity that uses the liquidation basis of accounting is required to make all disclosures required by GAAP that are relevant to an understanding of the following information:

- The entity's statement of net assets in liquidation and statement of changes in net assets in liquidation
- The amount of cash or other consideration that an entity expects to collect and the amount that the entity is obligated or expects to be obligated to pay during the course of liquidation

At a minimum, an entity shall disclose all of the following when it prepares financial statements using the liquidation basis of accounting:

- That the financial statements are prepared using the liquidation basis of accounting, including the facts and circumstances surrounding the adoption of the liquidation basis of accounting and the entity's determination that liquidation is imminent.
- A description of the entity's plan for liquidation, including a description of each of the following:

  - The manner by which it expects to dispose of its assets and other items it expects to sell that it had not previously recognized as assets (e.g., trademarks)

  - The manner by which it expects to settle its liabilities

  - The expected date by which the entity expects to complete its liquidation

- The methods and significant assumptions used to measure assets and liabilities, including any subsequent changes to those methods and assumptions
- The type and amount of costs and income accrued in the statement of net assets in liquidation and the period over which those costs are expected to be paid or income earned

Do the fair value disclosures apply to financial statements prepared on the liquidation basis of accounting?

Although ASU 2013-07 is silent on the matter, there is no indication that fair value disclosures are required. The ASU states that assets shall be measured to reflect the estimated amount of cash or other consideration that it expects to collect in settling or disposing of those assets in carrying out its plan for liquidation. The ASU further notes that in some cases, fair value may approximate the amount that an entity expects to collect. However, an entity shall not presume this to be true for all assets. What this means is that assets and liabilities are not recorded at fair value even though the values measured under ASU 2013-07 may approximate fair value.

Another source of authority on this issue is found in ASC 820-10-50-9 which states the following regarding fair value disclosures:

> *"The reporting entity is encouraged, but not required, to . . . .disclose information about other similar measurements (for example, inventories measured at market value under Topic 330), if practicable."*

Thus, an entity is encouraged to include disclosures similar to fair value disclosures in situations in which market value, current value, liquidation basis, or other similar measurements are used to record assets or liabilities. However, the entity is not required to do so.

Following are examples, some of which are included within ASU 2013-07, as modified by the author.

EXAMPLE 1: Unplanned Liquidation

Facts: Company A is a manufacturer of goods. In 20X3, Company A began experiencing financial difficulty because of declining market demand for its goods.

On September 19, 20X3, Company A's board of directors approved a plan for liquidation. The board of directors had the authority to make the plan effective. There were no other parties that could block the execution of the plan, and the likelihood that the entity would return from liquidation was remote.

Conclusion: Company A should begin applying the liquidation basis of accounting as of September 19, 20X3, which is the date that Entity A's board of directors approved the plan for liquidation.

EXAMPLE 2: Liquidation That Follows a Plan Specified at an Entity's Inception

Facts: On January 1, 20X1, Company B is established and its governing documents at inception specify that its contractual life would end on December 31, 20X10 (10 years).

On April 5, 20X10, Company B's board of directors approve a plan to liquidate the assets at approximate fair value, consistent with the 10-year plan specified at the entity's inception. It is remote that execution of the plan for liquidation will be blocked by other parties, and it is remote that the entity will return from liquidation.

Conclusion: B should not use the liquidation basis of accounting. This is because the liquidation follows a plan for liquidation that was specified in B's governing documents at B's inception. Moreover, the plan of liquidation is commensurate with the fair value of the assets.

EXAMPLE 3: Liquidation That Does Not Follow a Plan Specified at an Entity's Inception- Early Liquidation at an Amount that is Commensurate with Fair Value

Facts: On January 1, 20X1, Company B is established and its governing documents at inception specify that its contractual life would end in on December 31, 20X10 (10 years).

On September 30, 20X6, Company B's board of directors approve a plan to liquidate the assets at an amount that is commensurate with fair value. Although at inception the liquidation plan was 10 years, the market is strong and the board of directors believes it can maximize consideration that is commensurate with fair value if it liquidates early. It is remote that execution of the plan for liquidation will be blocked by other parties, and it is remote that the entity will return from liquidation.

Conclusion: B should *not* use the liquidation basis of accounting. This is because the liquidation follows a plan for liquidation that was specified in B's governing documents at B's inception.

Although it is true that the liquidation plan is being executed early (six years versus the original plan of 10 years), the ASU states that the key factor that determines whether an entity follows a plan of liquidation is whether the entity expects to receive consideration that is commensurate with fair value. Thus, the fact that the actual plan of liquidation at six years differs from the original plan of 10 years, does not, in and of itself, mean that the plan of liquidation was not followed. The key factor is whether the liquidation in year six is expected to be made at an amount that is commensurate with fair value, and not at a forced amount that differs significantly from fair value.

EXAMPLE 4: Liquidation That Does Not Follow a Plan Specified at an Entity's Inception- Early Liquidation at Less Than Fair Value

Facts: On January 1, 20X1, Company B is established and its governing documents at inception specify that its contractual life would end in on December 31, 20X10 (10 years).

On March 11, 20X6, B's board of directors determined that B would not be able to meet its debt obligations and voted to begin liquidating the entity earlier than planned.

Company B required approval from Company C, a third party, to make its plan of liquidation effective. Company B obtained approval from Entity C on April 10, 20X6. No other parties could block the execution of the plan of liquidation, and the likelihood that B would return from liquidation was remote. Under the plan of liquidation, because of B's financial situation, B does not anticipate that it will have sufficient time to sell its assets at an amount that is commensurate with fair value of those assets. Therefore, net assets are anticipated to be sold at less than an amount that is commensurate with fair value.

Conclusion: B should use the liquidation basis of accounting starting on April 10, 20X6, the date on which the plan is approved, and it is remote that any parties could block the execution of the plan, and the likelihood that B would return from liquidation is remote.

Although it is true that there is a liquidation plan, B did not follow that original plan on two accounts: First, B did not follow the original timeframe for liquidation (10 years). Second, the liquidation is expected to result in consideration received that is less than an amount that is commensurate with fair value of the assets. ASU 2013-07 states that the key factor that determined whether an entity follows the plan of liquidation found in the original documents is whether the entity expects to receive consideration that is commensurate with fair value. If not, the plan of liquidation is not followed and the liquidation basis of accounting should be used at the time the plan is approved by the board of directors.

In this example, because B does not expect to receive consideration that is commensurate with fair value of the assets, the original plan is not being followed. Therefore, B should use the liquidation basis of accounting on April 10, 20X6 until the end of the liquidation. The timeframe of the liquidation plan (six years versus the original 10-year plan at inception), is not a strong factor in determining whether the plan was followed. Instead, whether the company expects to receive an amount that is commensurate with fair value for the liquidation of assets is the key determinant of whether the plan was followed.

> **OBSERVATION:** In Examples 1 through 4, the key factor in determining whether the original plan of liquidation is followed is whether, in liquidation, the company expects to receive consideration that is commensurate with fair value. The term *commensurate with fair value* does not mean that the company plans to receive precisely fair value. What it means is that the company expects to receive an amount that is close to fair value.

STUDY QUESTION

3. Company Y and X enter into a joint venture that provides for a limited life of 10 years in the original governing documents. Which of the following is correct?

a. Y should use the liquidation basis of accounting throughout the 10-year period.

b. Y should use the liquidation basis of accounting if it follows the 10-year plan of liquidation.

c. Y should use the liquidation basis of accounting if it has a forced sale of the assets in year six.

d. Y should not use the liquidation basis of accounting under any circumstances because entities with limited lives are precluded from using this basis.

Effective Date and Transition

ASU 2013-07 is effective for entities that determine liquidation is imminent during annual reporting periods beginning after December 15, 2013, and interim reporting periods therein. Entities should apply the requirements prospectively from the day that liquidation becomes imminent. Early adoption is permitted.

An entity reporting on the liquidation basis of accounting as of the effective date need not apply the ASU if the entity had been applying guidance from another Topic about when and how to apply the liquidation basis of accounting (e.g., terminating employee benefit plans). Otherwise, an entity reporting on the liquidation basis of accounting as of the effective date shall record a cumulative-effect adjustment as of the date of adoption to account for any differences between the following:

- The entity's recognized assets and the measurements of its assets and liabilities (including measurement changes resulting from changes in assumptions) under other GAAP
- The entity's recognized assets and other items (e.g., previously unrecognized trademarks) and the measurements of its assets, other items, and liabilities (including measurement changes resulting from changes in assumptions).

OBSERVATION: The FASB did not provide any guidance as to how to transition to the liquidation basis of accounting. Therefore, if an entity changes to the liquidation basis of accounting on the date of approval of the plan by its board of directors, all assets and liabilities are adjusted to the liquidation basis of accounting. However, there is no guidance as to what the offsetting entry is. The ASU does not provide for presenting the adjustment as a restatement of the beginning net assets, similar to a restatement of retained earnings under other GAAP. Thus, it appears that in the statement of changes in net assets in liquidation, the beginning net assets is already restated and there is no transition from the ending net equity in the going concern GAAP statements, and the beginning net asset amount in the statement of changes in net assets in liquidation. The one exception where a "catch-up" adjustment is presented is where an entity is already using the liquidation basis of accounting at the time of ASU 2013-07's effective date. In such a situation, the ASU requires that a cumulative effect adjustment be made to adjust the net assets to conform with ASU 2013-07, if there is any adjustment. That adjustment should be presented as an adjustment to the beginning net assets presented in the statement of changes in net assets in liquidation.

Sample Financial Statements

XYZ Company, Inc. Statement of Net Assets in Liquidation December 31, 20X1	
Assets:	
Cash	$XX
Investments	XX
Accounts receivable, less allowance for doubtful accounts	XX
Equipment and fixtures	XX
Patents and tradenames not previously recognized	XX
Total assets	XX
Liabilities:	
Accounts payable	XX
Accrued disposal costs	XX
Accrued operating costs through liquidation	XX
Total liabilities	XX
NET ASSETS IN LIQUIDATION	$XX

XYZ Company, Inc. Statement of Changes in Net Assets in Liquidation For the Year Ended December 31, 20X1	
Net assets in liquidation -Beginning of year	$XX
Changes in net assets attributable to liquidation:	
Net income	XX
Adjustments to liquidation value of net assets	(XX)
Distributions to shareholders	(XX)
Net assets in liquidation-End of year	$XX

STUDY QUESTION

4. Which of the following is correct as to which costs should be accrued by an entity using the liquidation basis of accounting?

a. Costs should be accrued for the current year only using the matching principle.

b. An entity shall accrue costs it expects to incur through the end of the liquidation, not to exceed two years.

c. Costs should be accrued through the end of the liquidation.

d. An entity must accrue all costs using its best estimate even if there is no reasonable basis for the estimation.

MODULE 2: FINANCIAL STATEMENT REPORTING—CHAPTER 5: Comprehensive Income (ASC 220)

¶ 501 WELCOME

This chapter covers ASC 220, *Comprehensive Income* (formerly FAS 130), which was issued to address the presentation of certain items (other comprehensive income items) that historically have bypassed the income statement and were recorded directly to equity.

¶ 502 LEARNING OBJECTIVES

Upon completion of this chapter, the reader will be able to:

- Identify what is included in other comprehensive income
- Define comprehensive income
- Distinguish the differences that exist currently between U.S. GAAP and IFRS in regard to how other comprehensive income is presented
- Recognize the allowed presentation formats for other comprehensive income in the financial statements and notes
- Identify the ASC 220 requirements regarding reclassification adjustments
- Recognize how a non-controlling interest in another entity is presented in comprehensive income

¶ 503 BACKGROUND

ASC 220, *Comprehensive Income* (formerly FAS 130), was issued to address the presentation of certain items (other comprehensive income items) that bypass the income statement and were recorded directly to equity.

Without a means to present these other comprehensive income items, financial statement users who focused on net income as the prime measurement of results of operations would not be taking into account these other comprehensive income items in measuring the entity's financial performance.

Other comprehensive income items that previously bypassed the income statement and were recorded directly to stockholders' equity were:

- Certain foreign exchange transactions under ASC 830, *Foreign Currency Matters*
- Certain derivative transactions under ASC 815, *Derivatives and Hedging*
- Certain transactions involving available-for-sale securities under ASC 320, *Investments - Debt and Equity Securities*
- Certain pension transactions under ASC 715, *Compensation-Retirement Benefits*

Prior to the issuance of FAS 130 (now codified as ASC 220), an entity was required to present only the accumulated balances of the above list of other comprehensive income items in the statement of stockholders' equity. Yet, there were no standards on how to present these items. Moreover, an entity was not required to present one total for these items such as a caption "other comprehensive income."

ASC 220 now requires that comprehensive income be presented in a financial statement format using one of two options:

1. Present a separate statement of comprehensive income.

2. Combine the statement of income and comprehensive income.

¶ 504 GAAP VS. IFRS

Currently, there are differences between how U.S. GAAP and IFRS present comprehensive income, as follows:

U.S. GAAP	IFRS
Does not require a consecutive presentation of the statement of income and comprehensive income	Requires consecutive presentation of the statement of income and comprehensive income
Reclassification adjustments from other comprehensive income to net income may be displayed *either* on the face of the financial statement in which comprehensive income is reported, or may be presented in the notes to financial statements.	Reclassification adjustments from other comprehensive income to net income *must* be presented on the face of the financial statements.

There are also U.S. GAAP-IFRS differences in the types of items reported in other comprehensive income.

¶ 505 DEFINITION OF COMPREHENSIVE INCOME

The definition of comprehensive income has been around for some time and is defined in ASC 220-10-20 as follows:

> . . . the change in equity (net assets) of a business enterprise during a period from transactions and other events and circumstances from non-owner sources.

In other words, comprehensive income consists of the sum of those changes in equity, the source of which has *nothing to do with the owners (shareholders)*.

Following is a formula that depicts the computation of comprehensive income:

Formula: Comprehensive Income:

(changes in equity that are from non-owner sources):

	Net income and all of its components
+(-)	*Other comprehensive income*
=	Comprehensive income

Comprehensive income consists of changes in equity that are from non-owner sources.

One of the components of comprehensive income is net income, which is a change in equity from a non-owner source. There are also other changes in equity that are from non-owner sources, which are captured under the heading "other comprehensive income." ASC 220 defines "other comprehensive income as revenues, expenses, gains, and losses that under GAAP are included in comprehensive income but excluded from net income.

There are essentially four categories of other comprehensive income items:

1. Certain foreign exchange transactions (ASC 830)
2. Certain derivative transactions (ASC 815)
3. Certain transactions involving available-for-sale securities (ASC 320)
4. Certain pension transactions (ASC 715)

The following chart summarizes comprehensive income, consisting of net income (loss) and other comprehensive income:

COMPREHENSIVE INCOME

1. Net income (loss) + (-)

2. Other comprehensive income:

a. Certain foreign exchange transactions (ASC 830):

- Foreign exchange translation adjustments
- Gains/losses on foreign currency transactions that are designated as economic hedges of a net investment in a foreign entity
- Gains and losses on intra-entity foreign currency transactions that are of a long-term investment nature, when the entities to the transaction are consolidated, combined, or accounted for by the equity method

b. Certain derivative transactions (ASC 815):

- Gains or losses on derivative instruments that are designated as cash flow hedges

c. Certain transactions involving available-for-sale securities (ASC 320)

- Unrealized gains and losses on securities available for sale
- Unrealized gains and losses from transfers of securities from the held-to-maturity category to available-for-sale category
- Amounts recognized in other comprehensive income for debt securities classified as available-for-sale and held-to-maturity related to an other-than-temporary impairment recognized if a portion of the impairment was not recognized in earnings
- Subsequent decreases (if not an other-than-temporary impairment) or increases in the fair value of available-for-sale securities previously written down as impaired

d. Certain pension transactions (ASC 715)

- Gains or losses associated with pension or other postretirement benefits that are not recognized immediately as a component of net periodic benefit cost
- Prior service costs or credits associated with pension or other postretirement benefits
- Transition assets or obligations associated with pension or other postretirement benefits that are not recognized immediately as a component of net periodic benefit cost

= Comprehensive Income

EXAMPLE: Facts. Company A has the following at year-end:

Net income	$1,000,000
Other comprehensive income:	
Foreign exchange transaction adjustments	100,000
Unrealized gain on available-for-sale securities	50,000

Conclusion. Comprehensive income is computed as follows:

Net income	$1,000,000
Other comprehensive income:	
Foreign exchange transaction adjustments	100,000
Unrealized gain on available-for-sale securities	50,000
Total comprehensive income	$1,150,000

Comprehensive income *excludes:*

1. Changes in equity from investments by owners or distributions to owners:
   a. Issuance of stock or equity interests
   b. Payment of dividends or owners' draws
2. Items reported as direct adjustments to paid-in capital, retained earnings, or other non-income related equity accounts such as:
   a. A reduction of equity related to employee stock ownership plans (ESOP)
   b. Taxes not payable in cash
   c. Net cash settlement resulting from a change in the value of a contract that gives an entity a choice of net cash settlement or settlement in its own shares
   d. Prior-period adjustments

OBSERVATION: Even though the previous list of items in (2)(a), (b) and (c) does consist of items that are recorded directly to equity, these items are specifically excluded from the definition of comprehensive income because the FASB chose to do so.

By way of example, the FASB concluded that a reduction in equity related to an ESOP is not part of comprehensive income because such a transaction involves the company's own stock, so such a transaction could be considered a transaction with the owners excluded from the definition of comprehensive income.

The FASB also excluded from the definition of comprehensive income taxes not paid in connection with an entity reorganization under ASC 852, *Reorganizations.* These taxes not paid may result from a reorganized enterprise suffering net operating losses prior to reorganization that provide it with significant tax advantages going forward. ASC 852 requires that a reorganized enterprise record a "full tax rate" on its pretax income although its actual cash taxes paid are minimal because of those net operating loss carryforwards. Taxes not payable in cash are reported in the income statement as an expense with a corresponding increase to additional paid-in capital (APIC) in stockholders' equity. Although the credit to APIC resulting from taxes not payable in cash is not a transaction with an owner, it does not qualify as comprehensive income because the APIC credit stems from transactions and accounting that took place upon reorganization. In effect, the APIC credit adjusts transactions that were recorded in equity in an earlier period and does not result from the current period debit to income tax expense.

¶ 506 SCOPE OF THE STATEMENT

ASC 220 applies *to* all entities that provide a *full set of financial statements* including a statement of financial position, results of operations and cash flows.

> **NOTE:** Investment companies, defined benefit pension plans and other employee benefit plans that are exempt from providing a statement of cash flows are not exempt from the requirements of comprehensive income, even though there is not a full set of financial statements.

ASC 220 does *not* apply to:

- An entity that does not have any items of other comprehensive income items in any period presented.
- A not-for-profit organization that is required to follow the provisions of ASC Subtopic 958-205, *Not-for-Profit Entities, Presentation of Financial Statements*

> **EXAMPLE:** Company A is presenting comparative financial statements for 20X2 and 20X1. Its only change in stockholders' equity for 20X2 and 20X1 is net income. There are no other comprehensive income items (e.g., foreign exchange gains/losses, unrealized gains/losses on securities, etc.).

Conclusion. The Company is exempt from the requirements of ASC 220 because it does not have any items of other comprehensive income. Consequently, there is no requirement to present other comprehensive income or comprehensive income in a statement format.

Change the facts. Same facts as above, except Company A has an unrealized gain on available-for-sale securities in the amount of $100,000 in 20X2.

Conclusion: The Company must comply with the requirements of ASC 220 because it has an item of other comprehensive income (unrealized gain on available-for-sale securities). Therefore, the Company is required to present comprehensive income in a financial statement format.

What happens when there are compiled financial statements that omit a statement of cash flows?

SSARS 19, *Compilation and Review Engagements*, provides that an entity may elect to omit a statement of cash flows (and also substantially all disclosures) required by GAAP. In such a situation, the entity is not presenting a full set of financial statements (e.g., the statement of cash flows is not included).

> **EXAMPLE:** Company A has the following changes in stockholders' equity for 20X1:

Net income	$500,000
Other comprehensive income:	
Unrealized gains on securities available for sale	50,000
Foreign exchange translation adjustments	20,000

The company's financial statements are being compiled and management has elected to omit substantially all disclosures and the statement of cash flows.

Conclusion. The company is *exempt* from complying with ASC 220 because it is not presenting a full set of financial statements. Consequently, even though the company has two other comprehensive income items (unrealized gains and foreign exchange adjustments), it is not required to present comprehensive income in a financial statement.

Further, in accordance with Interpretation 10 of AR § 80 (SSARS 19): *Omission of the Display of Comprehensive Income in Compiled Financial Statements*, the compilation report should be modified to reflect the fact that a statement of comprehensive income is not presented even though there are other comprehensive income items.

The Interpretation requires the compilation report to be modified to reflect the fact that a statement of comprehensive income is not displayed.

The following is suggested modified wording (shown in italic) to the paragraph in the compilation report:

> Management has elected to omit substantially all the disclosures, the statement of cash flows, *and the display of comprehensive income* required by accounting principles generally accepted in the United States of America. If the omitted disclosures, the statement of cash flows, *and the display of comprehensive income* were included in the financial statements, they might influence the user's conclusions about the company's financial position, results of operations, and cash flows. Accordingly, these financial statements are not designed for those who are not informed about such matters.

Change the facts. The company is issuing a full set of financial statements including a statement of cash flows.

Conclusion. Because the company has other comprehensive income items (unrealized gains and foreign exchange adjustments), the company must comply with the requirements of ASC 220. That means that comprehensive income must be presented in a financial statement format (one or two statements).

Do the requirements to display comprehensive income apply when OCBOA statements are presented?

No. ASC 220 only applies if a full set of financial statements is presented, including a statement of cash flows. When Other Comprehensive Basis of Accounting (OCBOA) statements are presented (e.g., income tax basis), a statement of cash flows is *not required* in accordance with ASC 230, *Statement of Cash Flows*. Therefore, OCBOA statements do not provide a full set of financial statements and are not subject to the comprehensive income requirements. Even if the entity elects to include a cash flow statement in a set of OCBOA financial statements, the statement would still not apply; that is, a statement of comprehensive income would not be required. This is because, in general, OCBOA statements do not have any other comprehensive income items.

OCBOA income tax basis financial statements would not have any of the other comprehensive income items (e.g., unrealized gains/losses on securities, foreign translation gains/losses) posted directly to equity.

STUDY QUESTIONS

---

1. Which of the following is an example of another comprehensive income item?

    a. Certain transactions involving trading securities

    b. Certain transactions involving available-for-sale securities

    c. Certain transactions involving debt securities held to maturity

    d. Certain transactions involving non-security investments

2. The formula for comprehensive income is which of the following?

  a. Net income +/- change in equity

  b. Net income +/- other comprehensive income

  c. Net income +/- non-cash transactions

  d. Net income +/- change in working capital

3. Which of the following is an example of a transaction involving available-for-sale securities that would be part of other comprehensive income?

  a. Unrealized gains and losses from transfers of securities from the available-for-sale category to the held-to-maturity category

  b. Subsequent increase in the fair value of available-for sale securities previously written down as an other-than-temporary impairment

  c. Amounts recognized in other comprehensive income for debt securities classified as available-for-sale and held-to-maturity related to an other-than-temporary impairment recognized if a portion of the impairment was recognized in earnings

  d. Unrealized gains on securities available-for-sale

4. ASC 220 requires that comprehensive income be presented in a format. Which of the following is one of the format options available?

  a. Disclose comprehensive income only

  b. Present a single continuous statement of income and comprehensive income

  c. Present comprehensive income as a section within the statement of stockholders' equity

  d. Present comprehensive income as an asset.

¶ 507 REQUIREMENTS OF THE STATEMENT

The Statement requires the following:

Comprehensive income. All components of comprehensive income must be presented in the financial statements in the period in which they are recognized segregated as follows:

Net income	$XX
Other comprehensive income:	
Certain foreign exchange transactions	XX
Certain derivative transactions	XX
Certain transactions involving available-for-sale securities	XX
Total comprehensive income	$XX

Presentation. An entity with other comprehensive income items must report comprehensive income either in:

- A single continuous statement of income and comprehensive income
- Two separate but consecutive financial statements consisting of:
  - Statement of income, followed by a
  - Statement of comprehensive income

Regardless of whether a single or two financial statements approach is used, all items that meet the definition of comprehensive income shall be presented for the period in which those items are recognized. An entity reporting a *single continuous financial statement* (statement of income and comprehensive income) shall present the following components in two sections; net income and other comprehensive income:

- A total amount for net income together with the components that make up net income (e.g., revenue, expenses, etc.)
- A total amount for other comprehensive income together with the components that make up other comprehensive income
- Total comprehensive income

An entity reporting comprehensive income in *two separate but consecutive statements* shall present the following:

In the statement of income:

- Components of and the total for net income in the statement of net income

In the statement of comprehensive income:

- Components of and the total for other comprehensive income
- Total comprehensive income

> **NOTE:** If two separate statements are presented, the statement of comprehensive income shall be presented immediately after the statement of income. Moreover, the statement of comprehensive income may (but is not required to) start with net income.

The terms "comprehensive income" or "other comprehensive income" do not have to be used in the financial statements even though they are used throughout ASC 220.

If an entity has an outstanding noncontrolling interest, the following must be presented in the financial statements in which net income and comprehensive income are presented:

- Amounts for both net income and comprehensive income attributable to the parent
- Amounts for net income and comprehensive income attributable to the noncontrolling interest in a less-than-wholly owned subsidiary
- Consolidated net income and comprehensive income

Tax effect of other comprehensive income items. An entity shall present components of other comprehensive income in the statement in which other comprehensive income is reported either:

- Net of tax effects
- Before the tax effects with one amount shown for the total income tax expense allocated to total other comprehensive income

An entity shall present the amount of income tax expense (or benefit) allocated to each component of other comprehensive income, including reclassification adjustments, either in the statement in which those components are presented, or disclose it in the notes to financial statements.

NOTE: In lieu of disclosing in the notes the income tax expense allocated to each component of other comprehensive income, that information can be presented parenthetically for each component of other comprehensive income in the statement in which other comprehensive income is presented.

Balance sheet and statement of equity. The total of other comprehensive income must be presented as a separate component in the equity section of the balance sheet under a caption similar to *accumulated other comprehensive income.*

Accumulated other comprehensive income shall be presented separately from retained earnings and additional paid-in capital in the equity section of the balance sheet at the end of the accounting period. An entity shall present on the face of the financial statements or disclosure in the notes the changes in the accumulated *balance* for each component of *accumulated other comprehensive income.* The components must correspond to those used in the presentation of other comprehensive income.

The following example illustrates the options available for presenting comprehensive income under ASC 220:

EXAMPLE: Facts. The following financial data applies to XYZ Corporation for the year ended December 31, 20X1.

Revenue	$1,000,000
Expenses	800,000
Income from operations	200,000
Income taxes	80,000
Net income	120,000
Retained earnings:	
Beginning of year	2,000,000
End of year	$2,120,000

Other comprehensive income items:	
Unrealized gains on available-for-sale securities	$50,000
Income taxes allocated	(20,000)
Net gain	$30,000
Foreign currency translation adjustments	$40,000
Income taxes allocated	(16,000)
Net amount	$24,000

Format 1: Single Continuous Statement Approach
(Combined Statement of Income and Comprehensive Income)

XYZ Corporation Statement of Income and Comprehensive Income For The Year Ended December 31, 20X1

Revenue		$1,000,000
Expenses		800,000
Income from operations		200,000
Income taxes		80,000
Net income		120,000
Other comprehensive income:		
Unrealized gain on securities available for sale (net of tax of $20,000)		30,000
Foreign currency translation adjustments (net of tax of $16,000)		24,000
Total other comprehensive income		54,000
Comprehensive income		$174,000

Alternatively, the tax effect of other comprehensive income could be presented as follows:

Unrealized gain	50,000	
Foreign currency adjustments	40,000	
Other comprehensive income, before taxes		90,000
Income tax expense allocated	(36,000)	
Other comprehensive income		54,000

Format 2: Two-Statement Approach

(Two separate but consecutive financial statements)

- Statement of income, followed by a
- Statement of Comprehensive Income

Separate Statement of Income

XYZ Corporation Statement of Income For The Year Ended December 31, 20X1

Revenue	$1,000,000
Expenses	800,000
Income from operations	200,000
Income taxes	80,000
Net income	120,000

Separate Statement of Income	
XYZ Corporation Statement of Income For The Year Ended December 31, 20X1	
Retained earnings:	2,000,000
Beginning of year	
End of year	$2,120,000

Separate Statement of Comprehensive Income	
XYZ Corporation Statement of Comprehensive Income For The Year Ended December 31, 20X1	
Net income	$120,000
Other comprehensive income:	
Unrealized gain on securities available for sale (net of tax of $20,000)	30,000
Foreign currency translation adjustments (net of tax of $16,000)	24,000
Total other comprehensive income	54,000
Comprehensive income	$174,000

¶ 508 PRESENTATION OF CHANGES IN COMPONENTS OF ACCUMULATED OTHER COMPREHENSIVE INCOME IN THE STATEMENT OF STOCKHOLDERS' EQUITY

Regardless of whether a single or two-statement format is used to present comprehensive income, ASC 220 requires an entity to present on the face of the financial statements or in the notes to financial statements, the changes in the accumulated *balance* for each component of *accumulated other comprehensive income*.

The changes may be shown either in the statement of stockholders' equity or in the notes to financial statements. Continuing with the previous example, the two presentation options are presented below:

Option 1: Present the changes in each component of accumulated other comprehensive income in the statement of stockholders' equity.

			Accumulated Other Comprehensive Income		
XYZ Corporation Statement of Stockholders' Equity For The Year Ended December 31, 20X2					
	Total	Retained Earnings	Unrealized gains on securities	Foreign currency adjustments	Common Stock
Beginning balance	$2,525,000	$2,000,000	$10,000	$15,000	$500,000
Comprehensive income					
Net income	120,000	120,000			

XYZ Corporation Statement of Stockholders' Equity For The Year Ended December 31, 20X2					
			Accumulated Other Comprehensive Income		
	Total	Retained Earnings	Unrealized gains on securities	Foreign currency adjustments	Common Stock
Unrealized gains on securities available for sale	30,000		30,000		
Foreign currency translation adjustments	24,000	0	0	24,000	0
Ending balance	$2,699,000	$2,120,000	$40,000	$39,000	$500,000

NOTE: The requirement is to present the changes in each component of accumulated other comprehensive income. The two changes in accumulated other comprehensive income (unrealized gains and foreign currency adjustments) are shown net of tax. However, there is no requirement to disclose the tax effect of these changes when presenting the changes in accumulated other comprehensive income. Notice also that there is no labeling required such as "other comprehensive income" or "comprehensive income."

Option 2: Present the changes in each component of accumulated other comprehensive income in the notes to financial statements.

XYZ Corporation Statement of Stockholders' Equity For The Year Ended December 31, 20X2				
			Accumulated Other Comprehensive Income	
	Total	Retained Earnings		Common Stock
Beginning balance	$2,525,000	$2,000,000	$25,000	$500,000
Comprehensive income				
Net income	120,000	120,000		
Other comprehensive income- current year	54,000	.	54,000	.
Ending balance	$2,699,000	$2,120,000	$79,000	$500,000

NOTE X: CHANGES IN ACCUMULATED OTHER COMPREHENSIVE INCOME

Changes in each component of accumulated other comprehensive income follow:

	Accumulated Other Comprehensive Income		
	Unrealized gains (losses) - available-for-sale securities	Foreign exchange translation adjustments	Total
Beginning balance	$10,000	$15,000	$25,000
Other comprehensive income- current year	30,000	24,000	54,000
End balance	$40,000	$39,000	$79,000

NOTE: An entity is required to present the changes in accumulated other comprehensive income either in a statement (statement of stockholders' equity) or in the notes to financial statements. The author believes that the best place to present this change is in the statement of stockholders' equity and not in the notes which is represented by Option 1 above. Option 2 provides for presentation in the notes to financial statements. Under Option 2, the total accumulated other comprehensive income is shown in one column in the statement of stockholders' equity because GAAP requires that all changes in equity be presented. Because the changes in the two components of accumulated other comprehensive income (unrealized gains and foreign currency adjustments) are disclosed in the notes (NOTE X), only the total change in accumulated other comprehensive income is presented in the statement of stockholders' equity.

¶ 509 PRESENTATION OF BALANCE SHEET: ALL FORMATS

Regardless of the format for presenting comprehensive income, *accumulated other comprehensive income* must be presented as a *separate component* on the balance sheet as follows:

XYZ Corporation Balance Sheet December 31, 20X1	
Assets:	
Cash	$XX
Accounts receivable	XX
Securities, available-for sale	XX
Property and equipment, net	XX
Total assets	$XX
Liabilities:	
Accounts payable	$XX
Accrued expenses	XX
Deferred income taxes	XX
Total liabilities	XX
Stockholders' equity:	
Common stock	XX
Retained earnings	XX
Accumulated other comprehensive income	**79,000**
	(Unrealized gains on securities ($40,000) plus foreign exchange adjustments (39,000) (total $79,000).
Total stockholders' equity	XX
Total liabilities and stockholders' equity	$XX

NOTE: ASC 220 requires that accumulated other comprehensive income be presented as a separate component in the equity section of the balance sheet. It does not require that the individual components be presented as long as they are presented elsewhere such as in the statement of stockholders' equity or in the notes to financial statements.

¶ 510 ALTERNATIVE PRESENTATION OF TAX EFFECT OF OTHER COMPREHENSIVE INCOME ITEMS

ASC 220 requires disclosure of the tax effect of each item of other comprehensive income. In each of the preceding three formats, this requirement has been achieved by presenting the tax effect parenthetically next to each item of other comprehensive income. Alternatively, this requirement can be satisfied by presenting the total tax expense as one line item assigned to other comprehensive income, with a separate note provided that discloses the breakout of income tax expense assigned to each other comprehensive income component.

Facts. Assume Format 1 (a single continuous statement) is selected to present comprehensive income, except that the tax effect of each item of other comprehensive income is not parenthetically presented, as follows:

XYZ Corporation Statement of Income and Comprehensive Income For The Year Ended December 31, 20X1	
Revenue	$1,000,000
Expenses	800,000
Income from operations	200,000
Income taxes	80,000
Net income	120,000
Other comprehensive income *(before taxes):*	
Unrealized gain on securities available for *sale (no tax effect disclosed)*	50,000
Foreign currency translation adjustments *sale (no tax effect disclosed)*	40,000
Other comprehensive income before taxes	90,000
Income tax expense related to items of other comprehensive income	**(36,000)**
Other comprehensive income, net of taxes	54,000
Comprehensive income	$174,000

NOTE X: COMPREHENSIVE INCOME

The following summarizes the tax effect, by component, of other comprehensive income:

	Unrealized gains - available-for-sale securities	Foreign exchange translation adjustments	Total other comprehensive income
Amount before tax effect	$50,000	$40,000	$90,000
Tax effect	(20,000	(16,000)	(36,000)
Amount, net of tax effect	$30,000	$24,000	$54,000

STUDY QUESTIONS

5. Which of the following is an acceptable presentation of the tax effect related to components of other comprehensive income?

    a. Present each component net of tax effects.

    b. Present total other comprehensive income with one total allocation of income taxes, and no allocation or disclosure as to the individual components.

    c. The tax effects are not required to be allocated to other comprehensive income.

    d. Present other comprehensive income in the financial statements without the tax effect and disclose the tax effect in the notes to financial statements.

6. ASC 220 requires which of the following?

    a. If a single format is used to present comprehensive income, an entity must present the changes in the accumulated balance for each component of accumulated other comprehensive income. This is not required for the two-statement format.

    b. The changes in the accumulated balance for each component of accumulated other comprehensive income may be shown in the statement of stockholders' equity.

    c. Changes in accumulated other comprehensive income must be shown either in the notes to financial statements.

    d. Individual components of accumulated other comprehensive income must be presented in the equity section of the balance sheet.

¶ 511 RECLASSIFICATION ADJUSTMENTS

If applicable, adjustments must be made to avoid double counting of comprehensive income items that are presented as part of net income in one period, and as part of other comprehensive income in that period or earlier periods. ASC 220 refers to such adjustments as reclassification *adjustments*.

    EXAMPLE: In year 1, an entity records an unrealized gain on securities available for sale which is shown as part of stockholders' equity and other comprehensive income.

    In year 2, the company sells the security which results in a realized gain on the income statement.

Conclusion. In year 2, the gain must be deducted from other comprehensive income to avoid including the gain in comprehensive income twice—once as a realized gain on the sale, and once as an unrealized holding gain.

Rules for Reclassification Adjustments

An entity shall present separately for each component of other comprehensive income:

- Current-period reclassifications out of accumulated other comprehensive income
- Other amounts of current-period other comprehensive income

The reclassification adjustment for foreign currency translation adjustments is limited to translation gains and losses realized upon sale or upon complete or substantially complete liquidation of an investment in a foreign entity.

An entity shall separately provide information about the effects on net income of significant amounts reclassified out of each component of accumulated other comprehensive income, if those amounts are required under GAAP to be classified to net income in the same reporting period. An entity shall provide this information together, in one location, in either of the following ways:

- On the face of the statement where net income is presented
- As a separate disclosure in the notes to the financial statements

If an entity chooses to present information about the effects of significant amounts reclassified out of accumulated other comprehensive income on net income, on the face of the statement, the entity shall present parenthetically, by component of other comprehensive income, the effect of significant reclassification amounts on the respective line items of net income.

An entity also shall present parenthetically the aggregate tax effect of all significant reclassifications on the line item for income tax benefit or expense in the statement where net income is presented. If an entity is unable to identify the line item of net income affected by any significant amount reclassified out of accumulated other comprehensive income in a reporting period, the entity must follow the guidance for presentation in the notes.

If an entity chooses to present information about significant amounts reclassified out of accumulated other comprehensive income in the notes to the financial statements, it shall present the significant amounts by each component of accumulated other comprehensive income, and provide a subtotal of each component of comprehensive income.

The subtotals for each component shall agree with the other presentations. Both before-tax and net-of-tax presentations are permitted provided the entity complies with the other requirements.

For each significant reclassification amount, the entity shall identify, for those amounts that are required under other GAAP to be reclassified to net income, each line item affected by the reclassification on the statement where net income is presented. For any significant reclassification for which other GAAP does not require that reclassification to net income, the entity shall cross-reference to the note where additional details about the effect of the reclassifications are disclosed.

Required Disclosures

An entity is required to disclose the effect of reclassifications on the line items in the statement in which net income is presented on either a before-tax or a net-of-tax basis consistent with the entity's method of presentation for the line items in that statement. In either case, the total for this disclosure should agree with the total amount of reclassifications for each component of other comprehensive income that complies with the presentation requirements.

> **EXAMPLE:** The following example extracted from ASC 220 illustrates the application of the reclassification adjustment when presented on the face of the income statement.

Facts. On December 31, 20X1, Company X purchases 1,000 shares of equity securities at $10 per share (total purchase price is $10,000). The securities are classified as available for sale.

Fair value of these securities at December 31, 20X3 and 20X2 follows:

Year End	Fair value/ share	Total fair value	Total cost	Unrealized gain	30% tax effect	Unrealized net gain
12-31-X2	$12	$12,000	$10,000	$2,000	$(600)	$1,400
12-31-X3	15	15,000	10,000	5,000	(1,500)	3,500

- Federal and state tax rate is 30 percent.
- On December 31, 20X3, the securities were sold for $15,000.

Conclusion. Because the security is categorized as available for sale, it is recorded at fair value with any unrealized gain or loss recorded as a component of other comprehensive income, net of the tax effect.

Entries as follows:

December 31, 20X1:

	dr	cr
Investment in equity security	10,000	
Cash		10,000
To record purchase of 1,000 shares at $10 per share		

December 31, 20X2 and 20X3 entries:

	20X2 Entries		20X3 Entries	
	dr	cr	dr	cr
Allowance for unrealized gain	2,000		3,000	
Unrealized gain on securities (equity)		2,000		3,000
Unrealized gain on securities (30%) (equity)	600		900	
Deferred income tax liability		600		900
To record unrealized holding gains on securities available for sale, net of related tax effect				

	20X3 Entries	
	dr	cr
Cash	15,000	
Investment in equity security		10,000
Gain on sale of securities		5,000
To record sale of investment on 12-31-X3		
Unrealized gain on securities	3,500	
Allowance for unrealized gain		5,000
Deferred income tax liability	1,500	
To reverse the unrealized gain and related tax effect related to the sale of investments.		

Presentation on Financial Statements:

Company X Statements of Income and Comprehensive Income For The Years Ended December 31, 20X3 and 20X2		
	20X3	20X2
Revenue	$XX	$XX
Expenses	XX	XX
Income from operations	XX	XX
Other income:		
Gain on sale of securities	**5,000**	0
Income taxes	XX	XX
Net income (given)	400,000	300,000
Other comprehensive income *(before taxes):*		
Unrealized gain on securities available for *sale* (net of taxes $900 in 20X3 and $600 in 20X2)	2,100	1,400
Reclassification adjustment (net of tax effect of $1,500)	**(3,500)**	**0**
Other comprehensive income	(1,400)	1,400
Comprehensive income	$398,600	$301,400

What happens to the reclassification adjustment if there are purchases and sales of securities within the same year?

EXAMPLE: Assume in 20X1, a security is purchased and sold as follows:

March 1, 20X1 purchased	$10,000
November 1, 20X1 sold	13,000
Gain	3,000
Tax effect 40%	(1,200)
Net gain	$1,800

Should an unrealized gain be shown up to the date of sale ($1,800) with a corresponding reversal as a reclassification adjustment of $(1,800)? Or should the entire unrealized gain up to the date of sale be excluded with only the $3,000 realized gain shown?

Response: For ASC 320 purposes, there would be no unrealized gain recorded because the calculation is done at the balance sheet date. At that date, there were no securities owned. However, for ASC 220 presentation purposes, the unrealized gain must be reflected up to the date of the sale as follows:

Company X Statement of Income and Comprehensive Income For The Year Ended December 31, 20X1	
Revenue	$XX
Expenses	XX
Income from operations	XX
Other income:	
Gain on sale of securities	3,000
Income before income taxes	XX
Income taxes	XX
Net income	XX
Other comprehensive income:	
Unrealized gain on securities available for sale (net of taxes $1,200)	1,800
Reclassification adjustment (net of tax effect of $1,200)	(1,800)
Other comprehensive income	(0)
Comprehensive income	$XX

¶ 512 CESSATION OF A CONTROLLING FINANCIAL INTEREST

When a reporting entity (a parent) ceases to have a controlling financial interest in a subsidiary or group of assets that is either a nonprofit activity or a business (other than a sale of in-substance real estate or conveyance of oil and gas mineral rights) within a foreign entity, the parent is required to apply the guidance in ASC 830-30, *Translation of Financial Statements*, to release any related cumulative translation adjustment into net income.

Under ASC 830-30, upon sale or upon complete or substantially complete liquidation of an investment in a foreign entity, the cumulative translation adjustment component of equity shall be both:

- Removed from the separate component of equity
- Reported in net income as part of the gain or loss on sale or liquidation of the investment for the period during which the sale or liquidation occurs

The sale of an investment in a foreign entity includes both:

- Events that result in the loss of a controlling financial interest in an investment in a foreign entity
- Events that result in an acquirer obtaining control of an acquiree in which it held an equity interest immediately before the acquisition date

Partial Sales

If a parent has an equity method investment in a foreign entity, the partial sale rules in ASC 830-30-40, *Foreign Currency Matter, Translation of Financial Statements, Derecognition*, should be followed. Under ASC 830-30-40, if a reporting entity sells part of its ownership interest in an equity investment that is a foreign entity, a pro rata portion of the cumulative translation adjustment component of equity attributable to that equity method investment shall be released into net income.

If the partial sale involves ownership in a non-foreign entity, the pro-rata portion rule does not apply. In those instances, the cumulative translation adjustment is released into net income only if the partial sale represents a complete or substantially complete liquidation of the foreign entity that contains the equity method investment.

¶ 513 PRESENTATION OF NON-CONTROLLING INTERESTS

If a company has a non-controlling interest in another entity, comprehensive income must be presented before and after the non-controlling interest.

Following is an example of a two-statement approach for a company that has a non-controlling interest in another entity.

Format 2: Two-Statement Approach

Separate Statement of Income
XYZ Corporation Consolidated Statement of Income For The Year Ended December 31, 20X1

Revenue	$1,000,000
Expenses	800,000
Income from operations	200,000
Income taxes	80,000
Net income	120,000
Less: net income attributable to noncontrolling interest	**(25,000)**
Net income attributable to XYZ Corporation	95,000
Retained earnings:	
Beginning of year	2,000,000
End of year	$2,095,000

Separate Statement of Comprehensive Income
XYZ Corporation Consolidated Statement of Comprehensive Income For The Year Ended December 31, 20X1

Net income	$120,000
Other comprehensive income:	
Unrealized gain on securities available for sale (net of tax of $20,000)	30,000

Separate Statement of Comprehensive Income XYZ Corporation Consolidated Statement of Comprehensive Income For The Year Ended December 31, 20X1	
Foreign currency translation adjustments (net of tax of $16,000)	24,000
Total other comprehensive income	54,000
Comprehensive income	174,000
Less: comprehensive income attributable to non-controlling interest	**(32,000)**
Comprehensive income attributable to XYZ Corporation	$142,000

XYZ Corporation Consolidated Balance Sheet December 31, 20X1	
Assets:	
Cash	$XX
Accounts receivable	XX
Securities, available-for sale	XX
Property and equipment, net	XX
Total assets	$XX
Liabilities:	
Accounts payable	$XX
Accrued expenses	XX
Deferred income taxes	XX
Total liabilities	XX
Stockholders' equity:	
Common stock	500,000
Retained earnings	2,095,000
Accumulated other comprehensive income	62,000
Total stockholders' equity- XYZ Corporation	2,657,000
Noncontrolling interest	**42,000**
Total equity	2,699,000
Total liabilities and stockholders' equity	$XX

XYZ Corporation Consolidated Statement of Stockholders' Equity For The Year Ended December 31, 20X1					
	Total	Retained Earnings	Accumulated Other Comprehensive Income	Common Stock	Non-controlling interest
Beginning balance (given)	$2,525,000	$2,000,000	$15,000	$500,000	$10,000
Comprehensive income					
Net income	120,000	95,000			(1)25,000
Other comprehensive income - current year	54,000		47,000		(1) 7,000
Ending balance	$2,699,000	$2,095,000	$62,000	$500,000	$42,000

(1) $25,000 + $7,000 = $32,000 comprehensive income attributable to noncontrolling interest.

¶ 514 INTERIM-PERIOD REPORTING

ASC 220-10-45-18, as amended by ASU 2013-02 states that for interim-period reporting, publicly traded companies must meet the reporting requirements in ASC 220 at each reporting period. Companies shall follow the guidance in Subtopic 270-10 for the level of detail required for condensed financial statements for interim-period financial statements. Nonpublic entities must meet the reporting requirements in ASC 220 at each reporting period, except for the requirements in paragraphs 220-10-45-17 through 45-17B. Nonpublic entities are not required to meet the requirements in paragraphs 220-10-45-17 through 45-17B for interim reporting periods but are required to meet them for annual reporting periods.

¶ 515 REPORTING ISSUES: COMPREHENSIVE INCOME

If a separate statement of comprehensive income or a combined statement of income and comprehensive income is chosen to present comprehensive income, the report wording must be changed to reflect the new statement.

SSARS 19 states that if the statement of comprehensive income is presented, reference to the statement should be made in the appropriate paragraphs. Thus, if a statement of comprehensive income is required, the compilation, review, and audit reports should be modified to include reference to the statement.

STUDY QUESTIONS

---

7. Reclassification adjustments are made to _____.

    a. Ensure that items are not classified in the wrong financial statement

    b. Avoid double counting of comprehensive income items

    c. Make sure disclosures thoroughly present information on comprehensive income

    d. Permit a company to present comprehensive income on the correct line in the statement of comprehensive income

8. Company X sells its investment in a foreign entity. How should X deal with the cumulative translation adjustment component?

   a. Retain that amount in equity.

   b. Remove that amount from equity in its entirety.

   c. Remove a portion of the component and retain the remainder in equity.

   d. Reclassify the component to a separate section of equity and re-label it.

9. Company Y makes a partial sale of its investment in a non-foreign entity that is accounted for using the equity method. The sale does not represent a complete or substantially complete liquidation. Which of the following is correct?

   a. The pro rata portion rule applies.

   b. The entire cumulative transaction adjustment should be released into income.

   c. None of the adjustment should be released into income.

   d. The adjustment should be reclassified into a separate section of equity.

MODULE 2: FINANCIAL STATEMENT REPORTING - CHAPTER 6: Other Comprehensive Bases of Accounting (OCBOA) Issues

¶ 601 WELCOME

This chapter covers questions concerning Other Comprehensive Bases of Accounting and provides practical answers for these often-asked questions. It includes numerous examples and illustrations.

¶ 602 LEARNING OBJECTIVES

Upon completion of this chapter, the reader will be able to:

- List and describe three bases of accounting that are considered Other Comprehensive Bases of Accounting
- Identify how certain transactions should be presented, recorded, and disclosed when an entity uses the income tax basis of accounting

¶ 603 DISREGARDED ENTITIES AND INCOME TAX BASIS FINANCIAL STATEMENTS

Question 1: There are instances in which an accountant is required to report on income tax basis financial statements related to a disregarded entity, such as a:

- Grantor Trust
- One-member LLC

If the entity is disregarded for federal income tax purposes, is an accountant permitted to report on that entity as it is not recognized for tax purposes?

Response: Yes.

The definition of an *Other Comprehensive Basis of Accounting* (OCBOA) is found in SSARS No. 19, and includes any of the following:

- *Income tax basis:* A basis of accounting that the reporting entity *uses or expects to use* to file its income tax return for the period covered by the financial statements
- *Cash or modified basis:* Cash basis of accounting and modifications of the cash basis having substantial support
- *Regulatory basis:* A basis of accounting that the reporting entity uses to comply with the requirements or financial reporting provisions of a governmental regulatory agency to whose jurisdiction the entity is subject

The income tax basis is defined as:

"A basis of accounting that the reporting entity uses or expects to use to file its income tax return for the period covered by the financial statements."

However, if an entity is disregarded for tax purposes, it does not file income tax returns.

SSARS No. 19 does not address the issue of what happens if the reporting entity does not directly file income tax returns. However, there is a similar example found in a non-authoritative AICPA Technical Practice Aid, *TIS Section 1400, Consolidated Financial Statements: Combining Financial Statements Prepared in Accordance With the Income Tax Basis of Accounting.*

The TIS addresses the issue of whether an auditor is permitted to report on OCBOA financial statements that differ from the way in which tax returns are filed.

The example found in the TIS deals with brother-sister entities each of which files its own tax return. Yet, for financial statement purposes, the entities are combined and OCBOA financial statements are issued on a combined basis, which is not the same way in which the tax returns are filed.

The nonauthoritative conclusion reached in the TIS is that nothing precludes an auditor from reporting on the combined OCBOA presentations as long as the basis of accounting for each of the underlying entities is the one each *uses or expects to use* to file its income tax return for the reporting period.

Although the facts are not quite the same in the previous example, it would appear that the similar conclusion is reached; that is, as long as the LLC's or grantor trust's financial statements are issued in the format used to file the LLC's or trust's net income (taxable income) on the tax return of the individual who is the beneficiary or member (typically on schedule E and C), OCBOA financial statements may be issued for the trust or LLC and the accountant may report on them.

STUDY QUESTION

---

1. Which of the following is *not* an example of an other comprehensive basis of accounting (OCBOA) under SSARS No. 19?

    a. Regulatory basis

    b. Income tax basis

    c. GAAP basis

    d. Cash basis

Question 2: Because the entity is disregarded, should the financial statements be titled as those related to a sole proprietorship (Schedule C or E) or as an entity (LLC or trust)?

There is no authority to address this matter. Some commentators believe that because the LLC or grantor is a disregarded entity, the entity form should be ignored in preparing the financial statements and should be titled as a sole proprietorship (schedule C or E).

Others believe that the substance of the transaction is that it is a separate LLC or trust and therefore, the identity of the entity should be retained even though the entity is disregarded for tax purposes.

    EXAMPLE: John James is the grantor and sole beneficiary of the JSM Realty Trust, a grantor trust for income tax purposes. The trust holds title to one piece of residential rental property.

    Mary Smith, CPA, is asked to issue a compilation report on the trust using the income tax basis of accounting.

Mary does not prepare a tax return for the grantor trust. Instead, the net rental income of the trust is recorded on Schedule E of John's Form 1040.

Conclusion: Assume Mary wishes to recognize the tax entity in the financial statements. The format would look like the following:

Accountants' Compilation Report

Trustee

JSM Realty Trust

Nowhere, Massachusetts

We have compiled the accompanying statement of assets, liabilities and trust equity- income tax basis of JSM Realty Trust as of December 31, 20X1, and the related statement of revenue, expenses and trust equity- income tax basis, for the year then ended. We have not audited or reviewed the accompanying financial statements and, accordingly, do not express an opinion or provide any assurance about whether the financial statements are in accordance with the income tax basis of accounting.

Trust management is responsible for the preparation and fair presentation of the financial statements in accordance with the income tax basis of accounting, and for designing, implementing, and maintaining internal control relevant to the preparation and fair presentation of the financial statements.

Our responsibility is to conduct the compilation in accordance with Statements on Standards for Accounting and Review Services issued by the American Institute of Certified Public Accountants. The objective of a compilation is to assist **trust management** in presenting financial information in the form of financial statements without undertaking to obtain or provide any assurance that there are no material modifications that should be made to the financial statements.

Trust management has elected to omit substantially all of the disclosures *ordinarily included* in financial statements prepared in accordance with the income tax basis of accounting. If the omitted disclosures were included in the financial statements, they might influence the user's conclusions about the trust's assets, liabilities, equity, revenue, and expenses. Accordingly, the financial statements are not designed for those who are not informed about such matters.

Smith and Smyth, CPA

March 18, 20X2

JSM Realty Trust Statement of Assets, Liabilities and Trust Equity-Income Tax Basis December 31, 20X1 (See Accountants' Compilation Report)	
ASSETS	
Current assets:	
Cash	$40,000
Accounts receivable	10,000
Total current assets	50,000

Property and equipment:

Land	200,000
Building	2,000,000
Equipment	100,000
	2,300,000
Less accumulated depreciation	400,000
Total property and equipment	1,900,000

Other assets:

Utility deposits	5,000
Financing costs, net of amortization	8,000
Total other assets	13,000
	$1,963,000

LIABILITIES AND TRUST EQUITY

Current liabilities:

Accounts payable and accrued expenses	$70,000
Current portion of long-term debt	40,000
Total current liabilities	110,000
Long-term debt	1,600,000
Trust equity	253,000
	$1,963,000

JSM Realty Trust Statement of Revenue, Expenses and Trust Equity-Income Tax Basis For the Year Ended December 31, 20X1 (See Accountants' Compilation Report)

Revenue:

Rental income	$800,000
Laundry income	30,000
	830,000

Expenses:

Advertising	10,000
Depreciation	85,000

Amortization	1,000
Real estate taxes	30,000
Repairs and maintenance	45,000
Cleaning	6,000
Utilities	25,000
Interest	92,000
Sundry other	5,000
	299,000
Net income- income tax basis	531,000
Trust equity:	
Beginning of year	122,000
Distributions	(400,000)
End of year	$ 253,000

Change the facts: Assume the entity is JSM Realty LLC, a one-member LLC, and a disregarded entity.

Accountants' Compilation Report

Managing Member

JSM Realty LLC

Nowhere, Massachusetts

We have compiled the accompanying statement of assets, liabilities and member's equity- income tax basis of **JSM Realty LLC** as of December 31, 20X1, and the related statement of revenue expenses and member's equity- income tax basis for the year then ended. We have not audited or reviewed the accompanying financial statements and, accordingly, do not express an opinion or provide any assurance about whether the financial statements are in accordance with the income tax basis of accounting.

Management is responsible for the preparation and fair presentation of the financial statements in accordance with the income tax basis of accounting, and for designing, implementing, and maintaining internal control relevant to the preparation and fair presentation of the financial statements.

Our responsibility is to conduct the compilation in accordance with Statements on Standards for Accounting and Review Services issued by the American Institute of Certified Public Accountants. The objective of a compilation is to assist management in presenting financial information in the form of financial statements without undertaking to obtain or provide any assurance that there are no material modifications that should be made to the financial statements.

Management has elected to omit substantially all of the disclosures *ordinarily included* in financial statements prepared in accordance with the income tax basis of accounting. If the omitted disclosures were included in the financial statements, they might influence the user's conclusions about the entity's assets, liabilities, equity, revenue, and expenses. Accordingly, the financial statements are not designed for those who are not informed about such matters.

Smith and Smyth, CPA

March 18, 20X2

JSM Realty LLC Statement of Assets, Liabilities and Member's Equity-Income Tax Basis December 31, 20X1 (See Accountants' Compilation Report)

ASSETS

Current assets:	
Cash	$40,000
Accounts receivable	10,000
Total current assets	50,000
Property and equipment:	
Land	200,000
Building	2,000,000
Equipment	100,000
	2,300,000
Less accumulated depreciation	400,000
Total property and equipment	1,900,000
Other assets:	
Utility deposits	5,000
Financing costs, net of amortization	8,000
Total other assets	13,000
	$1,963,000

LIABILITIES AND MEMBER'S EQUITY

Current liabilities:	
Accounts payable and accrued expenses	$70,000
Current portion of long-term debt	40,000
Total current liabilities	110,000
Long- term debt	1,600,000
Member's equity	253,000
	$1,963,000

JSM Realty LLC Statement of Revenue, Expenses and Member's Equity-Income Tax Basis For the Year Ended December 31, 20X1 (See Accountants' Compilation Report)	
Revenue:	
Rental income	$800,000
Laundry income	30,000
	830,000
Expenses:	
Advertising	10,000
Depreciation	85,000
Amortization	1,000
Real estate taxes	30,000
Repairs and maintenance	45,000
Cleaning	6,000
Utilities	25,000
Interest	92,000
Sundry other	5,000
	299,000
Net income- income tax basis	531,000
Member's equity:	
Beginning of year	122,000
Distributions	(400,000)
End of year	$253,000

Change the facts again: Assume the entity is JSM Realty LLC, is a one-member LLC, and Mary CPA decides to present the financial statements as a sole proprietorship (Schedule E), thereby ignoring the entity.

Accountants' Compilation Report

Mr. John James

JSM Realty LLC

Nowhere, Massachusetts

We have compiled the accompanying statement of assets, liabilities and **proprietor's equity**-income tax basis of JSM Realty LLC (**a sole proprietorship**) as of December 31, 20X1, and the related statement of revenue and expenses- income tax basis for the year then ended. We have not audited or reviewed the accompanying financial statements and, accordingly, do not express an opinion or provide any assurance about whether the financial statements are in accordance with the income tax basis of accounting.

The owner is responsible for the preparation and fair presentation of the financial statements in accordance with the income tax basis of accounting, and for designing, implementing, and maintaining internal control relevant to the preparation and fair presentation of the financial statements.

Our responsibility is to conduct the compilation in accordance with Statements on Standards for Accounting and Review Services issued by the American Institute of Certified Public Accountants. The objective of a compilation is to assist management in presenting financial information in the form of financial statements without undertaking to obtain or provide any assurance that there are no material modifications that should be made to the financial statements.

The owner has elected to omit substantially all of the disclosures *ordinarily included* in financial statements prepared in accordance with the income tax basis of accounting. If the omitted disclosures were included in the financial statements, they might influence the user's conclusions about the trust's assets, liabilities, equity, revenue, and expenses. Accordingly, the financial statements are not designed for those who are not informed about such matters.

Smith and Smyth, CPA

March 18, 20X2

JSM Realty LLC Statement of Assets, Liabilities and Proprietor's Equity-Income Tax Basis December 31, 20X1 (See Accountants' Compilation Report)

ASSETS

Current assets:	
Cash	$40,000
Accounts receivable	10,000
Total current assets	50,000
Property and equipment:	
Land	200,000
Building	2,000,000
Equipment	100,000
	2,300,000
Less accumulated depreciation	400,000
Total property and equipment	1,900,000
Other assets:	
Utility deposits	5,000
Financing costs, net of amortization	8,000
Total other assets	13,000
	$1,963,000

LIABILITIES AND PROPRIETOR'S EQUITY

Current liabilities:

Accounts payable and accrued expenses	$70,000
Current portion of long-term debt	40,000
Total current liabilities	110,000
Long-term debt	1,600,000
Proprietor's equity	253,000
	$1,963,000

JSM Realty LLC Statement of Revenue, Expenses and Proprietor's Equity- Income Tax Basis For the Year Ended December 31, 20X1 (See Accountants' Compilation Report)

Revenue:

Rental income	$800,000
Laundry income	30,000
	830,000

Expenses:

Advertising	10,000
Depreciation	85,000
Amortization	1,000
Real estate taxes	30,000
Repairs and maintenance	45,000
Cleaning	6,000
Utilities	25,000
Interest	92,000
Sundry other	5,000
	299,000
Net income- income tax basis	531,000

Proprietor's equity:

Beginning of year	122,000
Distributions	(400,000)
End of year	$ 253,000

OBSERVATION: In the previous example, if the accountant decides to report on the one-member LLC (or grantor trust) as a sole proprietorship, the legal name of the entity does not change, which is, in this case, JSM Realty LLC.

Question 3: Does the decision to report on a grantor trust as a trust (instead of a sole proprietorship) change if the accountant files a Form 1041 Grantor Trust information return for the grantor trust?

Response: Although a grantor trust generally is a disregarded entity, the entity is permitted to file a Form 1041 grantor trust return with grantor information. If a Form 1041 trust return is filed for the grantor trust, the accountant should report on the trust as a trust and not a sole proprietorship.

Question 4: What if a one-member LLC makes a check-the-box election to be taxed as a C corporation or an S corporation?

Response: If the LLC is going to be taxed as a C or S corporation, this means that a Form 1120 or 1120S tax return will be filed. In such a case, the LLC should be reported on as an LLC and not as a sole proprietorship. If there is a tax provision because the LLC is taxed as a C corporation, that tax provision should be reflected in the income tax basis financial statements even though the entity is an LLC.

STUDY QUESTION

2. A one-member LLC makes a check-the-box election to be taxed as a C corporation. How should the LLC be reported if financial statements are issued using the income tax basis of accounting?

    a. As an LLC without a tax provision

    b. As a sole proprietorship

    c. As an LLC with a tax provision for the entity tax

    d. As a partnership

¶ 604 PRESENTING INSOLVENCY IN INCOME TAX BASIS FINANCIAL STATEMENTS

Question 1: Internal Revenue Code (Code) Sec. 108 provides for a portion or all of cancellation of debt (COD) income to be excluded from taxable income under various tests, one of which is the "insolvency exception."

If an entity has Code Sec. 108 income that is excluded from taxable income under the insolvency exception, should that income be presented on income tax basis financial statements?

Response: Nothing has been written authoritatively on this matter. However, there are parallel situations that have become generally accepted within income tax basis financial statements, involving nontaxable and nondeductible items (permanent differences).

First, let's understand Code Sec. 108.

Code Sec. 108 deals with COD income. Under this section, the amount of COD income recognized generally is equal to the excess of the amount of debt forgiven over the fair value of the asset.

Code Sec. 108 provides certain exclusions under which COD income is excludable from taxable income. One of those exclusions is the insolvency exception.

The insolvency exception states that COD income is excludable from taxable income to the extent that "immediately before the discharge," total liabilities exceed the fair value of total assets. Code Sec. 108 also has rules under which an entity (or taxpayer) must reduce its tax attributes (NOLs, credits, etc.) by the amount of excludable COD income.

Insolvency is determined at different levels depending on the type of entity:

- Partnership or LLC: Insolvency is determined at the member or partner level

- S or C corporation: Insolvency is determined at the entity level

> **EXAMPLE:** Company X has $1,000,000 of COD income.

Immediately before the discharge of the debt that created the COD income, total liabilities exceeded the fair value of X's assets by $600,000.

Conclusion: $600,000 of the $1,000,000 is excludable from taxable income, while the remaining $400,000 is taxable.

> Now let's address the issue of income tax basis financial statements.

Question 2: If an entity has COD income, a portion of which is excludable from taxable income, should that excluded income be presented on the income statement of income tax basis financial statements?

Response: Although there is no specific authority dealing with Code Sec. 108 COD income, there is similar guidance that has been followed by most practitioners in connection with nontaxable income and nondeductible expenses, otherwise known as permanent differences. Examples include nondeductible meals and entertainment expense, penalties and fines, life insurance, and nontaxable interest.

It has become generally accepted that although these permanent differences are not included in taxable income (and are treated as Schedule M-1 items), income tax basis financial statements include these items as income and expense items. Thus, net income on income tax basis financial statements does not agree with taxable income on the tax return.

The portion of Code Sec. 108 COD income that is excluded from taxable income is nothing more than a permanent difference just like other nontaxable income, such as nontaxable municipal interest income. Thus, such excluded COD income should probably be presented on a statement of income as income in the income tax basis financial statements.

> **EXAMPLE:** Company X, a C corporation, has the following information for year ended December 31, 20X1:

COD income	*$1,000,000*
Portion excludable from taxable income under the insolvency exception	*(600,000)*
Taxable portion of COD income	*$400,000*

Conclusion: X's statement of revenue and expenses- income tax basis would present the COD income as follows:

¶604

Option 1: Present the COD income as part of other income, in total

Company X Statement of Revenue and Expenses- Income Tax Basis For the Year Ended December 31, 20X1	
Net sales	$20,000,000
Cost of sales	15,000,000
Gross profit on sales	5,000,000
Operating expenses	7,000,000
Net operating loss	(2,000,000)
Other income:	
Forgiveness of debt income	**1,000,000**
Interest income	100,000
Net loss before income taxes	(900,000)
Income taxes (credit)	(300,000)
Net loss- income tax basis	$(600,000)

Option 2: Present the portion of COD income that is not taxable in a separate section

Company X Statement of Revenue and Expenses- Income Tax Basis For the Year Ended December 31, 20X1	
Net sales	$20,000,000
Cost of sales	15,000,000
Gross profit on sales	5,000,000
Operating expenses	7,000,000
Net operating loss	(2,000,000)
Other income:	
Forgiveness of debt income	**400,000**
Interest income	100,000
Net taxable loss before income taxes	(1,500,000)
Non-taxable items:	
Non-taxable portion of forgiveness of debt income	**600,000**
Net loss before income taxes	(900,000)
Income taxes (credit)	(300,000)
Net loss- income tax basis	$ (600,000)

OBSERVATION: Either Option 1 or 2 is an acceptable presentation although Option 2 offers the user the additional information on the portion of the COD income that is excludable from taxable income.

STUDY QUESTION

3. How is the portion of Code Sec. 108 cancellation of debt (COD) income that is *not* taxable treated on income tax basis financial statements?

    a. Excluded from the statement of income

    b. Disclosed only

    c. Presented as income

    d. Presented as part of comprehensive income

¶ 605 DISCLOSURES OF FAIR VALUE- INCOME TAX BASIS FINANCIAL STATEMENTS

Question 1: If an entity presented financial statements on the income tax basis of accounting, must fair value disclosures be included in the notes?

Response: Generally not.

GAAP requires an entity to record fair value disclosures as follows:

- *Items recorded on the balance sheet at fair value*—all entities must include fair value disclosures for items recorded on the balance sheet at fair value.

- *Financial instruments not recorded at fair value*—SEC companies, and nonpublic entities with either 1) total assets of $100 million or more or 2) recorded derivatives, must include fair value disclosures for financial instruments even if they are not recorded at fair value on the balance sheet.

With respect to income tax basis financial statements, assets and liabilities that would otherwise be recorded at fair value (such as investments in equity securities, derivatives, etc.), are recorded at cost. Therefore, an entity would not be required to include disclosures about fair value information with respect to those items.

However, if a nonpublic entity has total assets of $100 million or more or recorded derivatives, GAAP requires that entity to include fair value disclosures for all financial instruments even if those instruments are not recorded at fair value. A similar disclosure would be required if that same large nonpublic entity ($100 million or more, or derivatives) issued income tax basis financial statements.

EXAMPLE: Company X, a nonpublic entity, has total assets of $20 million for which income tax basis financial statements are issued. X has an investment in bonds that is recorded at cost in accordance with the Code.

Conclusion: Regardless of the type of financial statements presented (GAAP, OCBOA, etc.), fair value disclosures are not required because X has no assets or liabilities recorded at fair value. X is a nonpublic entity and its total assets do not exceed $100 million and it has no derivatives. Thus, under GAAP rules, fair value disclosures would not be required unless an asset or liability is recorded on the balance sheet at fair value.

EXAMPLE 2: Company X is a nonpublic entity with total assets of $150 million for which income tax basis financial statements are issued. X has an investment in bonds that is recorded at cost.

Conclusion: Because X has total assets of $100 million or more, GAAP requires X to include fair value information about financial instruments *even if those instruments are not recorded at fair value*. That's the GAAP side of the rules.

When income tax basis financial statements are issued, such statements much include disclosures that are "similarly informative" to those disclosures required by GAAP. Thus, X would have to include fair value disclosures about its financial instruments (e.g., the bond investment) even though they are not recorded at fair value in the income tax basis financial statements.

Should the fact that fair value is not used be disclosed as a primary difference between income tax basis and GAAP financial statements?

Yes. When income tax basis financial statements are issued, SAS No. 122, AU-C Section 800, *Special Considerations—Audits of Financial Statements Prepared in Accordance With Special Purpose Frameworks*, provides guidance as to the extent of disclosures that are required when reporting on special purpose frameworks, which include income tax and cash basis financial statements.

The AU-C requires that financial statements prepared on a special-purpose framework (such as income tax basis) should include the following disclosures:

- Summary of significant accounting policies
- Basis of accounting and how it differs from GAAP
- Similar informative disclosures to those required by GAAP

One of the differences that should be disclosed is the fact that certain assets that would be recorded at fair value under GAAP are recorded at cost under the income tax basis.

> **NOTE X: BASIS OF ACCOUNTING**
>
> The accompanying financial statements present financial results on the accrual basis of accounting used for federal income tax purposes which **differs** from the accrual basis of accounting required under generally accepted accounting principles. The **primary differences** between the Company's method and the method required by generally accepted accounting principles is that a) depreciation has been recorded using accelerated methods authorized in the Code, b) uncollectible accounts on accounts receivable are recorded when deemed uncollectible without use of an allowance account, c) certain accruals for compensation and other expenses are recorded when paid rather than when incurred, d) certain costs are capitalized to inventory that are not typically capitalized under generally accepted accounting principles, and *e) certain investments are recorded at cost when such investments are recorded at fair value under generally accepted accounting principles.*

The above element (e) would only apply if the entity has investments that, under GAAP, would be recorded at fair value.

¶ 606 USING OCBOA BASED ON A METHOD THAT DIFFERS FROM THE INCOME TAX RETURN

Question 1: May an entity that uses the cash basis of accounting to prepare its federal income tax return issue financial statements on the income tax basis of accounting using the accrual basis?

Response: SSARS No. 19 defines OCBOA to include income tax basis financial statements. However, the income tax basis is defined as "a basis of accounting that the reporting entity *uses or expects to use to file its income tax return* for the period covered by the financial statements."

What this means is that the entity must use the basis used or expected to be used to prepare its tax return. Thus, if the tax return is prepared on the cash basis, the income tax basis financial statements must also be on a cash basis. Further, if the entity wishes to prepare income tax basis financial statements on an accrual basis, it must file its income tax return on an accrual basis.

This situation is problematic for many companies who file their income tax return on a cash basis, yet wish to prepare income tax basis financial statements on an accrual basis, as it is more meaningful to do so. Such a scenario is not authorized by SSARS No. 19.

The solution—the income tax basis of accounting departure!

One way to issue income tax basis financial statements on an accrual basis, while continuing to file cash basis income tax returns, is to issue a report with an income tax basis of accounting departure, similar to a GAAP departure. The difference is that there is a departure from the rules for the income tax basis of accounting (found in SSARS No. 19 rather than GAAP.) SSARS No. 19 requires the basis to be the same as the one used for filing the income tax return. By preparing accrual basis financial statements, the entity is violating SSARS No. 19.

Following are sample reports:

Compilation Report- Income Tax Basis of Accounting with Report Exception

Accountant's Compilation Report

Board of Directors

XYZ Company

55 North Street,

Boston, Massachusetts 02113

We have compiled the accompanying statement of assets, liabilities and stockholders' equity- income tax basis of XYZ Company as of December 31, 20XX, and the related statement of revenue, expenses and retained earnings-income tax basis for the year then ended. We have not audited or reviewed the accompanying financial statements and, accordingly, do not express an opinion or provide any assurance about whether the financial statements are in accordance with the income tax basis of accounting.

Management is responsible for the preparation and fair presentation of the financial statements in accordance with the *income tax basis of accounting* and for designing, implementing, and maintaining internal control relevant to the preparation and fair presentation of the financial statements.

Our responsibility is to conduct the compilation in accordance with Statements on Standards for Accounting and Review Services issued by the American Institute of Certified Public Accountants. The objective of a compilation is to assist management in presenting financial information in the form of financial statements without undertaking to obtain or provide any assurance that there are no material modifications that should be made to the financial statements. *During our compilation, I (we) did become aware of a departure from the income tax basis of accounting that is described in the following paragraph.*

The income tax basis of accounting requires that financial statements prepared on the income tax basis of accounting use the same basis used or expected to be used to file the Company's income tax return. Management has informed us that the company has prepared the accompanying financial statements on the accrual basis of accounting while it files its federal income tax return on the cash basis of accounting. If the cash basis had been followed, net income and stockholders' equity would have decreased by $100,000.

Management has elected to omit substantially all of the disclosures ordinarily included in financial statements prepared in accordance with the income tax basis of accounting. If the omitted disclosures were included in the financial statements, they might influ-

¶606

ence the user's conclusions about the company's assets, liabilities, equity, revenue, and expenses. Accordingly, the financial statements are not designed for those who are not informed about such matters.

James J. Fox & Company, CPA

[Date (date of completion of compilation engagement)]

Review Report-Income Tax Basis of Accounting with Report Exception
Independent Accountant's Review Report

Board of Directors

XYZ Company

55 North Street

Boston, Massachusetts 02113

We have reviewed the accompanying statement of assets, liabilities, and stockholders' equity—income tax basis of XYZ Company as of December 31, 20XX, and the related statement of revenue, expenses and retained earnings, and cash flows—income tax basis for the year then ended. A review includes primarily applying analytical procedures to management's financial data and making inquiries of company management. A review is substantially less in scope than an audit, the objective of which is the expression of an opinion regarding the financial statements as a whole. Accordingly, we do not express such an opinion.

Management is responsible for the preparation and fair presentation of the financial statements in accordance with the income tax basis for accounting and for designing, implementing, and maintaining internal control relevant to the preparation and fair presentation of the financial statements.

Our responsibility is to conduct the review in accordance with Statements on Standards for Accounting and Review Services issued by the American Institute of Certified Public Accountants. Those standards require us to perform procedures to obtain limited assurance that there are no material modifications that should be made to the financial statements. We believe that the results of my (our) procedures provides a reasonable basis for our report.

Based on our review, **with the exception of the matter described in the following paragraph**, we are not aware of any material modifications that should be made to the accompanying financial statements in order for them to be in **conformity with the income tax basis of accounting, as described in Note 1**.

As described in Note 2, the income tax basis of accounting requires that financial statements prepared on the income tax basis of accounting use the same basis used or expected to be used to file the Company's income tax return. Management has informed us that the company has prepared the accompanying financial statements on the accrual basis of accounting while it files its federal income tax return on the cash basis of accounting. If the cash basis had been followed, net income and stockholders' equity would have decreased by $100,000.

James J. Fox & Company, CPA

[Date]

> **NOTE:** Effective in 2012, auditing standards eliminated the term "OCBOA" and replaced it with the term "special purpose framework", as found in AU-C Section 800, *Special Considerations—Audits of Financial Statements Prepared in Accordance With Special Purpose Frameworks*.

¶606

In January 2013, the Auditing Standards Board issued SAS No. 127, *Omnibus Statement on Auditing Standards—2013*. SAS No. 127 added a new category to the definition of a special purpose framework (formerly OCBOA) which is defined as:

> Other basis: A basis of accounting that uses a definite set of logical, reasonable criteria that is applied to all material items appearing in financial statements.

This new category appears to capture any framework that has a set of logical, reasonable criteria and could include a framework based on income tax basis financial statements prepared on a method other than the one used to file the entity's tax return. For example, an entity prepares its tax return on the cash basis but wishes to issue income tax basis financial statements on the accrual basis.

The definition of income tax basis financial statements found in SSARS No. 19 has not yet been modified to include the SAS No. 127 definition that includes the "other basis" category.

¶ 607 INCOME TAX BASIS AND THE "EXPECTS TO USE" CRITERION

Question 1: An accountant has Company X's December 31, 20X1 tax return on extension and "expects" to file it on the accrual basis of accounting.

On March 18, 20X2, the accountant decides to issue a compilation report on income tax basis financial statements that X prepared on the accrual basis of accounting, which is the method on which the accountant expects to file the tax return.

On October 15, 20X2, the accountant actually files X's income tax return on the cash basis.

Is the fact that the accountant filed the report on the accrual basis and then files the return on the cash basis mean that the originally issued financial statements were erroneously issued under the income tax basis of accounting?

Response: SSARS No. 19 defines OCBOA to include income tax basis financial statements. However, the income tax basis is defined as "a basis of accounting that the reporting entity uses *or expects to use* to file its income tax return for the period covered by the financial statements."

At the time the accountant issued the financial statements, presumably the client expected to file the tax return using the accrual basis. The fact that in the end the client changed his or her mind and chose to file the tax return on the cash basis, does not mean that the financial statements were improperly prepared using the accrual basis. The term "expects to use to file" must take into account the intent of the reporting entity. At the time the financial statements were issued, the client intended to file tax returns using the accrual basis.

Now, this scenario can apply in one year but probably cannot occur from year to year. In theory, a client could inform the accountant that the entity expects to file its tax return in October using the accrual basis, and then actually file the return on a cash basis. If this situation occurs from year to year, it would raise a question as to whether the reporting entity actually "expects" to use the accrual basis of accounting to file its tax return.

¶ 608 INCOME TAX BASIS FINANCIAL STATEMENTS— STATE INCOME TAX BASIS OF ACCOUNTING

Question 1: Company X wishes to issue income tax basis financial statements. Because of the significant amount of depreciation taken for federal income tax purposes (due to Section 179 and bonus depreciation), X wishes to use the income tax basis of accounting based on its state income tax laws, not federal. By using the state tax basis, certain depreciation deductions are not allowed, thereby showing a slightly higher profit.

Is X permitted to issue state income tax basis financial statements?

Response: The definition of an *Other Comprehensive Basis of Accounting* (OCBOA) is found in two sections within accounting and auditing literature:

- SSARS No. 19 defines the income tax basis of accounting as:

  "A basis of accounting that the reporting entity *uses or expects to use* to file its income tax return for the period covered by the financial statements."

- AU-C 800, *Special Considerations* (formerly SAS No. 62), defined the "tax basis" as:

  "A basis of accounting that the entity *uses* to file its income tax return for the period covered by the financial statements."

Notice that the two definitions include the language "income tax return" with no distinction between a federal or state tax return.

Absent language to the contrary, there is no reason why an entity cannot issue income tax basis financial statements using the state income tax basis of accounting, provided the entity discloses that fact.

¶ 609 MISCELLANEOUS DISCLOSURES—INCOME TAX BASIS OF ACCOUNTING

Question 1: Do the disclosure and measurement requirements for uncertain tax positions in GAAP need to be included in income tax basis financial statements?

Response: The requirements to record a liability for the effect of an uncertain tax position do not apply to income tax basis financial statements because such a liability is not required or allowed under the Code.

However, certain disclosures that are required for GAAP statements also have to be included in income tax basis financial statements, as follows:

Tax Uncertainties

The Company's policy is to record interest expense and penalties in operating expenses. For the year ended December 31, 20XX, there was no interest and penalties expense recorded and no accrued interest and penalties.

The Company is subject to U.S. federal and state income tax examinations for tax years 20X1 to 20X5.

Question 2: Is an entity required to disclosure information on management's evaluation of subsequent events in income tax basis financial statements?

Response: Yes. Such a disclosure is required for all financial statement formats.

Question 3: Do the consolidation of variable interest entity rules and requirements found in FIN 46R apply to financial statements prepared using the income tax basis of accounting?

Response: No. Because the Code does not provide for consolidation of variable interest entities, the FIN 46R rules and their application do not apply to income tax basis financial statements.

¶ 610 PRESENTING SECTION 179 AND BONUS DEPRECIATION ON THE INCOME TAX BASIS INCOME STATEMENT

Question 1: XYZ Company has a large amount of Section 179 and bonus depreciation. X issues income tax basis financial statements (accrual basis) and is concerned that the large amount of depreciation distorts its income statement.

Is there a way in which X can present the Section 179 and bonus depreciation?

Response: Yes. Because the rules for income tax basis financial statements are limited, the company has flexibility as to how depreciation is presented. One way that may be effective is to present Section 179 and bonus depreciation as an other income/deduction item in the income statement. Below are two examples that illustrate this approach.

Statement of Revenues and Expenses-Income Tax Basis Section 179 and Bonus Depreciation Presented Separate from Other Depreciation C Corporation

XYZ Company Statement of Revenues, Expenses and Retained Earnings-Income Tax Basis For the Year Ended December 31, 20XX (See Accountant's Compilation Report)	
Net sales	$1,200,000
Cost of sales- tax return	800,000
Gross profit	400,000
Deductible expenses:	
Officer's compensation	25,000
Salaries and wages	25,000
Utilities	10,000
Advertising and promotion	5,000
Insurance	2,000
Uncollectible accounts	21,000
Payroll taxes and fringe benefits	12,000
State excise taxes	5,000
Interest	18,000
Depreciation	**20,000**
Sundry other expenses	5,000
Total deductible expenses	148,000
Taxable state income	252,000
State income taxes	(25,000)
Taxable federal income before accelerated depreciation	227,000

Additional first-year depreciation	(180,000)
Taxable federal income	**47,000
Non-taxable and non-deductible item:	
Federal income tax expense	(7,500)
Non-deductible life insurance	(12,000)
Nondeductible meals and entertainment	(2,500)
Non-taxable interest	3,000
Net income	28,000
Retained earnings:	
Beginning of year	71,900
End of year	$99,900

** Agrees with line 28 of tax return.

Statement of Revenues and Expenses-Income Tax Basis Section 179 and Bonus Depreciation Presented Separate from Other Depreciation S Corporation

XYZ Company (An S Corporation) Statement of Revenues and Expenses-Income Tax Basis For the Year Ended December 31, 20XX (See Accountant's Compilation Report)

Net sales	$1,300,000
Cost of sales- tax return	900,000
Gross profit	400,000
Deductible expenses:	
Officer's compensation	25,000
Salaries and wages	25,000
Utilities	10,000
Advertising and promotion	5,000
Insurance	2,000
Uncollectible accounts	21,000
Payroll taxes and fringe benefits	12,000
State excise taxes	5,000
Interest	18,000
Depreciation	**20,000**
Sundry other expenses	5,000
Total deductible expenses	148,000
Taxable ordinary income-state tax purposes	252,000**

State income taxes	(25,000)
Taxable ordinary income	227,000
Other taxable income (deductible expenses):	
Interest***	1,000
Dividends***	5,000
Additional first-year depreciation***	(180,000)
Total taxable income**	53,000
Non-taxable and non-deductible items:	
Non-deductible life insurance	(12,000)
Nondeductible meals and entertainment	(2,500)
Non-taxable interest	3,000
Net income	$41,500

** Agrees with Schedule K of Form 1120S.
*** Schedule K items.

MODULE 2: FINANCIAL STATEMENT REPORTING—CHAPTER 7: Joint and Several Liability Arrangements (ASC 405-40)

¶701 WELCOME

This chapter discusses ASC 405-40—*Liabilities (Topic 405): Obligations Resulting from Joint and Several Liability Arrangements*. It examines requirements of the ASC including the scope, disclosures, and transition rules. Numerous examples are included.

¶702 LEARNING OBJECTIVES

Upon completion of this chapter, the reader will be able to:

- Identify how a reporting entity measures an obligation under ASC 405-40
- State the obligations to which ASC 405-40 applies
- Describe the obligations to which ASC 460 applies

¶703 OVERVIEW

ASC 405-40 provides guidance for the recognition, measurement, and disclosure of obligations resulting from joint and several liability arrangements for which the total amount of the obligation within the scope of this guidance is fixed at the reporting date. It does not apply to obligations addressed within other U.S. GAAP.

¶704 BACKGROUND

In some instances, several entities may engage in a transaction in which each entity is jointly and severally liable for the joint obligations of the entities; that is, a liability is established that is shared by more than one party. Examples of such obligations include:

- Debt arrangements
- Contractual obligations
- Settled litigation and judicial rulings

Prior to the issuance of ASU 2013-04, now ASC 405-40, U.S. GAAP offered no specific guidance on accounting for such obligations, including the recognition, measurement, and disclosure of such obligations. Consequently, there were variations in practice.

Some entities recorded the entire amount of the obligation under the joint and several liability. This is on the basis of the concept of a liability and based on the premise that the amount recorded should equal the amount that must be satisfied to extinguish a liability under the guidance in ASC 405-20—*Liabilities—Extinguishments of Liabilities*.

Other entities recorded a portion of the total obligations allocated among all obligors. The allocation method may be based on the amount allocated among the entities, the amount of proceeds received, or the portion of the amount the entity agreed to pay among its co-obligors. This allocation method is based on guidance found in the contingent liabilities rules in ASC 450-20—*Contingencies—Loss Contingencies*, and ASC 410-30—*Asset Retirement and Environmental Obligations—Environmental Obligations*.

ASC 410-30 permits an entity to record its estimated portion of the total obligation subject to joint and several liability.

> **NOTE:** International standards also do not offer specific guidance on the accounting and disclosures related to obligations under joint and several liability arrangements. Instead, international standards require an entity to treat that portion of a joint and several liability that is expected to be met by other parties as a contingent liability under International Accounting Standards (IAS) 37, *Provisions, Contingent Liabilities and Contingent Assets*. Although the guidance of IAS 37 applies to contingent liabilities, contingent liabilities are not included within the scope of ASC 405-40. However, the measurement approach in IAS 37 for joint and several liabilities is rather consistent with the measurement approach in ASC 405-40. In effect, ASC 405-40 does not eliminate any existing differences that currently exist between U.S. GAAP and IFRS.

ASC 405-40 requires an entity to measure obligations resulting from joint and several liability arrangements for which the total amount of the obligation is fixed at the reporting date, as the sum of two components:

1. The amount the reporting entity agreed to pay on the basis of its arrangement among its co-obligors

2. Any additional amount the reporting entity expects to pay on behalf of its co-obligors

> **NOTE:** The FASB Emerging Issues Task Force (EITF) chose not to define the term "expects to pay." Consequently, an entity should weigh all facts and circumstances to determine the amount that an entity expects to pay on behalf of all co-obligors (co-borrowers).

If there is some amount within a range of the additional amount the reporting entity expects to pay that is a better estimate than any other amount within the range, that amount shall be the additional amount included in the measurement of the obligation. If no amount within the range is a better estimate than any other amount, then the minimum amount in the range shall be the additional amount included in the measurement of the obligation.

> **OBSERVATION:** Use of the "better estimate" within a range or, absent a better estimate, the minimum amount within the range, is consistent with the rules found in ASC 450, related to loss contingencies.

> **OBSERVATION:** ASC 410-30-30—*Asset Retirement and Environmental Obligations, Environmental Obligations-Initial Measurement*, offers a parallel to the accounting for the joint and several obligation situation found in ASC 405-40. In ASC 410-30-30, an entity is required to record an environmental remediation liability based on that entity's estimate of its allocable share of the joint and several remediation liability. In making that estimate, the entity is required to take certain actions that include assessing the likelihood that other parties will pay their full allocable share of the joint and several remediation liability. In ASC 405-40, the FASB EITF does not require that the co-borrower assessment the "likelihood" that other parties will pay. Instead, the company should calculate the amount it "expects to pay," which does not reflect likelihood.

The guidance in the ASC also requires an entity to disclose the nature and amount of the obligation as well as other information about those obligations.

Problem with Current Practice

One of the problems with existing practice that led to the issuance of ASC 405-40 was that several co-borrowers involved with each other under a joint and several liability arrangement would potentially record duplicate liabilities to account for the same liability obligation.

> **EXAMPLE:** Companies X, Y, and Z are co-borrowers of a loan in the amount of $3 million. Each of the companies receives one-third of the proceeds ($1 million) and each is jointly and severally liable for the entire $3 million. Because each company is potentially liable for $3 million, each company records the entire $3 million liability even though each only receives $1 million. The result is that the entire liability recorded among the three entities is:

	Liability Recorded
Company X	$3,000,000
Company Y	3,000,000
Company Z	3,000,000
	$9,000,000

Because of the fact that each company is jointly and severally liable for the entire $3 million, the companies collectively record total liabilities of $9 million. There is clearly redundancy.

¶ 705 SCOPE

ASC 405-40 applies to all entities, both public and nonpublic, that have obligations resulting from joint and several liability arrangements for which the total amount of the obligation is fixed at the reporting date and for which no specific guidance exists. The ASC applies to obligations that have the following two criteria:

1. There must be a joint and several liability arrangement.

2. The total amount under the arrangement must be fixed at the reporting date.

ASC 405-40 does not apply to obligations accounted for under the following ASC topics:

- *Asset Retirement and Environmental Obligations*, ASC 410
- *Contingencies*, ASC 450
- *Guarantees*, ASC 460
- *Compensation—Retirement Benefits*, ASC 715
- *Income Taxes*, ASC 740

In order for the total amount of an obligation to be considered fixed at the reporting date, there can be no measurement uncertainty at the reporting date relating to the total amount of the obligation. However, although the obligation must be fixed at the reporting date, the total amount of the obligation may change subsequent to the reporting date because of factors that are unrelated to measurement uncertainty.

> **EXAMPLE:** Company X has a line of credit obligation under a joint and several arrangement with another company. Both X and the other company have joint and several liability under the line of credit. At the reporting date, the amount of the line of credit outstanding is fixed. Although the amount of the line of credit outstanding is fixed at the reporting date, the total amount of the obligation (line of credit) may change in future periods because an additional amount is borrowed under the line of credit, or because the interest rate on the line of credit changes. The fact that the amount of the obligation might change subsequent to the reporting date does not negate the fact that the obligation is fixed at the reporting date.

ASC 405-40 applies to all joint and several liability arrangements for which the total amount of the obligation is fixed at the reporting date, regardless of the relationship among parties involved in the arrangement. A joint and several liability arrangement is not excluded from the scope of the ASC because the parties involved are unrelated or related.

ASC 405-40 does not apply to guarantors of an obligation. A joint and several liability arrangement involving an entity as a guarantor (instead of borrower) of an obligation must follow the guidance of ASC 460, *Guarantees*, and not ASC 405-40.

> **OBSERVATION:** ASC 405-40 applies only to situations in which the entity is a primary borrower under a joint and several obligation, and not as a guarantor. In situations in which the entity is a guarantor, that obligation is excluded from the scope of ASC 405-40, and, instead, is covered under ASC 460, *Guarantees*.

Liabilities subject to a measurement uncertainty (e.g., not fixed) are excluded from the scope of the ASC and should continue to be accounted for under the guidance in ASC 450, *Contingencies*, or other U.S. GAAP.

STUDY QUESTIONS

1. In order for ASC 405-40 to apply to an entity, the total amount under the arrangement must be _____.

   a. Predictable

   b. Calculable

   c. Fixed

   d. Variable

2. ASC 405-40:

   a. Does not apply to guarantors of an obligation

   b. Applies to guarantors as long as ASC 460 is followed

   c. Applies to a guarantor only if the guarantor is not the primary obligor

   d. Does not address whether it applies to guarantors

¶706 ADDITIONAL RULES

An arrangement may be included in the scope of the ASC at the inception of the arrangement (such as a debt arrangement), while in other circumstances, the arrangement may be included in the scope of the ASC after the inception of the arrangement (such as when the total amount of the obligation becomes fixed in a subsequent period).

ASC 460-10-25-4 states that at the inception of a guarantee, the guarantor shall recognize in its statement of financial position a liability for that guarantee. The initial measurement of the liability is the fair value of the guarantee. The fair value of the liability shall be based on a standalone arm's-length transaction. When a guarantee is issued in a standalone arm's-length transaction with an unrelated party, the liability recognized at the inception of the guarantee should be the premium received or receivable by the guarantor.

Related Party Guarantees

ASC 460 does not apply to related party guarantees. Therefore, if an entity guarantees the debt of a related party, the guarantor is not required to record a liability (at fair value) in accordance with ASC 460.

EXAMPLE 1: Company X guarantees the debt of its related party, Company Y. Because X is a guarantor of a related-party's debt, the rules found in ASC 460, *Guarantees*, apply. Under those 460 rules, X is exempt from having to record a liability for the guarantee obligation, because X is giving a related-party guarantee.

If, instead, X and Y were not related parties, X would be recorded to record a liability at the inception of the guarantee, based on the fair value of the guarantee on that date.

EXAMPLE 2: Company X is a co-borrower of the debt of its related party, Company Y. Because X is a co-borrower (and not a guarantor) of a related-party, joint and several obligation that is fixed in amount, X must comply with the provisions of ASC 405-40, which require X to record a liability. That liability is recorded on X's balance sheet at:

- The amount that X agreed to pay on the basis of its arrangement with Y, and
- Any additional amount that X expects to pay on behalf of its co-obligor, Y.

The corresponding entry or entries to recording the obligation depend on the facts and circumstances of the obligation. Examples of some corresponding (debit) entries include:

- Cash for proceeds from a debt arrangement
- An expense for a legal settlement
- A receivable (that is assessed for impairment) for a contractual right
- An equity transaction with an entity under common control where there is equity ownership

NOTE: In instances in which a legal or contractual arrangement exists to recover amounts funded under a joint and several obligation from the co-obligors, the FASB EITF noted that a receivable could be recognized at the time the corresponding liability is established. After recording, that receivable would need to be assessed for impairment. When no legal or contractual arrangement exists to recover the funded amounts from the co-obligors, the FASB EITF noted that an entity should consider all relevant facts and circumstances to determine whether the gain contingencies guidance found in ASC 450-30, *Gain Contingencies*, or other guidance would apply in recognizing a receivable for potential recoveries.

Disclosures

An entity shall disclose the following information about each obligation, or each group of similar obligations, resulting from joint and several liability arrangements:

- The nature of the arrangement, including:
  - How the liability arose
  - The relationship with other co-obligors
  - The terms and conditions of the arrangement
- The total outstanding amount under the arrangement, which shall not be reduced by the effect of any amounts that may be recoverable from other entities
- The carrying amount, if any, of an entity's liability and the carrying amount of a receivable recognized, if any

- The nature of any recourse provisions that would enable recovery from other entities of the amounts paid, including any limitations on the amounts that might be recovered

- In the period the liability is initially recognized and measured or in a period the measurement changes significantly:

  - The corresponding entry

  - Where the entry was recorded in the financial statements

NOTE: The disclosures required by the ASC do not affect the related-party disclosure requirements in ASC 850, *Related Party Disclosures*. The disclosure requirements in ASC 405-40 are incremental to those requirements.

Transition and Effective Date

ASC 405-40 is effective for fiscal years, and interim periods within those years, beginning after December 15, 2013. For nonpublic entities, it is effective for fiscal years ending after December 15, 2014, and interim and annual periods thereafter. Earlier application was permitted.

The ASC must be applied retrospectively to all prior periods presented for those obligations resulting from joint and several liability arrangements within the scope of the ASC that existed at the beginning of an entity's fiscal year of adoption. An entity may elect to use hindsight for the comparative periods presented in the initial year of adoption (if it changed its accounting as a result of adopting the ASC) and shall disclose that fact. The use of hindsight would allow an entity to recognize, measure, and disclose obligations resulting from joint and several liability arrangements within the scope of this Subtopic in comparative periods using information available at adoption rather than requiring an entity to make judgments about what information it had in each of the prior periods to measure the obligation.

An entity shall disclose information required in ASC 250, *Accounting Changes and Error Corrections*, within paragraphs 250-10-50-1 through 3, in the period the entity adopts the new content.

EXAMPLE 1: Company X and Y are co-borrowers of a $2 million loan, with each party receiving $1 million of cash from the loan. Under X and Y's agreement, X and Y agree to be co-borrowers on a 50-50 basis. To the extent that either party is required to pay more than 50 percent of any loan deficit in default, the other party agrees to indemnify that party for the percentage paid in excess of 50 percent. Both X and Y are financially solvent and have the financial wherewithal to satisfy each entity's share of the guarantee. At December 31, 20X1, the loan balance is $2 million. What is the amount of liability that X should record on its balance sheet?

Conclusion: Under ASC 405-40, obligations resulting from joint and several liability arrangements where the total amount under the arrangement is fixed at the report date shall be measured as the sum of the following:

1. The amount the reporting entity agreed to pay on the basis of its arrangement among its co-obligors, and

2. Any additional amount the reporting entity expects to pay on behalf of its co-obligors, using the guidance similar to the rules found in ASC 450, Contingencies.

In this example, the obligation is fixed at the December 31, 20X1 balance sheet date, which is $2 million. X should record a liability for its share of the obligation as follows:

The amount that X agrees to pay on the basis of its arrangement with Y: $1,000,000

Any additional amount that X expects to pay on behalf of Y: $0

Total liability $1,000,000

Entry:

Cash		1,000,000
	Liability	1,000,000

Because the amount of the total obligation is fixed at $2 million at the balance sheet date, X must record a liability for the joint and several obligation. The recorded amount has two parts. First is the amount that X agrees to pay under its debt obligation, which is $1 million. The second portion is any additional amount that X expects to pay on behalf of Y. Because Y is solvent, X should not expect to pay any additional amount beyond the $1 million.

EXAMPLE 2: Same facts as Example 1 except that Company Y is having financial problems at December 31, 20X1. X is concerned that if the $2 million loan is called, X may have to pay a portion of Y's share of the obligation. X believes that the range of possible exposure to Y's share of the liability is $500,000 to $1 million with no amount within the range being a better estimate.

Conclusion: X should record a liability for its share of the obligation as follows:

The amount that X agrees to pay on the basis of its arrangement with Y: $1,000,000

Any additional amount that X expects to pay on behalf of Y: 500,000

Total liability $1,500,000

Entry:

Receivable—Company Y		500,000
Cash	1,000,000	
Liability	1,500,000	

The amount of the liability related to the joint and several obligation is the sum of two parts. The first part is the amount that X agrees to pay under its joint venture agreement with Y, which is the $1 million that was received in cash. The second part consists of the additional amount that X expects to pay on behalf of Y. Because Y is having financial difficulties, X expects that if the total loan is called, X may have to pay an additional amount ranging from $500,000 to $1 million with no amount within the range being a better amount.

ASC 405-40 states that when there is a range of additional amounts, and there is no better estimate within the range, the entity should record the minimum amount within the range, which in this case is $500,000. Thus, the total liability that X should record under its joint and several obligation is $1,500,000.

Now to the debit side of the entry. X should record cash for the $1 million it received for its share of the loan proceeds. In addition, X should record a receivable for $500,000 due from Company Y for the additional amount that Y would owe X as reimbursement under X and Y's joint venture agreement.

Once the $500,000 receivable is recorded, it should be tested for impairment each period. In fact, given that Y has financial difficulties, it may be difficult for X to justify that it would be able to collect the $500,000 from Y.

What if X does not have a contractual right to recover the receivable from Y?

Assume that in Example 2, X and Y have not contractually agreed to indemnify each other for any portion of the total obligation that one entity has to pay beyond its 50 percent share.

If that is the case, would X have a right to recover the $500,000 receivable from Y if X had to pay that excess portion of the obligation belonging to Y?

Because there is no legal or contractual arrangement to recover the funded amounts from Y, as co-obligor, X should consider whether the $500,000 represents a gain contingency instead of a receivable. When there is a gain contingency, the guidance of ASC 450-30, Gain Contingencies, applies, which states that a gain contingency should not be recorded until realized. In this case, without a contractual right to recovery, the receivable becomes realized only once there is an agreement for recovery, either by settlement agreement or court order. The odd part of this situation is that if the $500,000 receivable cannot be recorded because it is a gain contingency, then what is the debit to the entry? (The FASB EITF did not opine as to the debit side of the entry.)

EXAMPLE 3: Companies C and D are sued as co-defendants and settle the case for $5 million. Under the settlement agreement, C and D agree to pay the $5 million to the plaintiff over the next five years. C and D have joint and several liability. C and D also consummate an agreement between themselves under which each party agrees to pay $2.5 million toward the $5 million. If either party fails to pay its $2.5 million share and the other party pays the shortfall, the paying entity will be indemnified by the other party.

The balance sheet date is December 31, 20X1. Company C is issuing financial statements and wants to know how much liability to record. Both entities are solvent.

Conclusion: Because the total obligation is fixed at $5 million at the December 31, 20X1 balance sheet date, the rules of ASC 405-40 apply. That means that C must record a liability for its share of the obligation as follows:

The amount that C agrees to pay on the basis of its joint and several obligation arrangement: $2,500,000

Any additional amount that C expects to pay on behalf of D: $0

Total liability $2,500,000

Entry:

Legal settlement expense	2,500,000	
Liability		2,500,000

C's share of the fixed obligation is $2,500,000. Because D is solvent, C does not expect to pay an additional amount for any shortfall by D. Thus, the total liability that C should record at December 31, 20X1 is $2,500,000.

EXAMPLE 4: Same facts as Example 3, except that D is having financial trouble. C is concerned that it may have to pay a portion of C's obligation under its joint and several obligation. C estimates the range of possible liability is $1 million to $2.5 million.

Conclusion: C should record $3.5 million for its share of the obligation, computed as follows:

The amount that C agrees to pay on the basis of its joint and several obligation arrangement: $2,500,000

Any additional amount that C expects to pay on behalf of D: 1,000,000

Total liability $3,500,000

Entry:

Receivable—Company D	1,000,000
Legal settlement expense	2,500,000
Liability	3,500,000

Because D is having financial trouble, C's liability should include not only its share of the settlement amount ($2.5 million) but also an additional amount that C expects to pay of D's $2.5 million obligation. C estimates that the range of possible payment that C may have to pay of D's share of the liability is $1 million to $2.5 million, with no better estimate within that range. Thus, C should record the lowest amount within the range, which is $1 million. Total estimated liability is $3.5 million.

The debit consists of $2.5 million of legal settlement expense, and a receivable due from Company D for the $1 million of estimated additional liability C expects to pay from D's share of the obligation. Once the receivable is recorded, C should evaluate that receivable for impairment.

EXAMPLE 5: Companies C and D are sued but at December 31, 20X1, there is no settlement with the plaintiff.

Conclusion: The rules of ASC 405-40 do not apply because the joint and several obligation is not fixed at the balance sheet date. Instead, C should follow the contingency rules found in ASC 450, Contingencies. Under those rules, C would record a liability if it meets the probable and estimable criteria.

STUDY QUESTION

3. In accordance with ASC 405-40, if an entity has no legal or contractual arrangement to recover the funded amounts from a co-obligor, the debit side of the transaction may be considered a _____.

    a. Loss contingency

    b. Gain contingency

    c. Deferred credit

    d. Operating expense

Dealing With Related Parties Involved in Joint and Several Obligations

ASC 405-40 applies to joint and several obligations where the obligation amount is fixed at the balance sheet date. It does not differentiate between those joint and several obligations among unrelated or related parties. Thus, related-party entities that are co-obligors (co-borrowers) must follow ASC 405-40's guidance.

It is not uncommon for one entity to act as a co-borrower for another related party that requires the financial strength of its affiliate.

EXAMPLE 1: Company E and F are related parties, both owned by Johnny James. Company F needs to borrow $5 million for its operations. Company E agrees to be a co-borrower with F in obtaining the $5 million loan. All of the proceeds from the loan are received by F to be used in F's operations.

E and F agree that each will be responsible for $2.5 million of the loan. Although E is financially stronger than F, E expects that F will be able to pay off its share of the $2.5

million loan. What is the amount of liability that E should record with respect to its co-borrowing under the $5 million loan?

Conclusion: E should record the following liability:

The amount that E agrees to pay on the basis of its joint and several obligation arrangement with F: $2,500,000

Any additional amount that E expects to pay on behalf of F: $0

Total liability $2,500,000

Entry—Company E:

Receivable—Company F	2,500,000	
Liability—bank loan		2,500,000

What entry should F make?

Entry—Company F:

Cash (loan proceeds)	5,000,000	
Liability—bank loan		2,500,000
Liability—Company E		2,500,000

Assuming F reaches the same conclusion as E, F would record $2,500,000, consisting of the portion of the $5 million loan that F agrees to pay on the basis of its joint and several obligation arrangement with E. The remainder of the $2.5 million is payable to Company E, representing its share of the loan proceeds that it did not receive.

> **EXAMPLE 1A:** Same facts as Example 1 except that F is financially weak and needs Company E to be a co-borrower in order for F to obtain the $5 million loan. E expects to pay all $2.5 million of F's share of the obligation if the loan is called.

E should record the following liability:

The amount that E agrees to pay on the basis of its joint and several obligation arrangement with F: $2,500,000

Any additional amount that E expects to pay on behalf of F: $2,500,000

Total liability: $5,000,000

Entry—Company E:

Receivable—Company F	5,000,000	
Liability—bank loan		5,000,000

Once the liability and related receivable are recorded, E would have to test the $5 million receivable for impairment and possible writedown. The fact that F is having financial difficulty may indicate that the receivable is not recoverable.

F's entry:

The amount that F agrees to pay on the basis of its joint and several obligation arrangement: $2,500,000

Any additional amount that F expects to pay on behalf of E: $0

Total liability $2,500,000

Entry—Company F

¶706

Cash (loan proceeds)	5,000,000	
Liability—bank loan		2,500,000
Liability—Company E		2,500,000

Notice that there is the potential for double recording of the same liability. Company E records a total liability of the bank loan of $5 million while F records an additional $2.5 million, for a total of $7.5 million. Yet, the total bank loan balance is only $5 million.

As E records an additional $2.5 million of the obligation to reflect that portion of F's obligation that E expects to pay, there is no corresponding reduction of the liability on F's books. The result is that the total liability recorded is $7.5 million.

This is a perfect example of a situation in which two parties can reach different conclusions that do not result in transactions being a mirror of each other.

> **OBSERVATION:** It is quite common for related parties to act as co-borrowers on one single bank loan. Typically the loan proceeds are scattered among the entities and all of the parties remain jointly and severally liable. In such situations, one or more of the related-party co-borrowers might be financially weak with no ability to repay its share of the loan obligation. When this occurs, a stronger entity might be required to record an additional liability for that portion of the total obligation that the entity "expects to pay" on behalf of a financially weaker related party entity.

> **EXAMPLE 1B:** Company E and F are related parties, both owned by Johnny James. F needs to borrow $5 million for its operations. Company E agrees to act as a guarantor (not a co-borrower) of F's $5 million bank loan. All of the proceeds from the loan are received by F to be used in F's operations. E and F have no formal agreement as to indemnification for the guarantee. What is the amount of liability that E should record with respect to its co-borrowing under the $5 million loan?

Conclusion: E should record no liability. Because the joint and several obligation involves E in the capacity as a guarantor, not a co-borrower, the rules of ASC 405-40 do not apply. Instead, E should follow the guarantee rules found in ASC 460, *Guarantees*. ASC 460 requires a guarantor to record a liability.

CPE NOTE: When you have completed your study and review of chapters 4-7, which comprise Module 2, you may wish to take the Quizzer for this Module. Go to **CCH-Group.com/PrintCPE** to take this Quizzer online.

MODULE 3: OTHER CURRENT DEVELOPMENTS—CHAPTER 8: Goodwill Amortization for Nonpublic Companies

¶ 801 WELCOME

This chapter explains the new optional method to amortize goodwill that is available to private (nonpublic) entities.

¶ 802 LEARNING OBJECTIVES

Upon completion of this chapter, the reader will be able to:

- Recall the accounting treatment for an intangible asset with a finite life
- Identify the life over which a private company may elect to amortize goodwill under ASU 2014-02
- Recognize an example of goodwill transactions to which ASU 2014-02's accounting alternative applies
- Identify a private company's new, single-step quantitative test for goodwill impairment loss authorized by ASU 2014-02

¶ 803 INTRODUCTION

ASU 2014-02—*An Amendment of the FASB Accounting Standards Codification® Intangibles—Goodwill and Other (Topic 350): Accounting for Goodwill (a consensus of the Private Company Council)* was issued in January 2014. The objective of this ASU was to address the new optional method to amortize goodwill that is available to private (nonpublic) entities.

¶ 804 BACKGROUND

Under current GAAP, goodwill and intangible assets are accounted for as follows:

Accounting for Impairments of Assets			
Type of Intangible Asset	Authority for impairment	Accounting treatment	Impairment test approval
Goodwill	ASC 350 (formerly FASB No. 142)	Not amortized	Tested annually for impairment
Intangibles with indefinite lives (tradenames, etc.)	ASC 350 (formerly FASB No. 142)	Not amortized	Tested annually for impairment
Intangibles with finite lives (patents, agreement not to compete, etc.)	ASC 360 (formerly FASB No. 144)	Amortized	Tested for impairment only if there is an indication that an impairment might exist

Currently, GAAP does not permit an entity to amortize goodwill. Because goodwill is not amortized, GAAP requires that goodwill be tested for impairment at least annually or more frequently if certain conditions exist.

For years, the only method by which an entity could perform its annual impairment test was to perform a quantitative assessment that involved measuring fair value. More recently, the FASB issued ASU 2011-08—*Intangibles—Goodwill and Other (Topic 350): Testing Goodwill for Impairment.* ASU 2011-08 adds an optional qualitative assessment that can be used in lieu of the quantitative assessment.

Thus, current GAAP permits an entity, in performing its annual goodwill impairment test, to now choose to either:

- **Use a qualitative assessment**: Perform a *qualitative assessment* to determine whether it is more likely than not (more than 50 percent probability) that a reporting unit's fair value is less than its carrying amount

- **Use a quantitative assessment**: Proceed directly to step one of the *quantitative impairment test*, which is to compare the carrying amount of the reporting unit with its fair value.

Using the quantitative method, if the carrying amount of an entity's stockholders' equity exceeds the fair value of its stockholders' equity, the entity must determine the extent of a goodwill impairment, if any. In calculating the amount of the impairment, an entity must compare the implied fair value of the reporting unit's goodwill with its carrying amount. (The test is done at the reporting unit level but In practice, most nonpublic entities have only one reporting unit, which is the entity as a whole.)

ASU 2014-02 represents the Private Company Council's first standard that modifies GAAP for nonpublic (private) companies.

The Private Company Council (PCC) added this issue to its agenda in connection with a related issue addressing whether private companies should obtain relief in recording certain identifiable intangible assets acquired in a business combination. Because goodwill is a residual asset calculated after recognizing other (tangible and intangible) assets and liabilities acquired in a business combination, any modifications to the initial recognition and measurement guidance for identifiable intangible assets would correspondingly change the goodwill amount recognized in the business combination.

During its research and outreach efforts on this issue, the PCC obtained feedback from private company stakeholders, including accountants and auditors. From that outreach, the PCC gathered comments which included the following:

- The annual goodwill impairment test is required because goodwill is not amortized.

- The costs of the annual goodwill test far exceed its benefit for most private companies for several reasons:

  - The goodwill impairment test provides limited useful information because most users of private company financial statements generally disregard goodwill and goodwill impairment losses in their analysis of a private company's financial condition and operating performance.

  - Many users of private company financial statements do not use goodwill impairment charges in their analysis of a private company's operating performance because they focus on tangible net assets, cash flows, and/or some form of adjusted earnings before income taxes, depreciation, and amortization (EBITDA).

  - In performing the current annual goodwill impairment test, GAAP requires an entity to first determine its reporting units, a unit of account concept that requires a private company to identify operating segments. Most private company preparers generally are not familiar with the operating segment concept which is primarily used by public companies in complying with segment reporting.

- Although the recently new qualitative assessment option has reduced some of the cost of performing the annual impairment test, that annual test is still too costly.

Private company stakeholders acknowledge that the FASB's recent introduction of the optional qualitative assessment in ASU 2011-08 has provided some cost reduction in testing goodwill for impairment, but many of those stakeholders stated that the level of cost reduction has not been significant.

ASU 2014-02 makes a few key changes for private (nonpublic) entities:

- It permits a private (nonpublic) entity to elect to amortize goodwill on a straight-line basis over 10 years or a shorter period if such a shorter period can be justified.

- It eliminates the annual goodwill impairment test and replaces it with an impairment test that is required *only if* there is a triggering event.

- It replaces the two-step quantitative assessment impairment test with a single-step quantitative goodwill impairment test.

- It retains the current option to use the qualitative assessment impairment test for goodwill, or an entity can now bypass the qualitative assessment and proceed directly to a single quantitative test by comparing the carrying amount of the entity (or the reporting unit) with its fair value.

- It requires a company to make an accounting policy election to test goodwill either at the reporting unit or entity level.

- It reduces some of the goodwill disclosures, including elimination of the tabular goodwill activity reconciliation.

STUDY QUESTION

1. An intangible asset with an indefinite life _____.
    a. Should be amortized over its estimated useful life
    b. Should not be amortized
    c. May be amortized if certain conditions are satisfied
    d. Must be amortized over a 15-year period

¶ 805 DEFINITIONS

ASU 2014-02 provides specific definitions of a private company and public business entity.

A *private company* is an entity *other than*:

- A public business entity
- A not-for-profit entity
- An employee benefit plan on plan accounting

A public business entity is a business entity meeting any one of the criteria below. (Neither a not-for-profit entity nor an employee benefit plan is a business entity.)

- It is required by the SEC to file or furnish financial statements, or does file or furnish financial statements (including voluntary filers), with the SEC (including other entities whose financial statements or financial information are required to be or are included in a filing).

- It is required by the Securities Exchange Act of 1934 to file or furnish financial statements with a regulatory agency other than the SEC.
- It is required to file or furnish financial statements with a foreign or domestic regulatory agency in preparation for the sale of, or for purposes of issuing securities that are not subject to contractual restrictions on transfer.
- It has issued, or is a conduit bond obligor for, securities that are traded, listed, or quoted on an exchange or an over-the-counter market.
- It has one or more securities that are not subject to contractual restrictions on transfer.
- It is required by law, contract, or regulation to prepare U.S. GAAP financial statements (including footnotes) and make them publicly available on a periodic basis (e.g., interim or annual periods).

An entity may meet the definition of a public business entity solely because its financial statements or financial information is included in another entity's filing with the SEC. In that case, the entity is only a public business entity for purposes of financial statements that are filed or furnished with the SEC.

¶ 806 SCOPE

The scope of ASU 2014-02 applies to a private company. It is *not available* for any of the following entities:

- A public business entity
- Not-for-profit entity
- Employee benefit plan

¶ 807 RULES

A private company may make an accounting policy election to apply the accounting alternative in ASU 2014-02 to amortize goodwill. A private company that makes the election should continue to follow the applicable requirements in ASC 350, *Intangibles— Goodwill and Other,* for other accounting and reporting matters related to goodwill that are not addressed in the accounting alternative.

The accounting alternative applies to the following goodwill transactions:

- Goodwill that an entity recognizes in a business combination in accordance with ASC Subtopic 805-30, *Business Combinations,* after it has been initially recognized and measured
- Amounts recognized as goodwill in applying the equity method of accounting in accordance with ASC 323, *Investments-Equity Method and Joint Ventures,* on:
  - Investments- equity method
  - Joint ventures
  - The excess reorganization value recognized by entities that adopt fresh-start reporting in accordance with ASC 852, *Reorganizations*

An entity that elects the accounting alternative for goodwill shall apply it to all goodwill related subsequent measurement, derecognition, other presentation matters, and disclosure requirements upon election.

The accounting alternative, once elected, shall be applied to:

- Existing goodwill
- All additions to goodwill recognized in future transactions

Under the accounting alternative for goodwill:

- Goodwill relating to each business combination or reorganization event resulting in fresh-start reporting (amortizable unit of goodwill) shall be amortized on a straight-line basis over 10 years, or less than 10 years if the entity demonstrates that another useful life is more appropriate.
- An entity may revise the remaining useful life of goodwill upon the occurrence of events or changes in circumstances that warrant a revision to the remaining amortization period.

Rules related to revising the remaining useful life follow:

- The cumulative amortization period of goodwill cannot exceed 10 years (e.g., number of years amortized plus the revised estimated remaining number of years cannot exceed 10 years).
- If the estimate of the remaining useful life of goodwill is revised, the remaining carrying amount of goodwill shall be amortized prospectively on a straight-line basis over the revised remaining useful life.

> **OBSERVATION:** The PCC notes that an entity does not need to justify its selection of a 10-year amortization period as this period is the default period. Justification is required only if an entity uses a useful life that is less than 10 years.

Some PCC members supported the amortization model because, in their view, goodwill should be expensed to achieve an allocation of its cost to future operations. Those members noted that acquired goodwill is an asset that is consumed and replaced with internally generated goodwill. Therefore, acquired goodwill should be amortized, and the internally generated goodwill that is replacing it should not be recognized as an asset (because goodwill generally cannot be recognized as an asset outside a business combination). One PCC member noted that amortizing goodwill "levels the playing field" among those entities that grow through acquisitions and those that grow internally, because those that grow internally are not able to capitalize internally generated goodwill. Accordingly, those PCC members voted for the amortization model because, in their view, amortization (with impairment tests, if necessary) is a better representation of the underlying economics of goodwill than the current impairment-only model.

Why Didn't the PCC Require Use of the 15-year Tax Life for Goodwill Amortization to Save Private Companies the Burden of Having to Establish Deferred Income Taxes for the Temporary Difference?

In the ASU, the PCC states that it decided that the useful life should be limited to 10 years on the basis that a significant portion of the assets and liabilities acquired in a business combination involving private companies, would be fully used up or satisfied by the 10th year.

> **EXAMPLE:** If a business enterprise calculation assumed a three percent growth rate and a 15 percent discount rate, approximately 70 percent of the present value of the cash flows would be generated in the first 10 years. A higher discount rate (which would not be unusual, particularly if significant growth was projected) would increase the percentage of the present value of cash flows expected to be generated in the first 10 years.

The PCC also considered a longer amortization period, such as a 15-year period. While some stakeholders supported a 15-year period to align with amortization of goodwill for U.S. federal tax purposes (which would reduce the amount of deferred taxes recognized by a taxable entity electing this alternative), the PCC concluded that a period of 15 years is no less arbitrary than a period of 10 years and that a longer amortization period would increase the risk of impairment.

> **NOTE:** In its Financial Reporting Framework (FRF) for Small to Medium-Sized Entities (FRF For SMEs), the AICPA chose a 15-year life to amortize goodwill.

Testing for Impairment

Upon adopting the accounting alternative to amortize goodwill, an entity shall make an accounting policy election to test goodwill for impairment at the entity level or the reporting unit level. An entity that elects to perform its impairment test at the reporting unit level shall refer to ASC 350-20-35, *Intangibles—Goodwill and Other Goodwill, Subsequent Measurement*, paragraphs 33 to 38, and 350-20-55, *Intangibles—Goodwill and Other Goodwill, Implementation Guidance and Illustrations,* paragraphs 1 to 9, to determine the reporting units of an entity.

> **NOTE:** ASC 350-20-35, paragraphs 33 to 38, and ASC 350-20-55, paragraphs 1 to 9, provide rules on how an entity should determine its reporting units. Most nonpublic (private) companies have only one reporting unit, which is the entity as a whole. Therefore, the reporting unit concept is typically moot for most nonpublic entities so that any impairment test is performed at the entity level, not at the reporting-unit level.

The existing requirement to test goodwill annually for impairment is eliminated if the entity elects to amortize goodwill under the accounting alternative, and is replaced with a "triggering event" threshold.

> **OBSERVATION:** Because goodwill is amortized, under the amortization alternative, the PCC decided that a goodwill impairment test is necessary only when a *triggering event* exists, similar to other long-lived assets that are subject to periodic amortization. The PCC concluded that the amortization method (and the option to test at the entity level, if elected) generally should result in testing goodwill for impairment less frequently than once a year, especially in the later years of the useful life of goodwill.

Triggering Events

A triggering event exists if an event occurs or circumstances change that indicate that the fair value of the entity (or the reporting unit) may be below its carrying amount. Following are examples of events or circumstances that could be a triggering event and may indicate that the fair value of the entity is below its carrying amount:

- Macroeconomic conditions such as:
    - Deterioration in general economic conditions
    - Limitations on accessing capital
    - Fluctuations in foreign exchange rates
    - Other developments in equity and credit markets
- Industry and market considerations such as:
    - Deterioration in the environment in which an entity operates
    - An increased competitive environment
    - A decline in market-dependent multiples or metrics (consider in both absolute terms and relative to peers)
    - A change in the market for an entity's products or services, or a regulatory or political development

- Cost factors such as increases in raw materials, labor, or other costs that have a negative effect on earnings and cash flows
- Overall financial performance such as:
  - Negative or declining cash flows
  - A decline in actual or planned revenue or earnings compared with actual and projected results of relevant prior periods
- Other relevant entity-specific events such as changes in management, key personnel, strategy, or customers; contemplation of bankruptcy; or litigation
- Events affecting a reporting unit such as:
  - A change in the composition or carrying amount of its net assets
  - A more-likely-than-not expectation of selling or disposing all, or a portion, of a reporting unit
  - Testing for recoverability of a significant asset group within a reporting unit
  - Recognition of a goodwill impairment loss in the financial statements of a subsidiary that is a component of a reporting unit
- If applicable, a sustained decrease in share price (consider in both absolute terms and relative to peers)

Upon the occurrence of a triggering event, an entity may assess goodwill for impairment using *either* the qualitative or quantitative approach found in ASC 350.

If an entity determines that there are no triggering events, then further testing is unnecessary.

The Qualitative Approach

If the qualitative approach is used, the entity shall assess qualitative factors to determine whether it is *more likely than not* (i.e., a likelihood of more than 50 percent) that the fair value of the entity (or the reporting unit) is less than its carrying amount. Examples of qualitative factors to consider if the qualitative approach is used include the possible triggering events listed previously.

The PCC stated that under the accounting alternative, an entity should consider the same examples of events and circumstances for the assessment of triggering events as those considered for the qualitative assessment. However, the PCC intends for the nature and extent of those two assessments to be different. The assessment of triggering events should be similar to the current practice of how an entity evaluates goodwill impairment between annual tests.

The triggering event is the event that makes an entity stop and think about impairment. In contrast, the optional qualitative assessment is part of an entity's documented goodwill impairment test requiring the entity to positively assert its conclusion as to whether it is more likely than not that goodwill is impaired based on consideration of all events and circumstances, not just one triggering event.

The ASU states that in performing the qualitative assessment, an entity shall consider other relevant events and circumstances that affect the fair value or carrying amount of the entity (or of the reporting unit) in determining whether to perform the quantitative goodwill impairment test. In making the determination, an entity should:

- Consider the extent to which each of the adverse events and circumstances identified could affect the comparison of fair value with the carrying amount of the entity's stockholders' equity (or of the reporting unit's fair value with the reporting unit's carrying amount).

- Place more weight on the events and circumstances that most affect its fair value or the carrying amount of its stockholders' equity (or the reporting unit's fair value, or the carrying amount of the reporting unit's net assets).

- Consider positive and mitigating events and circumstances that may affect its determination of whether it is more likely than not that the fair value of its stockholders' equity is less than its carrying amount (or the fair value of the reporting unit is less than the carrying amount of the reporting unit)

If an entity has a recent fair value calculation (or recent fair value calculation for the reporting unit), it also should include that calculation as a qualitative factor in its consideration of the difference between the fair value and the carrying amount in reaching its conclusion about whether to perform the quantitative goodwill impairment test.

NOTE: In making the qualitative assessment, an entity shall evaluate, on the basis of the weight of evidence, the significance of all identified events and circumstances in the context of determining whether it is more likely than not that the fair value of the entity (or the reporting unit) is less than its carrying amount.

The existence of positive and mitigating events and circumstances is not intended to represent a rebuttable presumption that an entity should not perform the quantitative goodwill impairment test.

If, after assessing the totality of events or circumstances during the qualitative assessment, an entity determines that it is *not* more likely than not that the fair value of the entity (or the reporting unit) is less than its carrying amount, then further testing is unnecessary.

The Quantitative Test

If, after assessing the totality of events or circumstances, an entity determines that it *is* more likely than not that the fair value of the entity (or the reporting unit) is less than its carrying amount, or if the entity elected to bypass the qualitative assessment, the entity shall perform a single-step *quantitative test* for impairment as follows:

- Fair value of the entity is compared with the carrying amount.

- If the carrying amount, including goodwill, exceeds the fair value of the entity, an impairment loss should be measured and recorded as the amount by which the carrying amount of an entity (or a reporting unit) including goodwill, exceeds its fair value. A goodwill impairment loss shall not exceed the entity's (or the reporting unit's) carrying amount of goodwill.

Formula for goodwill impairment loss:

Carrying amount of the entity's stockholder's equity

− Fair value of the entity's stockholder's equity
──────────────────────────────────────

= **IMPAIRMENT LOSS**

OBSERVATION: Some PCC members acknowledged that a single-step approach may not result in as theoretically accurate an amount of goodwill impairment as the current two-step approach, but it noted that a less precise calculation of impairment does not take away from the usefulness of financial statements. The PCC concluded that eliminating a costly aspect of the current two-step goodwill impairment test, that is, the hypothetical application of the acquisition method to calculate implied goodwill (step two), provides a benefit to private company preparers with minimal reduction in user relevance. The PCC also noted that this approach to impairment testing is similar to the single-step impairment test used for goodwill under IFRS.

EXAMPLE 1: Company Z has elected to amortize its goodwill over 10 years under ASU 2014-02. In 20XX, Z identifies a triggering event that suggests that there may be a goodwill impairment. That event is that Z has had several years of continued negative cash flows from operations and no indication of a turnaround in the near future. Now that Z has a triggering event, Z elects to use the qualitative assessment to determine whether it is more likely than not (more than 50 percent probability) that the fair value of Z is less than its carrying amount.

Based on Z's analysis of qualitative facts, Z concludes that it is more likely than not that the fair value is less than the carrying amount.

Details as of December 31, 20XX (in thousands):

Fair value of Z's stockholders' equity	$1,000
Carrying amount of Z's stockholder's equity	1,100
Carrying amount (book value) of goodwill	450

Conclusion: Because it is more likely than not that the fair value of Z is less than its carrying amount, Z should perform the single, quantitative test for impairment as follows:

Fair value of Z's stockholders' equity	$1,000
Less: Carrying amount of Z's stockholders' equity	1,100
IMPAIRMENT LOSS	**$ (100)**
Entry:	
Goodwill impairment loss	100
Goodwill	100

After the entry, the carrying amount of goodwill is reduced to $350,000.

The impairment loss is presented on the statement of income in the following manner:

Company Z Statement of Income For the Year Ended December 31, 20XX ($000s)	
Net sales	$xx
Cost of sales	xx
Gross profit	xx
Operating expenses	xx
Impairment loss on goodwill	**(100)**
Net income before income taxes	xx
Income taxes	xx
Net income	$xx

In deciding to use the single-step impairment calculation, the PCC settled on the theory that the goodwill impairment amount (loss) represents the excess of the entity's carrying amount over its fair value. Thus, if the carrying amount exceeds the fair value, that excess is an impairment loss.

For an entity subject to the requirements of ASC 740, *Income Taxes,* when determining the carrying amount of an entity (or a reporting unit), deferred income taxes shall be included in the carrying amount of an entity (or the reporting unit), regardless of whether the fair value of the entity (or the reporting unit) will be determined assuming it would be bought or sold in a taxable or nontaxable transaction.

The goodwill impairment loss, if any, shall be allocated to individual amortizable units of goodwill (or the reporting unit) on a pro-rata basis using their relative carrying amounts or using another reasonable and rational basis.

After a goodwill impairment loss is recognized, the adjusted carrying amount of goodwill shall be its new accounting basis, which shall be amortized over the remaining useful life of goodwill. Subsequent reversal of a previously recognized goodwill impairment loss is prohibited.

An entity has an unconditional option to bypass the qualitative assessment described and proceed directly to a quantitative calculation by comparing the entity's (or the reporting unit's) fair value with its carrying amount.

> **NOTE:** An entity may resume performing the qualitative assessment upon the occurrence of any subsequent triggering event.

If goodwill and another asset (or asset group) of the entity (or the reporting unit) are tested for impairment at the same time, the other asset (or asset group) shall be tested for impairment before goodwill.

> **NOTE:** If a significant asset group is to be tested for impairment under the impairment rules related to property, plant, and equipment (thus potentially requiring a goodwill impairment test), the impairment test for the significant asset group would be performed before the goodwill impairment test. If the asset group is impaired, the impairment loss would be recognized prior to goodwill being tested for impairment.

Equity Method Investments

The portion of the difference between the cost of an investment and the amount of underlying equity in net assets of an equity method investee that is recognized as goodwill in accordance with ASC 323, *Investments—Equity Method and Joint Ventures,* (equity method goodwill), shall be amortized on a straight-line basis over 10 years, or less than 10 years if the entity demonstrates that another useful life is more appropriate.

Equity method goodwill shall not be reviewed for impairment in accordance with this ASU. Instead, equity method investments shall continue to be reviewed for impairment in accordance with ASC 323, *Investments—Equity Method and Joint Ventures,* Subtopic 10-35-32. ASC 323-10-35, paragraph 32, provides that a loss in the value of an equity investment that is other than a temporary decline shall be recognized.

Disposal of a Portion of an Entity

When a portion of an entity (or a reporting unit) that constitutes a business is to be disposed of, goodwill associated with that business shall be included in the carrying amount of the business in determining the gain or loss on disposal. An entity shall use a reasonable and rational approach to determine the amount of goodwill associated with the business to be disposed of.

Financial Statement Display

An entity that elects the accounting alternative to amortize goodwill shall provide the following financial statement displays:

- The aggregate amount of goodwill, net of accumulated amortization and impairment, shall be presented as a separate line item in the statement of financial position.

- The amortization and aggregate amount of impairment of goodwill shall be presented in income statement line items within continuing operations (or similar caption) unless the amortization or a goodwill impairment loss is associated with a discontinued operation.

- The amortization and impairment of goodwill associated with a discontinued operation shall be included (on a net-of-tax basis) within the results of discontinued operations.

STUDY QUESTION

2. Which of the following is an example of a triggering event that may suggest that goodwill should be tested for impairment?

- **a.** Strong general economic conditions
- **b.** A decrease in the competitive environment
- **c.** A negative or declining cash flow trend
- **d.** A reduction in the cost of key raw materials

¶ 808 EFFECTIVE DATE AND TRANSITION

Effective Date

The ASU's accounting alternative, if elected, should be applied prospectively to goodwill existing as of the beginning of the period of adoption and new goodwill recognized in annual periods beginning after December 15, 2014, and interim periods within annual periods beginning after December 15, 2015.

Early application is permitted, including application to any period for which the entity's annual or interim financial statements have not yet been made available for issuance.

Transition Rules

Goodwill *existing* as of the beginning of the period of adoption shall be amortized prospectively on a straight-line basis over 10 years, or less than 10 years if an entity demonstrates that another useful life is more appropriate.

Upon adoption of the accounting alternative, an entity shall make an accounting policy election to test goodwill for impairment at either the entity level or the reporting unit level.

¶ 809 DISCLOSURES

The ASU eliminated several of the current goodwill disclosures if a nonpublic entity elects to amortize goodwill. Following are the new disclosures that apply for a nonpublic entity that elects to amortize goodwill under ASU 2014-02.

Additions to Goodwill

The following information shall be disclosed in the notes to financial statements for any additions to goodwill in each period for which a statement of financial position is presented:

- The amount assigned to goodwill in total and by a major business combination or by a reorganization event resulting in fresh-start reporting
- The weighted-average amortization period in total and the amortization period by major business combination or by reorganization event resulting in fresh-start reporting

Each Period for Which a Statement of Financial Position is Presented

The following information shall be disclosed in the financial statements, or the notes to financial statements, for each period for which a statement of financial position is presented:

- The gross carrying amounts of goodwill, accumulated amortization, and accumulated impairment loss
- The aggregate amortization expense for the period
- Goodwill included in a disposal group classified as held for sale in accordance with ASC 360, *Property, Plant and Equipment*, and goodwill derecognized during the period without having previously been reported in a disposal group classified as held for sale.

Goodwill Impairment Loss

For each goodwill impairment loss recognized, the following information shall be disclosed in the notes to financial statements that include the period in which the impairment loss is recognized:

- A description of the facts and circumstances leading to the impairment
- The amount of the impairment loss and the method of determining the fair value of the entity or the reporting unit (whether based on prices of comparable businesses, a present value or other valuation technique, or a combination of those methods)
- The caption in the income statement in which the impairment loss is included
- The method of allocating the impairment loss to the individual amortizable units of goodwill

> **NOTE:** The quantitative disclosures about significant unobservable inputs used in fair value measurements categorized within Level 3 of the fair value hierarchy required by ASC 820, are *not* required for fair value measurements related to the financial accounting and reporting for goodwill after its initial recognition in a business combination.

COMPARISON-ABBREVIATED DISCLOSURES UNDER ASU 2014-02 VERSUS FULL DISCLOSURES UNDER GAAP	
Full Disclosures of Goodwill Under GAAP (Full disclosures apply to all public entities and those nonpublic entities that do not elect to amortize goodwill under ASU 2014-02.)	**Abbreviated Disclosures for Nonpublic Entities Electing to Amortize Goodwill** (Accounting Alternative- ASU 2014-02)
DISCLOSURE 1:	DISCLOSURE 1:
Information for each period for which a statement of financial position is presented:	Information for each period for which a statement of financial position is presented:
Tabular disclosure of changes in the carrying amount of goodwill during the period, showing separately:	ELIMINATED
Gross amount and accumulated impairment losses at beginning of period	

COMPARISON-ABBREVIATED DISCLOSURES UNDER ASU 2014-02 VERSUS FULL DISCLOSURES UNDER GAAP

Additional goodwill recognized during the period	
Adjustments resulting from subsequent recognition of deferred tax assets during the period	
Goodwill included in a disposal group classified as held for sale and goodwill derecognized during the period without having previously been reported in a disposal group classified as held for sale	Goodwill included in a disposal group classified as held for sale and goodwill derecognized during the period without having previously been reported in a disposal group classified as held for sale.
Impairment losses recognized during the period	
Net exchange differences arising during the period	
Any other changes in the carrying amounts during the period	
Gross amount and accumulated impairment losses at the end of the period	Gross carrying amounts of goodwill, accumulated amortization, and accumulated impairment loss at the end of the period
	The aggregate amortization expense for the period

Full Disclosures of Goodwill Under GAAP (Full disclosures apply to all public entities and those nonpublic entities that do not elect to amortize goodwill under ASU 2014-02.)	**Abbreviated Disclosures for Nonpublic Entities Electing to Amortize Goodwill** (Accounting Alternative- ASU 2014-02)
DISCLOSURE 2: For each goodwill impairment loss recognized:	DISCLOSURE 2: For each goodwill impairment loss recognized:
A description of the facts and circumstances leading to the impairment	A description of the facts and circumstances leading to the impairment
The amount of the impairment loss and the method of determining the fair value of the associated reporting unit	The amount of the impairment loss and the method of determining the fair value of the entity or the reporting unit
If a recognized impairment loss is an estimate that has not yet been finalized, that fact and the reasons therefore and, in subsequent periods, the nature and amount of any significant adjustments made to the initial estimate of the impairment loss	
	The caption in the income statement in which the impairment loss is included
	The method of allocating the impairment loss to the individual amortizable units of goodwill

DISCLOSURE 3:	DISCLOSURE 3:
None	Disclosures about additions to goodwill:
	The following information shall be disclosed in the notes to financial statements for any additions to goodwill in each period for which a statement of financial position is presented:
	• The amount assigned to goodwill in total and by major business combination or by reorganization event resulting in fresh-start reporting
	• The weighted-average amortization period in total and the amortization period by major business combination or by reorganization event resulting in fresh-start reporting

Full Disclosures of Goodwill Under GAAP (Full disclosures apply to all public entities and those nonpublic entities that do not elect to amortize goodwill under ASU 2014-02.)	**Abbreviated Disclosures for Nonpublic Entities Electing to Amortize Goodwill** (Accounting Alternative- ASU 2014-02)
DISCLOSURE 4: None	DISCLOSURE 4: Disclosure of an entity's accounting policy election to test goodwill for impairment at the entity level or the reporting unit level
DISCLOSURE EXCLUSION: The quantitative disclosures about significant unobservable inputs used in fair value measurements categorized within Level 3 of the fair value hierarchy are not required for fair value measurements related to the financial accounting and reporting for goodwill after its initial recognition in a business combination.	DISCLOSURE EXCLUSION: The quantitative disclosures about significant unobservable inputs used in fair value measurements categorized within Level 3 of the fair value hierarchy are not required for fair value measurements related to the financial accounting and reporting for goodwill after its initial recognition in a business combination.

OBSERVATION: In modifying the disclosures required for nonpublic entities that elect to amortize goodwill, the PCC decided that for amortizable goodwill, disclosures in the period of acquisition should be similar to disclosures for other finite-lived intangible assets for which an entity would disclose, for example, the weighted-average useful life of the asset.

The ASU does not carry forward the existing requirement in ASC 350 to include a tabular reconciliation of the beginning balance, ending balance, and activity (major additions and subtractions) in the goodwill balance from period to period. The tabular reconciliation was eliminated based on comment letter feedback and consideration of the *Private Company Decision-Making Framework*, which indicates that the PCC and the FASB generally should consider excluding tabular reconciliations from the disclosure requirements. The PCC concluded that information about changes in goodwill could be important to users (e.g., knowing the amount of amortization expense so that it can be added back to net income) but that it is not necessary to include that information in a tabular reconciliation. Further, some elements of the tabular reconciliation can be found elsewhere in the notes to the financial statements. For example, the amount of new goodwill is included as a part of the business combination note. When there is a goodwill impairment loss, the disclosure requirements in ASC 350 continue to apply, except for those disclosures related to step two of the test and those related to reporting units (if the option to test at the entity level is elected).

STUDY QUESTION

3. ASU 2014-02 eliminates which disclosure for private companies electing to amortize goodwill?

    a. Tabular reconciliation

    b. Aggregate amortization expense for the period

    c. Gross carrying amounts of goodwill at the end of the period

    d. Accumulated amortization at the end of the period

¶ 810 EXAMPLE: GOODWILL DISCLOSURES—ASU 2014-02

Facts: On January 1, 20X2, Company A, a non-public entity, acquired 100% of the assets Company B for $10 million.

At December 31, 20X2, the financial statements of Company A and B look like this:

Company A Balance Sheet December 31, 20X2 ($000s)			
Current assets:		*Current liabilities:*	
Cash	$xx	Accounts payable	$xx
Accounts receivable	xx	Accrued expenses	xx
Inventory	xx	Current portion of debt	xx
Other current assets	xx	Other current liabilities	xx
Total current assets	xx	Total current liabilities	xx
Property, plant and equipment, net	xx	*Long-term debt*	xx
Goodwill	**2,700**	*Stockholder's equity*	xx
Other intangibles assets, net	8,000		
Total assets	$xx	Total liabilities and equity	$xx

Company A elects to amortize goodwill over 10 years as authorized by ASU 2014-02.

The following disclosures are required by ASC 350 and 805, as amended by ASU 2014-02.

Disclosures in 20X2:

NOTE 1: SUMMARY OF SIGNIFICANT ACCOUNTING POLICIES

Goodwill and Other Intangible Assets:

Intangible assets include patents, customer lists, licenses and trademarks related to certain acquisitions.

Intangible assets are amortized over the following estimated useful lives using primarily straight-line basis.

Intangible asset	Life in years
Patents	7
Customer list	5

Licenses and certain trademarks acquired are not amortized as they are considered to have indefinite useful lives.

The excess of the purchase price over the fair value of identifiable tangible and intangible assets is allocated to goodwill. **For year 20X1, goodwill is not amortized and is tested for impairment annually.**

In accordance with Accounting Standards Update (ASU) 2014-02— *Intangibles— Goodwill and Other (Topic 350): Accounting for Goodwill,* effective in 20X2, **the Company elected to amortize goodwill on a straight-line basis over 10 years.** Beginning in 20X2, goodwill is tested for impairment *at the entity level only* when an event occurs or circumstances change that indicate that the fair value of the entity may be less than its carrying amount. Impairment losses, if any, are recorded in the statement of income as part of income from operations. No impairment losses were measured and recorded in 20X2 and 20X1.

NOTE 2: ACQUISITIONS

(Required in the year in which a material business combination is completed)

On January 1, 20X2, Company A acquired the net assets of Company B. The results of Company B's operations have been included in Company A's financial statements since the acquisition date, January 1 to December 31, 20X2.

Company B is a leading provider of data networking products and services in 18 states and Canada, and was acquired because it would provide Company A with the leader position in B's markets and result in reduced costs of both companies through economies of scale.

The aggregate acquisition cost was $10 million, consisting of $6 million of cash, and $4 million of acquisition financing.

The fair value of the assets acquired at the date of acquisition is summarized below:

	Fair value
Inventory	$2,800
Property and equipment	2,200
Identifiable intangible assets	2,000
Goodwill	**3,000**
Total assets acquired	$10,000

At the date of acquisition, the identified intangible assets and goodwill included the following:

	Fair value ($000s)	Weighted-average amortization period
Intangible assets subject to amortization:		
Patents	$ 400	7 years
Customer list	700	5 years
Total	1,100	5.6 years
Intangible assets not subject to amortization:		
Trademarks	900	Indefinite
Total identifiable intangible assets	$2,000	
Goodwill	**$3,000**	10 years

Significant elements of goodwill include the expected synergies between Company A and B (related to economies of scale and process improvements), competitive advantage, and distribution channels that will provide a market reach in both communications and networking.

The amount of goodwill that is expected to be deductible for income tax purposes is $3,000.

NOTE 3: GOODWILL AND OTHER INTANGIBLE ASSETS

(This note is shown for each year for which there is a balance sheet):

Intangible assets other than goodwill:

The following is a summary of goodwill and other intangible assets at December 31, 20X2 and 20X1.

	December 31, 20X2		December 31, 20X1	
	Gross carrying amount	Accumulated amortization	Gross carrying amount	Accumulated amortization
Intangible assets subject to amortization:				
Patents	$2,500	$1,200	$2,100	$800
Customer lists	2,600	1,400	1,900	1,000
	5,100	2,600	4,000	1,800
Intangible assets not subject to amortization:				
Licenses	3,000	0	3,000	0
Trademarks	2,500	0	1,600	0
	5,500	0	4,600	0
Goodwill	**3,000**	**300**	**0**	**0**
	$13,600	$2,900	$8,600	$1,800

Amortization expense was $1,100 in 20X2 and $500 in 20X1.

A summary of estimated amortization expense for the five years subsequent to 20X2 follows:

Year	Amortization expense
20X3	$1,200
20X4	1,200
20X5	1,200
20X6	1,200
20X7	1,200

-end of disclosure-

OBSERVATION: Note 2 related to acquisitions would be eliminated altogether in years subsequent to the acquisition unless the acquisition year is presented comparatively.

MODULE 3: OTHER CURRENT DEVELOPMENTS—CHAPTER 9: Changes Coming with Lease Accounting

¶ 901 WELCOME

This chapter discusses the changes that would be made to accounting for leases based on the May 2013 exposure draft, and the effects those changes may have.

¶ 902 LEARNING OBJECTIVES

Upon completion of this chapter, the reader will be able to:

- Identify the changes that will be made under the proposed lease standard
- Recall how lessees would account for leases under the new standard
- Identify the items that are considered part of the lease payment under the new standard
- Recall how the lessee calculates the liability for a lease under the new standard
- Recognize how existing leases will be handled when the new statement is adopted
- Determine the effect the new standard may have on future lease terms
- Recognize how the new standard may affect book/tax differences, EBITA, and debt-equity ratios

¶ 903 INTRODUCTION

Since the Sarbanes-Oxley Act became effective, the FASB has focused on standards that enhance transparency of transactions and that eliminate off-balance-sheet transactions. Accounting for leases is one of the areas that the FASB has concentrated on. The FASB added to its agenda a joint project with the IASB that would replace existing lease accounting rules found in ASC 840 and its counterpart in Europe, IASB No. 17. The FASB and IASB started deliberations on the project in 2007, and issued a discussion memorandum in 2009, followed by the issuance of an exposure draft in 2010 entitled, *Leases (Topic 840)*.

The 2010 exposure draft was met with numerous criticisms that compelled the FASB to issue a second, replacement exposure draft on May 16, 2013 entitled, *Leases (Topic 842)*, a revision of the 2010 proposed FASB Accounting Standards Update, *Leases (Topic 840)*. Given the fact that the FASB has now issued two exposure drafts and received extensive public comments, the second exposure draft is likely to pass as a final statement, with minor further edits.

This course discusses the changes that would be made to accounting for leases based on the May 2013 exposure draft, and the effects those changes may have.

¶ 904 BACKGROUND

Under current GAAP, ASC 840, *Leases* (formerly FAS 13), divides leases into two categories: operating and capital leases. Capital leases are capitalized while operating leases are not. In order for a lease to qualify as a capital lease, one of four criteria must be met:

- The present value of the minimum lease payments must equal or exceed 90 percent or more of the fair value of the asset.
- The lease term must be at least 75 percent of the remaining useful life of the leased asset.
- There is a bargain purchase at the end of the lease.
- There is a transfer of ownership.

In practice, it is common for lessees to structure leases to ensure they do not qualify as capital leases, thereby removing both the leased asset and obligation from the lessee's balance sheet. This approach is typically used by restaurants, retailers, and other multiple-store facilities.

EXAMPLE: Lease 1: The present value of minimum lease payments is 89 percent of the fair value of the asset and the lease term is 74 percent of the remaining useful life of the asset.

Lease 2: The present value of minimum lease payments is 90 percent of the fair value of the asset or the lease term is 75 percent the remaining useful life of the asset.

Lease 1 is an operating lease not capitalized, while Lease 2 is a capital lease under which both the asset and lease obligation are capitalized.

¶ 905 THE SEC PUSHES TOWARD CHANGES IN LEASE ACCOUNTING

In its report entitled *Report and Recommendations Pursuant to Section 401(c.) of the Sarbanes-Oxley Act of 2002 On Arrangements with Off-Balance-Sheet Implications, Special Purpose Entities, and Transparency of Filings by Issuer*, the SEC targeted lease accounting as one of the areas that resulted in significant liabilities being off-balance-sheet.

According to the SEC Report that focused on U.S. public companies and a U.S. Chamber of Commerce Report:

- Sixty-three percent of companies record operating leases while 22 percent record capital leases.
- U.S. companies have approximately $1.25 trillion in operating lease obligations that are off-balance-sheet.
- European companies have a total of approximately $928 billion in off-balance sheet operating lease obligations.
- Seventy-three percent of all leases held by U.S. public companies ($1.1 trillion) involve the leasing of real estate. (**CFO.com**)

In its Report, the SEC noted that because of ASC 840's bright-line tests (90 percent, 75 percent, etc.), small differences in economics can completely change the accounting (capital versus operating) for leases.

Keeping leases off the balance sheet while still retaining tax benefits is an industry unto itself. So-called synthetic leases are commonly used to maximize the tax benefits of a lease while not capitalizing the lease for GAAP purposes. In addition, lease accounting abuses have been the focus of restatements with approximately 270 companies, mostly restaurants and retailers, restating or adjusting their lease accounting in the wake of Section 404 implementation under Sarbanes-Oxley.

Retailers have the largest amount of operating lease obligations outstanding that are not recorded on their balance sheets, as noted in the following table:

Operating Leases Obligations Outstanding- Major Retailers	
Retailer	Lease Obligations (in millions)
Office Depot Inc.	$ 1,104
Walgreens Co.	27,434
CVS	38,917
Whole Foods	6,322
Sears	7,608
Source: Credit Suisse, August 2010	

The above table shows the amount of off-balance-sheet lease obligations for some of the largest U.S. retailers. These numbers are significant and bring to the forefront the pervasive impact the proposed lease standard would have on the larger retailers.

¶ 906 FASB-IASB LEASE PROJECT

Since the Sarbanes-Oxley Act became effective, the FASB has focused on standards that enhance transparency of transactions and that eliminate off-balance-sheet transactions, the most recent of which was the issuance of ASC 810, *Consolidation of Variable Interest Entities* (formerly FIN 46R). The FASB added to its agenda a joint project with the IASB that would replace existing lease accounting rules found in ASC 840 and its counterpart in Europe, IASB No. 17. The FASB and IASB started deliberations on the project in 2007, and issued a discussion memorandum in 2009, followed by the issuance of an exposure draft in 2010 entitled, *Leases (Topic 840)*.

The 2010 exposure draft was met with numerous criticisms that compelled the FASB to issue a second, replacement exposure draft on May 16, 2013 entitled, *Leases (Topic 842)*, a revision of the 2010 proposed FASB Accounting Standards Update, *Leases (Topic 840)*. Given the fact that the FASB has now issued two exposure drafts and received extensive public comments, the second exposure draft is likely to pass as a final statement, with minor further edits.

Following are some of the changes that the FASB and IASB have included it their proposed new lease model as outlined in the May 2013 Exposure Draft.

¶ 907 BASIC CONCEPTS OF THE 2013 LEASE EXPOSURE DRAFT

The core principle of the proposed requirements found in the 2013 Exposure Draft is that an entity should use the *right-of-use model* to account for leases which would require the entity to recognize assets and liabilities arising from a lease. Thus, most existing operating leases would be brought onto the balance sheet.

In accordance with the right-of-use model, a lessee would recognize assets and liabilities for any leases that have a maximum possible lease term of more than 12 months. Leases with terms of 12 months or less would have the option of remaining as operating leases.

Following is a summary of the key elements of the proposed lease standard.

STUDY QUESTIONS

1. Under existing GAAP (*Leases (ASC 840)* (formerly FASB No. 13)), in order for a lease to qualify as a capital lease, which one of the following conditions must be satisfied?

a. The future value of the minimum lease payments must be equal to or exceed 10 percent or more of the fair value of the asset.

b. The lease term must be no more than 50 percent of the remaining useful life of the leased asset.

c. There must be a bargain purchase at the end of the lease.

d. There must not be a transfer of ownership.

2. Which of the following models does the proposed lease standard use?

a. Right-of-use model

b. Operating lease model

c. Capital lease model

d. True lease model

¶ 908 LESSEE

At the commencement date, a lessee would measure both of the following:

- A lease liability (liability to make lease payments)
- A right-of-use asset (right to use the leased asset for the lease term)

Lease Liability

The lease liability would be recorded at the present value of the lease payments over the lease term, discounted using the *rate the lessor charges the lessee* (the lessor's imputed rate) based on information available at the commencement date. If the lessor's imputed rate cannot be readily determined, the lessee would use its *incremental borrowing rate*.

Nonpublic entities would be permitted to use a *risk-free discount rate*, determined using a period comparable to that of the lease term, as an accounting policy election for all leases. The risk-free discount rate would be a U.S. Treasury instrument rate for the same term as the lease.

Right-of-use Asset

At the commencement date, the cost of the right-of-use asset would consist of all of the following:

- The amount of the initial measurement of the lease liability
- Any lease payments made to the lessor at or before the commencement date, less any lease incentives received from the lessor
- Any *initial direct costs* incurred by the lessee

At the commencement date, initial direct costs would be included as part of the cost of the lease asset capitalized and may include:

- Commissions
- Legal fees
- Evaluating the prospective lessee's financial condition
- Evaluating and recording guarantees, collateral, and other security contracts
- Negotiating lease terms and conditions

- Preparing and processing lease documents
- Payments made to existing tenants to obtain the lease

The following items are examples of costs that would *not* be initial direct costs:

- General overheads (e.g., depreciation, occupancy and equipment costs, unsuccessful origination efforts, and idle time)
- Costs related to activities performed by the lessor for advertising, soliciting potential lessees, servicing existing leases, or other ancillary activities

Lease Payments

At the commencement date, lease payments included in the lease liability would consist of the following payments related to the use of the underlying asset during the lease term that are not yet paid:

- Fixed payments, less any lease incentives receivable from the lessor
- Variable lease payments that depend on an index or a rate (such as the Consumer Price Index or a market interest rate), initially measured using the index or rate at the commencement date
- Variable lease payments that are in-substance fixed payments
- Amounts expected to be payable by the lessee under residual value guarantees
- The exercise price of a purchase option if the lessee has a *significant economic incentive* to exercise that option
- Payments for penalties for terminating the lease, if the lease term reflects the lessee exercising an option to terminate the lease

Variable lease payments would be included in lease payments used to calculation the lease liability if:

- The lease payments would depend on an index or rate, such as a CPI index. Each year, the lessee would adjust the lease obligation to reflect the present value of the remaining lease payments using latest index in effect at the end of that year.
- The lease payments would be in-substance, fixed payments, such as minimum annual increase of two percent per year.

Lease payments based on performance (such as a percentage of sales, with no minimum) would not be reflected in the lease payments in computing the lease obligation. Instead, such payments would be recorded annually as actual sales are generated.

Lease Term

An entity would determine the lease term as the *noncancellable period of the lease*, together with *both* of the following:

- Periods covered by an option to extend the lease if the lessee has a significant economic incentive to exercise that option
- Periods covered by an option to terminate the lease if the lessee has a significant economic incentive *not* to exercise that option.

Factors would be considered together, and the existence of any one factor would not necessarily signify that a lessee has a significant economic incentive to exercise, or not to exercise, the option. Examples of factors to consider would include, but would not be limited to, any of the following:

- Contractual terms and conditions for the optional periods compared with current market rates

- Significant leasehold improvements that are expected to have significant economic value for the lessee when the option to extend or terminate the lease or to purchase the asset becomes exercisable

- Costs relating to the termination of the lease and the signing of a new lease, such as negotiation costs, relocation costs, costs of identifying another underlying asset suitable for the lessee's operations, or costs associated with returning the underlying asset in a contractually specified condition or to a contractually specified location

- The importance of that underlying asset to the lessee's operations, considering, for example, whether the underlying asset is a specialized asset and the location of the underlying asset

   EXAMPLE: A retail lessee, a liquor store, has a five-year lease with two, five-year options. It would be very difficult for the lessee to move the liquor store due to neighborhood opposition. Thus, the store location is very important to the lessee and the lessee most likely has a significant economic incentive to exercise the options so that the lease term is probably 15 years.

An entity would reassess the lease term only if either of the following occurs:

- There is a *change in relevant factors* that would result in the lessee having or no longer having a significant economic incentive either to exercise an option to extend the lease or not to exercise an option to terminate the lease.

   NOTE: A change in market-based factors (such as market rates to lease a comparable asset) shall not, in isolation, trigger reassessment of the lease term.

- The lessee does either of the following:

   - Elects to exercise an option even though the entity had previously determined that the lessee did not have a significant economic incentive to do so

   - Does not elect to exercise an option even though the entity had previously determined that the lessee had a significant economic incentive to do so

Classification of Leases

The Exposure Draft establishes two types of leases:

Type A lease: Lease in which lessee expects to consume *more than an insignificant portion* of the economic benefits (life) of the asset:

- Would apply to most leases of assets other than property (e.g., equipment, aircraft, cars, trucks)

- Would recognize a right-of-use asset and a lease liability, initially measured at the present value of lease payments

- Would recognize the unwinding of the discount on the lease liability as interest separately from the amortization of the right-of-use asset

- Total expense would be accelerated and shown in two expense components:

- Interest expense (accelerated)

- Amortization expense (straight-line)

Type B lease: Lease in which the lessee expects to consume only an insignificant portion of the economic benefits (life) of the asset:

- Would apply to most leases of property (i.e., land and/or a building or part of a building)

- Would recognize a right-of-use asset and a lease liability, initially measured at the present value of lease payments (same as Type A lease)

- Would recognize a single lease expense, combining the unwinding of the discount on the lease liability (interest) with the amortization of the right-of-use asset, on a straight-line basis.
- Total expense would be recorded on a straight-line basis throughout the lease term.

The following chart compares the proposed standard with existing GAAP for leases.

Comparison of Existing GAAP Versus Proposed GAAP for Leases Lessee Side		
Description	**Current GAAP for Operating Leases**	**Proposed GAAP**
Lease type	Leases are classified as operating or capital leases (financing arrangements) based on satisfying one of four criteria: • 75% rule • 90% rule • Bargain purchase • Transfer of ownership	All leases classified as financing arrangements (as if asset purchases) Right-of-use asset and lease liability recorded at present value of payments over the lease term
Lease term	Non-cancellable periods Option periods generally not included in lease term	Non-cancellable period together with any options to extend or terminate the lease when there is a significant economic incentive for the lessee to exercise an option to extend the lease
Contingent/ variable rents	Contingent rents excluded from lease payments. When paid, they are period costs.	Variable rents included in lease payments in certain instances
Income statement	Operating leases: lease expense straight-line basis Capital leases: depreciation and interest expense	Two Approaches: *TYPE A LEASE*: Interest and amortization expense recorded—Accelerated expense *TYPE B LEASE:* Lease expense recorded as combination of interest and amortization—straight-line expense
Assessment	Terms are not re-assessed	Leases reassessed in certain instances

STUDY QUESTION

3. Facts: A company is a lessee of a lease with a lease term of 12 months. How may the lessee account for this lease under the proposed lease standard?

    a. The company is required to record a lease asset and liability.

    b. The company is required to record the lease as an operating lease.

    c. The company has the option to record the lease asset and liability, or record the lease as an operating lease.

    d. The proposed standard does not address lease terms of 12 months or less.

¶ 909 LESSOR

A lessor would account for leases using the following rules:

Type A lease: Lessee is expected to consume more than an insignificant portion of the economic benefits (life) of the asset:

- Most leases of assets other than property (e.g., equipment, aircraft, cars, trucks)
- Lessor would:
  - Derecognize (remove) the underlying asset and recognize two new assets:
    - Lease receivable: Reflecting the right to receive lease payments
    - Residual asset: Reflecting the right the lessor retains in the underlying asset at the end of the lease
  - Recognize the unwinding of the discount on both the lease receivable and the residual asset as interest income over the lease term; interest income recorded on an accelerated basis
  - Recognize any profit relating to the lease at the commencement date

Type B lease: Lessee is expected to consume only an insignificant portion of the economic benefits (life) of the asset:

For most leases of assets of property (i.e., land and/or a building or part of a building) lessor would:

- Apply an approach similar to existing operating lease accounting in which the lessor would do the following:
  - Retain the lease asset on the lessor's balance sheet, and
  - Recognize lease (rental) income over the lease term typically on a straight-line basis.

Short-term Leases

A lessee would not be required to recognize lease assets or lease liabilities for short-term leases. A short-term lease is defined as follows:

"A lease that, at the date of commencement of the lease, has a maximum possible term, including any options to renew, of 12 months or less."

For short-term leases, the lessee would recognize lease payments as rent expense in the income statement on a straight-line basis over the lease term, unless another systematic and rational basis is more representative of the time pattern in which use is derived from the underlying asset.

> **NOTE:** The proposal would treat short-term leases (12 months or less) as operating leases by not requiring the lessee to record the lease asset and liability. Instead, rent expense would be recorded on a straight-line basis as incurred, although the proposal would permit an entity to use another approach (other than a straight-line method) to record rent expense if that alternative is more representative of the time pattern in which the lessee uses the lease asset.
>
> A lessee would be permitted (but is not required) to record a lease asset and liability for a short-term lease. Lessors would be permitted to elect to account for all short-term leases by not recognizing lease assets or lease liabilities and by recognizing lease payments received in rental income on a straight-line basis over the lease term, or another systematic and rational basis that is more representative of the time pattern in which use is derived from the underlying asset.

¶910 DISCLOSURES

Both lessees and lessors would provide disclosures to meet the objective of enabling users of financial statements to understand the amount, timing, and uncertainty of cash flows arising from leases.

¶911 EFFECTIVE DATE AND TRANSITION

The FASB will set the effective date for the proposed requirements when it considers interested parties' feedback on the revised Exposure Draft. The effective date is likely to be no earlier than 2016, and possibly as late as 2017. Existing leases would not be grandfathered thereby requiring existing operating leases to be brought onto the balance sheet. All existing outstanding leases would be recognized and measured at the date of initial application using a simplified retrospective approach. On transition, a lessee and a lessor would recognize and measure leases at the beginning of the earliest period presented using either a modified retrospective approach or a full retrospective approach.

¶912 IMPACT OF PROPOSED CHANGES TO LEASE ACCOUNTING

The proposed lease accounting changes would be devastating to many companies and would result in many more leases being capitalized which would impact all financial statements. Retailers, in particular, would be affected the most. If leases of retailers, for example, are capitalized, the impact on financial statements would be significant, as noted below:

- Lessee's balance sheets would be grossed up for the recognized lease assets and the lease obligations for all lease obligations.

  NOTE: Including contingent lease payments and renewal options may result in overstated liabilities given the fact that contingent payments must be included in the lease payments and renewal options must be considered in determining the lease term.

- For Type A leases, lessee's income statements would be adversely affected with higher lease expense in the earlier years of new leases. On average, a 10-year lease would incur approximately 15-20% higher annual lease expense in the earlier years, if capitalized, as compared with an operating lease. That higher lease amount would reverse in the later years.

- For Type A leases, on the statement of cash flows, there would be a positive shift in cash flow to cash from operations from cash from financing activities. A portion of rent expense previously deducted in arriving at cash from operations would now be deducted as principal payments in cash from financing activities. Thus, companies would have higher cash from operating activities and lower cash from financing activities.

- In most cases, annual lease expense for GAAP (interest and amortization) would not match lease expense for income tax purposes thereby resulting in deferred income taxes.

Changes to both the balance sheets and income statements of companies would have rippling effects on other elements of the lessee companies. On the positive side, a lessee's earnings before interest, taxes, depreciation and amortization (EBITDA) may actually improve as there is a shift from rent expense under operating leases to interest and amortization expense under the proposed standard.

- Both interest and amortization expense is not deducted in arriving at EBITDA while rent expense is.
- Changes in EBIDTA may affect existing agreements related to compensation, earn outs, bonuses, and commissions.

On the negative side, for Type A and B leases, lessee debt-equity ratios would be affected with entities carrying significantly higher lease obligation debt than under existing GAAP. Higher debt-equity ratios could put certain loan agreements into default. Moreover, net income would be lower in the earlier years of the lease term due to higher interest and amortization expense replacing rental expense.

How significant would the change to the proposed lease standard be for U. S. companies?

As previously noted, there are approximately $1.5 trillion of operating lease obligations that are not recorded on public company balance sheets. That $1.5 trillion is magnified by the many nonpublic companies that have unpublished operating lease obligations that are unrecorded.

The author estimates that unrecorded lease obligations of nonpublic operating leases is at lease $6.3 trillion based on the following computation:

Computation of Estimated Unrecorded Lease Obligations of Nonpublic U.S. Companies	
Estimated annual lease payments ($5,000 × 12)	$60,000
Estimated average number of years remaining	5
Gross lease payments	$300,000
Present value factor, 5 years, 5%	4.212
Present value of lease obligation	$1,263,600
Estimated # nonpublic entities in the United States with leases that would be subject to the proposed standard: 20 million nonpublic companies × 25%	5,000,000
Unrecorded lease obligations- U. S. nonpublic companies	$6.3 trillion
Source: The Author	

Consider the following estimated impacts of shifting those operating leases to capitalized right-of-use leases (Report issued by Change & Adams Consulting, commissioned by the U.S. Chamber of Commerce, and others (2012)):

- Earnings of retailers would decline significantly. One recent study suggested that there would be a median drop in EPS of 5.3 percent and a median decline in return on assets of 1.7 percent.
- Public companies would face $10.2 billion of added annual interest costs.
- There would be a loss of U.S. jobs in the range of 190,000 to 3.3 million.
- Cost of compliance with the new standard would lower U.S. GDP by $27.5 billion a year.
- Lessors would lose approximately $14.8 billion in the value in their commercial real estate.
- Balance sheets would be loaded with significant lease obligations that would impact debt-equity ratios (Bear Stearns research study).

- Aggregate debt of nonfinancial S&P 500 companies would increase by 17 percent if all leases were capitalized.

- Return on assets would decline as total assets (the denominator) would increase by approximately 10 percent.

- The S&P 500 would record an estimate of $549 billion of additional liabilities under the proposed lease standard on existing operating leases (Leases Landing on Balance Sheet (Credit Suisse)).

- U. S. companies, as a whole (public and nonpublic), would record approximately $7.8 trillion of additional liabilities if operating leases are capitalized (Author's estimate: $1.5 trillion for public companies and $6.3 trillion for non-public companies).

According to a Credit Suisse study (Leases Landing on Balance Sheet (Credit Suisse)), there are 494 of the S&P 500 companies that are obligated to make $634 billion of total future minimum lease payments under operating leases. On a present value basis, including contingent rents, the $634 billion translates into an additional liability under the proposed standard of $549 billion. Of the $549 billion of additional liabilities, 15 percent of that total relates to retail companies on the S&P 500.

In some cases, the effect of capitalizing lease obligations under the proposed lease standard is that the additional liability exceeds stockholders' equity.

Consider the following table:

Impact of Capitalizing Leases -Selected Retailers Based on Annual Reports					
Retailer	Operating lease obligations	PV converter 5 years 4%[a]	Additional liability under new lease standard	Stockholders' equity	**% equity**
Office Depot Inc.	$ 2 B	.822	$1.6 B	$661M	**248%**
Walgreens Co.	35 B	.822	28.8 B	18 B	**160%**
CVS	28 B	.822	23.0 B	38 B	**61%**
Whole Foods	6.8 B	.822	5.6 B	3.8 B	**147%**
Sears	4.5 B	.822	3.7 B	3.1 B	**119%**

Source: Annual Reports, as obtained by the author.

[a] Assumes the weighted-average remaining lease term is five years, and the incremental borrowing rate is four percent

The previous table identifies the sizeable problem that exists for many of the U.S. retailers, which is that there are huge off-balance-sheet operating lease liabilities as a percentage of company market capitalization. Under the proposed lease standard, these obligations would be recorded, thereby having a devastating impact on those retailers' balance sheets. For example, look at Office Depot and its $1.6 billion lease liability that would represent 248% of its stockholders' equity of $661 million.

How would the proposed lease standard impact how leases are structured?

Companies are going to consider the balance sheet impact when structuring leases and in deciding whether to lease or buy the underlying asset. There are several likely actions that would come from the proposed standard:

Lease-versus-buy decision impacted: By implementing the proposed standard, the GAAP differences between leasing and owning an asset would be reduced. Having to capitalize all leases may have a significant effect on the lease versus purchase decision, particularly with respect to real estate. Tenants, in particular those in single-tenant buildings with long-term leases, may choose to purchase a building instead of leasing it:

- A similar amount of debt would be included on the tenant's balance sheet under a long-term lease as compared with a purchase.

- GAAP depreciation under a purchase may actually be lower than amortization under a lease because the amortization life under the lease (generally the lease term) is likely to be shorter than the useful life under a purchase.

   EXAMPLE: Assume there is a 10-year building lease with two, five-year lease options, resulting in a maximum lease term of 20 years. Assume further that the useful life of the building is 30 years for depreciation purposes. If the entity leases the real estate, the right-of-use asset would be amortized over a maximum of 20 years. If, instead, the entity were to purchase the real estate, the building would be depreciated over the useful life of 30 years.

   NOTE: In some instances, lessees may choose to purchase the leased asset rather than lease it, if the accounting is the same. In particular, the purchase scenario may be more appealing for longer-term leases that have significant debt obligations on the lessee balance sheets. Lessees with shorter-term leases will not be burdened with the extensive debt obligations and, therefore, may choose not to purchase the underlying lease asset.

Lease terms are likely to shorten: For many companies who do not wish to purchase the underlying leased asset, lease terms may shorten to reduce the amount of the lease obligation (and related asset) that is recorded at the lease inception. The proposed lease standard would affect not only the landlords and tenants, but also brokers, as there would be much greater emphasis placed on executing leases for shorter periods of times thereby increasing the paperwork over a period of time and the commissions earned.

Deferred tax assets would be created: Because many operating leases would now be capitalized for GAAP but not for tax purposes, total GAAP expense (interest and amortization) would be greater than lease expense for tax purposes, resulting in deferred tax assets for the future tax benefits that would be realized when the temporary difference reverses in later years.

   Under existing GAAP, most, but not all, operating leases are treated as operating leases for tax purposes. Therefore, rarely are operating leases capitalized for tax purposes. Now the game is about to change if operating leases are capitalized as right-of-use assets under GAAP, while they continue to be treated as operating leases for tax purposes. As we have seen in the previous examples, most leases capitalized under the proposed standard would result in the creation of a deferred tax asset.

STUDY QUESTIONS

---

4. Which of the following would be a probable effect of the proposed lease standard?

   a. The lessee's income statement would have lower total lease expense in the earlier years of new leases.

   b. There would be a negative shift in cash from operations from cash from financing activities in the statement of cash flows.

   c. In most cases, total expense for GAAP would be the same as total expense for income tax purposes.

   d. The lessee's EBITDA may increase as there is a shift from rent expense to interest and amortization expense.

5. One change that may occur as a result of the proposed lease standard being implemented is:

a. Companies that typically purchase a single-tenant building may choose to lease instead of buy.

b. Tenants in multi-tenant buildings would likely sign longer-term leases.

c. Tenants in single-tenant buildings with long-term leases may choose to buy.

d. There is likely to be no change.

6. Annual GAAP depreciation expense for a purchase of a leased asset may be _____ assuming there is a Type A lease.

a. Higher than annual amortization expense under a lease

b. Lower than annual amortization expense under a lease

c. The same as annual amortization expense under a lease

d. Either higher or lower than amortization expense under a lease, depending on whether options are part of the lease term

---

Dealing with Financial Covenants

The proposed lease standard would cast a wide web across the accounting profession. By capitalizing leases that were previously off-balance-sheet as operating leases, there may be consequences.

Examples:

- *Impact on state apportionment computations*: Many states compute the apportionment of income assigned to that state using a property factor based on real and tangible personal property held in that particular state.

  NOTE: When it comes to rent expense, most states capitalize the rents using a factor such as eight times rent expense. Although each state has its own set of rules, the implementation of the proposed standard may have a sizeable positive or negative impact on state tax apportionment based on shifting rent expense to capitalized assets.

- *Impact on tax planning*: Capitalizing leases might have a positive effect in tax planning.

  NOTE: One example is where there is a C corporation with accumulated earnings and exposure to an accumulated earnings tax (AET). The additional lease obligation liability would certainly help justify that the accumulation of earnings is not subject to the AET.

- *Impact on total asset and liability thresholds:* Companies should also be aware that not only would the proposed standard increase liabilities, but would also increase total assets.

  NOTE: In some states, there are total asset thresholds that drive higher taxes and reporting requirements.

A critical impact of the proposed standard would be that certain loan covenants may be adversely impaired, thereby forcing companies into violations of their loans.

Consider the following ratios:

Ratio	Likely impact of proposed lease standard
EBITDA:	
Earnings before interest, taxes, depreciation and amortization	*Type A Leases:* Favorable impact due to shift from rental expense to interest and amortization expense, both of which are added back in computing EBITDA
	Type B Leases: May be favorable impact depending on whether "lease expense" is added back to compute EBITDA
Interest coverage ratio:	May be negatively impacted from lower ratio
$\dfrac{\textit{Earnings before interest and taxes}}{\textit{Interest expense}}$	
Debt-equity ratio:	Negative impact from higher ratio
$\dfrac{\textit{Total liabilities}}{\textit{Stockholders' equity}}$	

There would be a favorable impact on EBITDA for Type A leases by implementing the proposed standard. Rent expense recorded for operating leases under existing GAAP would be reduced while interest expense and amortization expense would increase once the leases are capitalized.

However, the issue is what happens to EBITDA for Type B leases. Under the proposal, interest and amortization are combined as one line item on the income statement entitled "lease expense." The question is whether that line item is added back in arriving at EBITDA. Perhaps it should be added back because it represents interest and amortization despite the lease expense label.

As to the interest coverage ratio, the impact on the ratio depends on the whether there is a Type A or B lease. For a Type A lease, earnings before interest and taxes would likely be higher as rent expense is removed and replaced with interest and amortization expense. For Type A leases, the denominator increases significantly due to the higher interest expense. On balance, the slightly higher earnings before interest and taxes divided by a higher interest expense in the denominator yields a lower interest coverage ratio.

For a Type B lease, the impact on the ratio is unclear. Although interest expense, along with amortization expense, would be embedded in the caption line item "lease expense," most analysts would likely carve out the interest and amortization components and adjust the interest coverage ratio by the interest portion.

Perhaps the most significant impact of capitalizing leases under the proposed lease standard would be its effect on the debt-equity ratio. With sizeable liabilities being recorded, this ratio would likely turn quite negative and severely impact company balance sheets. In some cases, the debt-equity ratio would result in violation of existing loan covenants, thereby requiring a company to renegotiate the covenants with its lenders or at least notify lenders in advance of the likely lack of compliance with loan covenants.

What about the impact on smaller nonpublic entities?

One leasing organization noted that more than 90 percent of all leases involve assets worth less than $5 million and have terms of two to five years (Equipment Leasing and Financing Association (ELFA) "Companies: New Lease Rule Means Labor Pains" (CFO. com)). That means that smaller companies have a significant amount of leases, most of which are currently being accounted for as operating leases. Previously, the author estimated that the present value of unrecorded lease obligations under operating leases of nonpublic entities to be at least $6.3 trillion which is much higher than the estimated $1.5 trillion of unrecorded lease obligations of public companies.

Unless these smaller, nonpublic entities choose to use the income tax basis for their financial statements, under GAAP, these companies would be required to capitalize their operating leases.

What about related party leases?

Some, but not all, related party leases result in the lessee (parent equivalent) consolidating the lessor (subsidiary equivalent) under the consolidation of variable interest entity rules (ASC 810) (formerly FIN 46R). The common example of a related-party lease is where an operating company lessee leases real estate from its related party lessor. In general, under FIN 46R, if there is a related party lessee and lessor, consolidation is required if:

- The real estate lessor is a variable interest entity (VIE) (e.g., it is not self-sustaining), and,
- The lessee operating company and/or the common shareholder provide financial support to the real estate lessor in the form of loans, guarantees of bank loans, above-market lease payments, etc.

If these two conditions are met, it is likely that the real estate lessor must be consolidated in with the operating company lessee's financial statements. If there is consolidation, capitalizing the lease under the proposed standard would be moot because the asset, liability, and lease payments would be eliminated in the consolidation.

In 2014, the Private Company Council (PCC) issued ASU 2014-07 which provides private (nonpublic) entities an election not to apply the consolidation of VIE rules to a related-party lease arrangement. When implemented, the ASU should provide most private companies with relief from the VIE rules for related party leases. Thus, most private (nonpublic) entities involved in related-party leases will not be consolidating the lessor into the lessee.

When it comes to a related-party lease in which there is no consolidation, the parties would have to account for that lease as a right-of-use lease asset and obligation, just like any other lease transaction. Consequently, under the proposed standard, the operating company lessee would be required to record a right-of-use asset and lease obligation based on the present value of the lease payments.

Many related parties either do not have formal leases or the leases are short-term. If the operating company lessee is going to have to record a significant asset and liability, it may make sense to have a related-party lease that has a lease term of 12 months or less or is a tenant-at-will arrangement.

With respect to a related party lease that is 12 months or less, the proposed standard would permit (but not require) use of the short-term lease rules as follows:

- A lessee would treat the short-term lease as an operating lease with no recognition of the lease asset or lease liability. The rental payments would be recognized as rent expense on a straight-line basis.

- On the lessor side, the lessor would record rental income on a straight-line basis and not record the lease asset and liability.
- Either the lessee or lessor could elect to record the lease asset and liability using the proposed standard rules.

With many related-party leases, the operating company lessee may issue financial statements while the real estate lessor does not. Therefore, how the lessee accounts for the transaction under GAAP may be more important than the lessor's accounting for the transaction.

> **EXAMPLE:** Company X is a real estate lessor LLC that leases an office building to a related-party operating Company Y. X and Y are related by a common owner. The companies sign an annual 12-month lease with no renewals, and no obligations that extend beyond the twelve months. Monthly rents are $10,000. Y issues financial statements to its bank while X does not issue financial statements. Y chooses ASU 2014-07's election not to consolidate X into Y's financial statements.

> Because the entities have a short-term lease of 12 months or less, Y, as lessee, would qualify for the short-term lease rules. Therefore, Y *would not* record a lease asset and liability and, instead, would record the monthly rent payments and rent expense on a straight-line basis over the short-term lease period. Alternatively, Y could elect to treat the short-term lease as a standard lease by recording both the lease asset and liability.

> As to the lessor, it would also not record the lease asset and liability and, instead, would record rental income on a straight-line basis over the 12-month period.

> **OBSERVATION:** If the proposed standard is issued in final form, many nonpublic entities would take steps to avoid its arduous rules. One approach will likely be to make sure the related-party leases have terms that are 12 months or less so that the lease can be treated as an operating lease and not capitalized. Another approach would be to issue income tax basis financial statements.

MODULE 3: OTHER CURRENT DEVELOPMENTS—CHAPTER 10: Selected ASUs 2013 - 2014

¶ 1001 WELCOME

This chapter discusses several Accounting Standards Updates (ASUs) issued in 2013 and 2014, including ASU 2014-05 regarding service concession arrangements, ASU 2014-04 regarding troubled debt restructurings, ASU 2013-12 regarding the definition of a public business entity, ASU 2013-11, dealing with the presentation of unrecognized tax benefits, and ASU 2013-05 concerning foreign currency matters.

¶ 1002 LEARNING OBJECTIVES

Upon completion of this chapter, the reader will be able to:

- Identify the scope of GAAP to which service concession arrangements apply
- Recognize a situation in which an in-substance repossession or foreclosure occurs
- Recognize a public business entity
- Determine how to present an unrecognized tax benefit when a net operating loss carryforward, a similar tax loss, or a tax credit carryforward exists
- Recall the accounting rules concerning the sale of an investment in a foreign entity

¶ 1003 SERVICE CONCESSION ARRANGEMENTS (ASU 2014-05)

ASU 2014-05—*Service Concession Arrangements (Topic 853) (a consensus of the FASB Emerging Issues Task Force)* was issued in January 2014. The objective of ASU 2014-05 is to address whether an operating entity should account for a service concession arrangement as a lease in accordance with Accounting Standards Codification (ASC) 840, *Leases.*

Background

Service concession arrangements may become more prevalent in the United States as public-sector entities seek alternative ways to provide public services on a more efficient and cost-effective basis.

A service concession arrangement is an arrangement between a public-sector entity grantor and a private operating entity under which the operating entity operates the grantor's infrastructure (e.g., airports, roads, and bridges). The operating entity also may provide the construction, upgrading, or maintenance services on the grantor's infrastructure.

Current U.S. GAAP does not contain specific guidance for the accounting for service concession arrangements. Depending on the terms of a service concession arrangement, some operating entities have concluded that a service concession arrangement meets the lease criteria in ASC 840.

ASU 2014-05 clarifies that a service concession arrangement within the scope of this ASU should *not* be accounted for as a lease in accordance with ASC 840, *Leases*, and, thereby, alleviates the confusion that arises when determining whether a service concession arrangement is a lease.

Scope

ASU 2014-05 applies to the accounting by operating entities of a service concession arrangement under which a public-sector entity grantor enters into a contract with an operating entity to:

- Operate the grantor's infrastructure (such as airports, roads, bridges, tunnels, prisons, and hospitals) for a specified period of time, or
- Provide construction, upgrading, or maintenance services of the grantor's infrastructure

A public-sector entity includes:

- A governmental body
- An entity to which the responsibility to provide public service has been delegated

A service concession arrangement satisfies *both* of the following conditions:

- The grantor (public-sector entity) controls or has the ability to modify or approve:
  - The services that the operating entity must provide with the infrastructure
  - To whom it must provide them
  - At what price
- The grantor (public-sector entity) controls (through ownership, beneficial entitlement, or otherwise), any residual interest in the infrastructure at the end of the term of the arrangement.

NOTE: The infrastructure already may exist or may be constructed by the operating entity during the period of the service concession arrangement. If the infrastructure already exists, the operating entity may be required to provide significant upgrades as part of the arrangement.

NOTE: In a typical service concession arrangement, an operating entity operates and maintains for a period of time the infrastructure of the grantor that will be used to provide a public service. In exchange, the operating entity may receive payments from the grantor to perform those services. Those payments may be paid as the services are performed or over an extended period of time. Additionally, the operating entity may be given a right to charge the public (the third-party users) to use the infrastructure. The arrangement also may contain an unconditional guarantee from the grantor under which the grantor provides a guaranteed minimum payment if the fees collected from the third-party users do not reach a specified minimum threshold.

ASU 2014-05 does not apply to a service concession arrangement that meets the scope criteria in ASC 980, *Regulated Operations*. The scope criteria of a regulated operation that is exempt from ASU 2014-05 is found in ASC 980-10-15, which covers an entity that has regulated operations that satisfies certain conditions.

Those conditions include:

- There are regulatory rates that must be approved by a regulatory body.
- The rates are designed to recover the entity's regulated services or products.
- It is reasonable that the rates can be charged and collected.

Rules

An operating entity shall refer to other GAAP to account for various aspects of a service concession arrangement.

> **EXAMPLE:** An operating entity shall account for revenue and costs relating to construction, upgrade, or operation services in accordance with ASC 605, *Revenue Recognition.*

The infrastructure that is the subject of a service concession arrangement within the scope of ASU 2014-05 shall not be recognized as property, plant, and equipment of the operating entity. Service concession arrangements within the scope of ASU 2014-05 are not within the scope of ASC 840, *Leases.*

> **OBSERVATIONS:** The FASB Emerging Issues Task Force (EITF) reached the conclusion that service concession arrangements (within the scope of ASC 853, *Service Concession Arrangements)* should not be accounted for as leases. Some EITF members noted that in many service concession arrangements, the operating entity receives substantially all of the economic output from the infrastructure during the term of the arrangement but the price paid is not fixed per unit of output or at current market price per unit of output. As such, service concession arrangements generally do meet one or more of the conditions to qualify as a lease.
>
> The EITF concluded that the accounting for service concession arrangements should be determined on the basis of whether the operating entity controls the infrastructure that is being used to provide the public service. The operating entity may have managerial discretion in operating the infrastructure; however, the grantor determines the services the operating entity must provide with the infrastructure, to whom it must provide them, and at what price. Also, the grantor controls any residual interest in the infrastructure at the end of the term of the arrangement.
>
> The EITF also decided to clarify that the operating entity's rights over the infrastructure do not result in the infrastructure being recognized as property, plant, and equipment of the operating entity. That is because the operating entity does not control or have title to the infrastructure under the terms of the arrangement. Many service concession arrangements have a very long term. In such cases, the form and/or the substance of the arrangement may convey the responsibilities customary of ownership over the infrastructure to the operating entity during the term of the arrangement. Because the operating entity does not have control over the infrastructure, ASU 2014-05 states that the infrastructure should not be recognized as the operating entity's property, plant, and equipment.

Transition and Effective Date

ASU 2014-05 is effective for a public business entity for annual periods and interim periods within those annual periods, beginning after December 15, 2014.

For an entity other than a public business entity (e.g., nonpublic entity), the amendments shall be effective for annual periods beginning after December 15, 2014, and interim periods within annual periods beginning after December 15, 2015. Early adoption is permitted.

The changes made by ASU 2014-05 shall be applied on a modified retrospective basis to service concession arrangements that exist at the beginning of an entity's fiscal year of adoption. The cumulative effect of applying the ASU to arrangements existing at the beginning of the fiscal year of adoption shall be recognized as an adjustment to the opening balance of retained earnings in the fiscal year of adoption.

¶1003

An entity shall provide the disclosures in ASC 853, and ASC 250, *Accounting Changes and Error Corrections*, paragraphs 250-10-50-1 through 50-3 in the period the entity adopts ASU 2014-05.

STUDY QUESTION

1. Which of the following is an example of a public-sector entity as referenced in ASU 2014-05?

    a. A non-governmental body to which no responsibility to provide public service has been delegated

    b. A private closely held business to which no responsibility to provide public service has been delegated

    c. An non-governmental entity to which the responsibility to provide public service has been delegated

    d. An entity that is responsible for providing a private for-profit service

¶ 1004 RECEIVABLES—TROUBLED DEBT RESTRUCTURINGS BY CREDITORS (ASU 2014-04)

ASU 2014-04—*Receivables—Troubled Debt Restructurings by Creditors (Subtopic 310-40): Reclassification of Residential Real Estate Collateralized Consumer Mortgage Loans upon Foreclosure (a consensus of the FASB Emerging Issues Task Force)* was issued in January 2014. The objective of the amendments in ASU 2014-04 is to clarify when an in-substance repossession or foreclosure occurs, that is, when a creditor should be considered to have received physical possession of residential real estate property collateralizing a consumer mortgage loan such that the loan receivable should be derecognized and the real estate property recognized.

Background

The rate of default on loans collateralized by residential real estate properties resulting from general economic conditions, including weakness in the housing market, has affected the rate of residential real estate foreclosures and the levels of foreclosed real estate owned by banks or similar lenders (creditors). U.S. GAAP on troubled debt restructurings includes guidance on situations in which a creditor obtains one or more collateral assets in satisfaction of all or part of the receivable. That guidance indicates that a creditor should:

> "Reclassify a collateralized mortgage loan so that the loan should be derecognized and the collateral asset recognized when it determines that there has been *in substance, a repossession or foreclosure* by the creditor."

Existing GAAP indicates that there has been in substance a repossession or foreclosure when the creditor receives *physical possession* of the debtor's assets *regardless of whether formal foreclosure proceedings take place*.

More specifically, ASC 310, *Receivables,* Subtopic 310-40-40-6, addresses accounting for a troubled debt restructuring and states the following:

> ". . . a troubled debt restructuring that is in substance a repossession or foreclosure by the creditor, that is, the creditor receives physical possession of the debtor's assets regardless of whether formal foreclosure proceedings take place, or in which the creditor otherwise obtains one or more of the debtor's assets in place of all or part of the receivable, shall be accounted for

according to the provisions of paragraphs 310- 40-35-7; 310-40-40-2 through 40-4 and; if appropriate, 310-40- 40-8."

A creditor is considered to have received physical possession of residential real estate property collateralizing a consumer mortgage loan when it determines that it has, in substance, repossessed or foreclosed on the residential real estate property.

However, the terms *"in substance a repossession or foreclosure"* and *"physical possession"* are not defined in the accounting literature and there is confusion about when a creditor should derecognize the loan receivable and recognize the real estate property. That confusion has been exacerbated by extended foreclosure timelines and processes related to residential real estate properties.

The goal of ASU 2014-04 is to clarify when an in-substance repossession or foreclosure occurs, so that the creditor should be considered to have received physical possession of residential real estate property collateralizing a consumer mortgage loan. In such a case, the loan receivable should be derecognized and the real estate property recognized.

The amendments in ASU 2014-04 apply to all creditors who obtain physical possession (resulting from an in-substance repossession or foreclosure) of residential real estate property collateralizing a consumer mortgage loan in satisfaction of a receivable.

Scope

The guidance in the ASU applies to all consumer mortgage loans collateralized by residential real estate properties.

NOTE: The EITF decided to limit the scope of ASU 2014-4 to consumer mortgage loans collateralized by residential real estate properties. In doing so, the EITF noted that the prevalent differences in practice relate to those arrangements because of the extended foreclosure timelines and processes, including those resulting from regulatory and legal safeguards afforded to residential borrowers.

The EITF considered whether the scope of the amendments should be expanded to include commercial real estate loans and loans collateralized by nonfinancial assets other than real estate. The EITF decided not to extend the scope of ASU 2014-04 to commercial real estate loans because the foreclosure processes and applicable laws for those assets are significantly different from residential real estate.

Rules

Foreclosure. A troubled debt restructuring that is in substance a repossession or foreclosure by the creditor shall be accounted for according to the troubled debt restructuring rules found in ASC 310, *Receivables*, paragraphs 310-40-35-7; 310-40-40-2 through 40-4 and; if appropriate, 310-40-40-8, as summarized below.

ASC 310-40 provides the following general rules to account for a troubled debt restructuring when there is in substance a repossession or foreclosure of an asset, subject to exceptions:

- The loan receivable is eliminated (derecognized).
- The asset received is recorded at the fair value less costs to sell.
- A loss is recorded, if applicable.

ASC 310 includes rules to address situations in which there is a partial loan satisfaction.

An in-substance repossession or foreclosure occurs when the creditor either:

- Receives *physical possession* of the debtor's assets regardless of whether formal foreclosure proceedings take place
- Obtains one or more of the debtor's assets in place of all or part of the receivable

Physical Possession of Residential Real Estate Property Collateralizing a Consumer Mortgage Loan. A creditor is considered to have received physical possession (resulting from an in-substance repossession or foreclosure) of residential real estate property collateralizing a consumer mortgage loan only upon the occurrence of either of the following:

- The creditor *obtains legal title* to the residential real estate property upon completion of a foreclosure. A creditor may obtain legal title to the residential real estate property even if the borrower has redemption rights that provide the borrower with a legal right for a period of time after a foreclosure to reclaim the real estate property by paying certain amounts specified by law.
- The *borrower conveys all interest in the residential real estate property* to the creditor to satisfy the loan through completion of a deed in lieu of foreclosure or through a similar legal agreement. The deed in lieu of foreclosure or similar legal agreement is completed when agreed-upon terms and conditions have been satisfied by both the borrower and the creditor.

Disclosures. The ASU adds disclosures found in ASC 310. An entity shall also disclose the following:

- The carrying amount of foreclosed residential real estate properties held at the reporting date as a result of obtaining physical possession
- The recorded investment of consumer mortgage loans secured by residential real estate properties for which formal foreclosure proceedings are in process according to local requirements of the applicable jurisdiction

    NOTE: If publicly held companies report summarized financial information at interim dates (including reports on fourth quarters), the company should report the additional disclosures noted above.

Transition and Effective Date

ASU 2014-04 shall be effective as follows with early adoption permitted:

- **Public business entities:** For annual periods, and interim periods within those annual periods, beginning after December 15, 2014.
- **Non-public business entities:** For annual periods beginning after December 15, 2014, and interim periods within annual periods beginning after December 15, 2015.

An entity can adopt the new rules found in ASU 2014-04, on either a prospective basis or a modified retrospective basis as follows:

- **Prospective transition:** A reporting entity shall apply the changes made by ASU 2014-04 to all instances of an entity receiving physical possession of residential real estate property collateralized by consumer mortgage loans that occur after the date of adoption.
- **Modified retrospective transition:** A reporting entity shall adopt by means of a cumulative-effect adjustment to residential consumer mortgage loans and foreclosed residential real estate properties existing as of the beginning of the annual period for which ASU 2014-04 is effective.

    NOTE: Using the modified retrospective transition, assets reclassified from real estate to loans as a result of adopting the ASU shall be based on the carrying value of the real estate at the date of adoption. Assets reclassified from loans to real estate as a result of adopting the ASU shall be based on the lower of the net amount of loan receivable or the real estate's fair value less costs to sell at the date of adoption.

In the period ASU 2014-04 is adopted, an entity shall provide the change in accounting principle disclosures found in ASC 250, *Accounting Changes and Error Corrections*, paragraphs 250-10-50-1 through 50-3.

STUDY QUESTION

2. The scope of ASU 2014-04 applies to which of the following types of loans?

    a. Unsecured loans

    b. Collateralized by commercial real estate

    c. Collateralized by residential real estate

    d. Collateralized by securities

¶ 1005 DEFINITION OF A PUBLIC BUSINESS ENTITY (ASU 2013-12)

ASU 2013-12—*Definition of a Public Business Entity—An Addition to the Master Glossary* was issued in December 2013. The objective of the ASU is to amend the Master Glossary of the *FASB Accounting Standards Codification®* to include one definition of a public business entity for future use in U.S. GAAP. There is no actual effective date for this ASU.

Background

The ASC includes multiple definitions of the terms *nonpublic entity* and *public entity*. Recently, the definition of a nonpublic versus public entity has become important in light of the introduction of the Private Company Council (PCC).

In 2012, the FASB established the PCC to establish GAAP exceptions and modifications for private (nonpublic) companies. Subsequently, the *Private Company Decision-Making Framework: A Guide for Evaluating Financial Accounting and Reporting for Private Companies* (Guide) was issued.

The FASB decided it would minimize the inconsistency and complexity of having multiple definitions of what constitutes a nonpublic entity and public entity within U.S. GAAP on a going-forward basis. Specifically, stakeholders asked that the FASB clarify which nonpublic entities potentially qualify for alternative financial accounting and reporting guidance.

In December 2013, the FASB and the PCC issued a final document, *Private Company Decision-Making Framework: A Guide for Evaluating Financial Accounting and Reporting for Private Companies*. The primary purpose of the private company guide is to assist the FASB and the PCC in determining whether and in what circumstances to provide alternative recognition, measurement, disclosure, display, effective date, and transition guidance for private companies reporting under U.S. GAAP. Thus, there is the need to delineate between the public and private company definitions.

In August 2013, the FASB issued a proposed Accounting Standards Update, *Definition of a Public Business Entity: An Amendment to the Master Glossary,* which, in December 2013, was issued as a final statement in ASU 2013-12.

ASU 2013-12 addresses those issues by defining a "public business entity."

The ASU:

- Amends the Master Glossary of the *FASB Accounting Standards Codification*® to include one definition of a *public business entity* for future use in U.S. GAAP
- Identifies the types of business entities that are excluded from the definition of a public business entity

The ASU does not affect existing requirements. The definition of a public business entity will be used by the FASB, the PCC, and the EITF in specifying the scope of future financial accounting and reporting guidance.

Rules

The Master Glossary is amended to add the term "public business entity." A public business entity is a business entity meeting *any one* of the criteria below:

- It is required by the SEC to file or furnish financial statements, or does file or furnish financial statements (including voluntary filers), with the SEC (including other entities whose financial statements or financial information are required to be or are included in a filing).
- It is required by the Securities Exchange Act of 1934 to file or furnish financial statements with a regulatory agency other than the SEC.
- It is required to file or furnish financial statements with a foreign or domestic regulatory agency in preparation for the sale of or for purposes of issuing securities that are not subject to contractual restrictions on transfer.
- It has issued, or is a conduit bond obligor for, securities that are traded, listed, or quoted on an exchange or an over-the-counter market.
- It has one or more securities that are not subject to contractual restrictions on transfer, and it is required by law, contract, or regulation to prepare U.S. GAAP financial statements (including footnotes) and make them publicly available on a periodic basis (e.g., interim or annual periods). An entity must meet both of these conditions to meet this criterion.

An entity may meet the definition of a public business entity solely because its financial statements or financial information is included in another entity's filing with the SEC. In that case, the entity is only a public business entity for purposes of financial statements that are filed or furnished with the SEC.

A business entity *excludes*:

- A not-for-profit entity
- An employee benefit plan

A private company that controls and consolidates a U.S. public company in its financial statements is not considered a public business entity.

STUDY QUESTION

---

3. Company X is a conduit bond obligor. Which of the following entities is X?

   a. Public business entity

   b. Public nonbusiness entity

   c. Not-for-profit entity

   d. Private business entity

¶ 1006 INCOME TAXES (ASU 2013-11)

ASU 2013-11—*Income Taxes (Topic 740): Presentation of an Unrecognized Tax Benefit When a Net Operating Loss Carryforward, a Similar Tax Loss, or a Tax Credit Carryforward Exists (a consensus of the FASB Emerging Issues Task Force)*, was issued in July 2013. The objective of the ASU is to eliminate variations in practice as to how to present an unrecognized tax benefit on the balance sheet.

Background

ASC 740, *Income Taxes*, does not include explicit guidance on the financial statement presentation of an unrecognized tax benefit when a net operating loss carryforward, a similar tax loss, or a tax credit carryforward exists. There is variation in practice in the presentation of unrecognized tax benefits in those instances.

Some entities present unrecognized tax benefits as a liability unless the unrecognized tax benefit is directly associated with a tax position taken in a tax year that results in, or that resulted in, the recognition of a net operating loss or tax credit carryforward for that year and the net operating loss or tax credit carryforward has not been utilized.

Other entities present unrecognized tax benefits as a reduction of a deferred tax asset for a net operating loss or tax credit carryforward in certain circumstances.

Rules

General Rule

An unrecognized tax benefit, or a portion of an unrecognized tax benefit, shall be presented in the financial statements as a *reduction to a deferred tax asset* for a net operating loss carryforward, a similar tax loss, or a tax credit carryforward.

Exceptions to the General Rule

The unrecognized tax benefit *shall be presented as a liability* and *not* combined with deferred tax assets, to the extent that either of the following is true:

- A net operating loss carryforward, a similar tax loss, or a tax credit carryforward is *not available at the reporting date* under the tax law of the applicable jurisdiction to settle any additional income taxes that would result from the disallowance of a tax position.

- The tax law of the applicable jurisdiction does not require the entity to use, and the entity does not intend to use, the deferred tax asset for such purpose.

    NOTE: The assessment of whether a deferred tax asset is available is based on the unrecognized tax benefit and deferred tax asset that exist at the reporting date and shall be made presuming disallowance of the tax position at the reporting date.

An entity that presents a classified statement of financial position shall classify an unrecognized tax benefit that is presented as a liability as a current liability to the extent the entity anticipates payment (or receipt) of cash within one year or the operating cycle, if longer.

An unrecognized tax benefit presented as a liability shall *not* be classified as a deferred tax liability unless it arises from a taxable temporary difference.

Effective Date and Transition

The guidance found in ASU 2013-11 is effective as follows:

- For fiscal years, and interim periods within those years, beginning after December 15, 2013.

- For nonpublic entities, for fiscal years, and interim periods within those years, beginning after December 15, 2014.

Earlier adoption is permitted.

An entity shall apply the ASU prospectively to unrecognized tax benefits that exist at the effective date, but may elect to apply rules in the ASU retrospectively.

An entity shall provide the change in accounting principles disclosures found in ASC 250, *Accounting Changes and Error Corrections*, paragraphs 250-10-50-1 through 50-3, in the period the entity adopts the ASU.

STUDY QUESTION

4. The general rule in ASU 2013-11 is that an unrecognized tax benefit shall be presented in the financial statements as _____.

   a. A deferred tax credit

   b. A liability

   c. A reduction to the deferred tax asset

   d. A credit to other comprehensive income in stockholders' equity

¶ 1007 FOREIGN CURRENCY MATTERS (ASU 2013-05)

Overview

ASU 2013-05, issued in March 2013, is entitled *Foreign Currency Matters (Topic 830): Parent's Accounting for the Cumulative Translation Adjustment upon Derecognition of Certain Subsidiaries or Groups of Assets within a Foreign Entity or of an Investment in a Foreign Entity*. Its objective is to resolve the inconsistencies in practice about whether ASC Subtopic 810-10, *Consolidation—Overall*, or ASC Subtopic 830-30, *Foreign Currency Matters—Translation of Financial Statements*, applies to the release of the cumulative translation adjustment into net income when a parent either sells a part or all of its investment in a foreign entity, or no longer holds a controlling financial interest in a subsidiary or group of assets.

Background

Translation adjustments to convert an entity's financial statements from its functional currency to the currency used for financial statement reporting are presented as another comprehensive income item, included in stockholders' equity. Translation adjustments accumulate from year to year in stockholders' equity and are labeled "cumulative translation adjustment."

ASU 2010-02 (ASC Subtopic 810-10) *Consolidation: Accounting and Reporting for Decreases in Ownership of a Subsidiary—a Scope Clarification*, requires that a parent deconsolidate a subsidiary or derecognize a group of assets (other than a sale of in substance real estate or conveyance of oil and gas mineral rights), if the parent ceases to have a controlling financial interest in that group of assets.

The derecognition guidance in ASC 810-10 supports releasing the cumulative translation adjustment into net income upon the loss of a controlling financial interest in such a subsidiary or group of assets. However, the ASC 810-10 guidance does not distinguish between sales or transfers pertaining to an investment *in* a foreign entity and to a subsidiary or group of assets *within* a foreign entity.

Further, ASC 830-30, *Foreign Currency Matters—Translation of Financial Statements,* provides for the release of the cumulative translation adjustment into net income only if a sale or transfer represents a sale, or complete or substantially complete, liquidation of an investment *in* a foreign entity.

ASU 2013-05 resolves the variations in practice for the treatment of business combinations achieved in stages (referred to as step transactions) involving a foreign entity. In practice, some entities have treated step acquisitions as being composed of two events:

- The disposition of an equity method investment
- The simultaneous acquisition of a controlling financial interest

As part of the two-step transaction, those entities generally released the cumulative translation adjustment related to the equity method investment.

Other entities viewed step acquisitions as being composed of a single event (increasing an investment), and generally did not release the cumulative translation adjustment in practice. Thus, there was confusion in practice.

ASU 2013-05 addresses entities that cease to hold a controlling financial interest in a subsidiary or group of assets *within* a foreign entity when:

- The subsidiary or group of assets is a nonprofit activity or a business (other than a sale of in substance real estate or conveyance of oil and gas mineral rights), and
- There is a cumulative translation adjustment balance associated with that foreign entity.

ASU 2013-05 also includes amendments that affect entities that lose a controlling financial interest in an investment *in* a foreign entity, by sale or other transfer event. Additionally, it includes those that acquire a business in stages, such as in a step acquisition, by increasing an investment *in* a foreign entity from one accounted for under the equity method to one accounted for as a consolidated investment.

Rules

Cessation of a Controlling Financial Interest

When a reporting entity (a parent) ceases to have a controlling financial interest in a subsidiary or group of assets that is either a nonprofit activity or a business (other than a sale of in-substance real estate or conveyance of oil and gas mineral rights) *within* a foreign entity, the parent is required to apply the guidance in ASC Subtopic 830-30 *Translation of Financial Statements,* to release any related cumulative translation adjustment into net income.

Under ASC Subtopic 830-30, upon *sale or upon complete or substantially complete liquidation* of an investment in a foreign entity, the cumulative translation adjustment component of equity shall be *both*:

- Removed from the separate component of equity
- Reported in net income as part of the gain or loss on sale or liquidation of the investment for the period during which the sale or liquidation occurs

The sale of an investment in a foreign entity includes both:

- Events that result in the loss of a controlling financial interest in an investment in a foreign entity
- Events that result in an acquirer obtaining control of an acquiree in which it held an equity interest immediately before the acquisition date

Partial Sales

If a parent has an equity method investment in a foreign entity, the *partial sale rules* in ASC 830-30-40, *Foreign Currency Matter, Translation of Financial Statements, Derecognition,* should be followed. Under ASC 830-30-40, if a reporting entity sells part of its ownership interest in an equity investment that is a foreign entity, a *pro rata portion* of the cumulative translation adjustment component of equity attributable to that equity method investment shall be released into net income.

> **NOTE:** If the sale of part of the equity method investment results in a loss of significant influence, the entity should follow the rules found in ASC 323-10, *Investments—Equity Method and Joint Ventures,* paragraphs 35-39, for guidance on how to account for that pro-rata portion of the cumulative translation adjustment component of equity attributable to the remaining investment. That discussion is not addressed in this section.

If the partial sale involves ownership in a non-foreign entity, the pro-rata portion rule does not apply. In those instances, the cumulative translation adjustment is released into net income only if the partial sale represents a complete or substantially complete liquidation of the foreign entity that contains the equity method investment.

Transition and Effective Date

ASU 2013-05 is effective for fiscal years, and interim periods within those years, beginning after December 15, 2013. For nonpublic entities, it is effective for fiscal years beginning after December 15, 2014, and interim and annual periods thereafter. An entity shall provide the disclosures in ASC 250-10-50, *Accounting Changes and Error Corrections, Overall, Disclosure* (paragraphs 1 through 3) in the period the entity adopts the ASU.

The ASU shall be applied prospectively for the following:

- A sale or transfer of a subsidiary or group of assets that is a nonprofit activity or a business within a foreign entity after the effective date

- A sale of ownership interests in a foreign entity after the effective date

- A business combination achieved in stages after the effective date (Prior periods shall not be adjusted.)

Earlier application of the ASU is permitted. If early application is elected, an entity shall apply the ASU from the beginning of an entity's fiscal year of adoption to account for the release of the cumulative translation adjustment in the same manner for all disposition and deconsolidation events and step acquisitions within that fiscal year.

STUDY QUESTION

---

5. Company X sells its investment in a foreign entity. How should X deal with the cumulative translation adjustment component?

    a. Retain that amount in equity.

    b. Remove that amount from equity in its entirety.

    c. Remove a portion of the component and retain the remainder in equity.

    d. Reclassify the component to a separate section of equity and re-label it.

MODULE 3: OTHER CURRENT DEVELOPMENTS—CHAPTER 11: The Move to Fair Value Accounting

¶ 1101 WELCOME

This chapter discusses the accounting standards and proposals designed to move the accounting community toward fair value accounting.

¶ 1102 LEARNING OBJECTIVES

Upon completion of this chapter, the reader will be able to:

- Recall the arguments for and against fair value measurement
- Identify the levels in the three-level hierarchy developed by ASC 820
- Recognize the criteria that should be used in determining the classification and measurement of financial assets

¶ 1103 BACKGROUND

For the past decade, the historical cost model that has been the basis of GAAP accounting has slowly deteriorated, being gradually replaced by fair value accounting, but perhaps not fast enough for the investment community.

In one survey, investors noted 12 proposed changes to the business reporting model. Among them, was the need for *full fair value financial statements*.

Given the fact that the source of the survey is the end user of many financial statements, (that is, the investor), its results should be looked at seriously.

As stated in the survey (*A Comprehensive Business Reporting Model*, CFA Institute):

- "Fair value information is the only information relevant to financial decision making. ... ... Decisions about whether to purchase, sell or hold investments are based upon the fair values. Financial statements based on outdated historical costs are less useful for making such assessments."
- Because current financial statements include a mixture of historical cost and fair value, investors who rely on fair values for decision making must expend considerable effort to restate cost to fair value.
- Historic cost itself is in reality historic market value, the amount of a past transaction, and is never comparable on a firm-to-firm basis because the costs were incurred at different dates by different firms.
- Investor conversion of historical cost components to fair value would be eliminated if GAAP recorded assets and liabilities at fair value at inception with a periodic revaluation to fair value.
- The FASB should make a move to fair value accounting a priority.

The fact is that the historical cost model is inconsistent with the way in which investors and other third parties measure an entity, which is by the change in entity value. Presently, GAAP uses a fair value model to record the initial measurement of assets and liabilities. Thereafter, many assets are recorded at historical cost, such as fixed assets, while others are recorded at fair value or a hybrid of cost and fair value.

The following table illustrates the blend of historical cost, fair value, and other measurements presently used in GAAP.

Financial Measurements Under Existing GAAP	
Item and Standard	**Accounting Treatment**
Cash	Carrying amount
Trade receivables	Net realizable value
Inventories- ASC 330	Lower of cost or market
Securities including mortgage-backed securities- ASC 320	Measured at fair value or cost depending on category
Non-security investments- ASC 340	Historical cost, unless permanent writedown to market value
Loans receivable, including bank loans that are not securities-ASC 815	Carrying amount. Written down to fair value if the loan is impaired
Fixed assets	Historical cost, depreciated or amortized
Goodwill- ASC 350	Initially recorded at historical cost (purchase price) and written down if there is an impairment in value
Intangibles other than goodwill with finite lives- ASC 350	Initially recorded at historical cost (purchase price) and amortized over the estimated useful lives
Intangibles other than goodwill with indefinite lives- ASC 350	Historical cost and written down if there is an impairment in value
Hedging derivatives- ASC 815	Fair value
Accounts payable and accrued expenses	Estimated amount at which obligation will be settled
Notes payable	Settlement amount
Asset retirement obligations- ASC 410	Recorded at fair value
Guarantee liabilities- ASC 460	Fair value of the guarantee obligation at its inception
Stock options- ASC 718	External fair value model
Business combinations- ASC 805	Identified assets acquired, liabilities assumed, and noncontrolling interests in the acquiree at fair value at acquisition date
Disclosures	SEC companies are required to disclose the fair value of financial instruments even if not recorded at fair value

The historical cost model has worked in terms of providing a format by which accountants can apply systematic and rational allocations of cost (such as in the case of depreciation and amortization) without the ambiguity of determining fair value. That is, the existing historical cost GAAP model has allowed accountants to follow a set of standard rules in preparing financial statements. But are historical cost financial statements meaningful to third parties?

The FASB has suggested that the historical cost model no longer works and needs to be replaced or repaired with a fair value model whenever assets and liabilities can be reliably measured at fair value.

But simply measuring the change in entity wealth from period to period has its critics who note the following challenges to a fair value model:

- Fair value accounting is merely an appraisal of an entity's net assets from period to period. As a result, it may disguise the true performance of the entity as appreciation in certain assets and may reward management for value enhancement for which they should take no credit.

- Fair value accounting introduces a degree of volatility to the accounting model as sharp increases and decreases in values may distort comparisons from period to period.

- Fair value accounting is too subjective as many assets and liabilities cannot be easily measured without making valuation assumptions. Such assumptions can vary and result in entities not being comparable.
- Although fair value accounting may be more relevant, the historical cost model is more reliable.
- The costs of moving to fair value accounting may exceed the benefit as companies would be required to perform asset valuations on a period-to-period basis.

¶ 1104 HOW WOULD A FAIR VALUE MODEL BE IMPLEMENTED ON A PERIOD-TO-PERIOD BASIS?

There are certainly challenges in applying a full fair value model to financial statements. For assets and liabilities with observable values (such as securities), fair value accounting is relatively easy to apply. However, for those assets that do not have observable values, such as fixed assets and intangibles, measuring fair value from period to period is difficult and costly.

> **EXAMPLE:** A company with property and equipment would be required to revalue such assets from year to year and may require outside services from an appraiser. Such a valuation would not only be costly but could delay the timely issuance of financial statements. Moreover, for many smaller companies, such cost of application may exceed the benefit derived from fair value information.

¶ 1105 IS FAIR VALUE A BETTER SYSTEM?

There are arguments for and against a fair value system, but the historic cost model does not purport to display the way third parties think in evaluating their investment. Unrealized gains and losses on assets should be an important element of total earnings for a period. More particularly, a company's performance for a period of time should be measured by the change in the fair value of its net assets from period to period as demonstrated below:

Fair value of net assets:	
End of year	XX
Beginning of year	XX
Change = earnings for the period	XX

A common criticism of fair value accounting is that such a measurement may lack reliability and accuracy based on the fact that there is a range of fair value for each asset or liability. Yet, the counter-argument is that the worst fair value is far better than the best historical cost.

Another criticism is that use of fair value would introduce a high degree of volatility to financial statements from unrealized gains and losses on assets being recorded from year to year. However, volatility is an element of risk that an investor or third party should factor into its assessment of a company's value.

¶ 1106 STATUS OF THE FASB'S FAIR VALUE PROJECT

The fair value process started in September 2006, when the FASB issued ASC 820, *Fair Value Measurements* (formerly FAS 157). ASC 820 defines fair value, establishes a framework for measuring fair value under GAAP, and enhances disclosures about fair value measurements. More specifically, ASC 820 does the following:

- Defines fair value as the exit price which is:

"the price that would be received to sell an asset or paid to transfer a liability in an orderly transaction between market participants at the measurement date."

- The exit price (fair value) is market-based, determined from the perspective of a market participant (the seller) that holds the asset or liability. An internally generated fair value is not relevant.

- Develops a three-level hierarchy for valuation:

- Level 1: Observable market inputs that reflect quoted prices for identical assets or liabilities in *active markets* the reporting entity has the ability to access at the measurement date.

- Level 2: Observable market inputs other than quoted prices for identical assets or liabilities such as:

  - Quoted prices for similar assets and liabilities in active markets
  - Quotes prices for identical or similar assets and liabilities in markets that are not active
  - Market inputs other than quoted prices that are directly observable for the asset or liability, such as interest rates, yield curves, volatilities, and default rates

- Level 3: Unobservable market inputs, such as those derived through extrapolation or interpolation that are not able to be corroborated by observable market data.

- Requires that in the absence of quoted prices for identical or similar assets or liabilities, fair value should be estimated using multiple-valuation techniques consistent with the market approach, income approach, and cost approach whenever the information necessary to apply those techniques is available, without undue cost and effort. In all cases, the valuation techniques used for those estimates would emphasize relevant market inputs, including those derived from active markets.

- Requires expanded disclosures about the use of fair value to remeasure assets and liabilities recognized in the statement of financial position, including information about the fair value amounts, how those fair value amounts were determined, and the effect of the remeasurements on earnings.

STUDY QUESTIONS

1. In A Comprehensive Business Reporting Model, investors stated which of the following?

    a. FASB should not move toward a fair value model.

    b. Fair value information is the only information relevant for financial decision-making.

    c. Historical costs are more useful for making decisions about whether to purchase, sell or hold investments.

    d. The fair value model is inconsistent with the way in which investors measure an entity.

2. What inputs are placed into Level 3 in the fair-value hierarchy?

    a. Inputs that are derived principally from or corroborated by observable market data by correlation

    b. Observable inputs other than quoted prices included in Level 1 that are observable

    c. Observable, unadjusted, quoted market prices in active markets for identical assets or liabilities that are accessible

    d. Unobservable inputs that should be used when observable inputs are unavailable

---

¶ 1107 NEXT STEP—ASC 825 AND THE FAIR VALUE OPTION

After issuing ASC 820 (formerly FAS 157), the FASB introduced a project in ASC 825, *Financial Instruments* (the fair value option (FVO)) to consider whether to permit (but not require) entities a one-time election to report certain financial instruments (and certain non-financial assets) at fair value with the changes in fair value included in earnings.

In February 2007, the FASB issued FAS 159, *The Fair Value Option for Financial Assets and Financial Liabilities*, which is now codified in ASC 825. ASC 825, which is still in effect, provides the option of recording certain financial assets and liabilities at fair value for initial and subsequent measurement.

It applies to financial asset and liabilities that, in general, are not otherwise subject to fair value accounting. Further, ASC 825 is *optional*; that is, an entity may choose (but is not required) to record certain financial assets and liabilities at fair value, contrary to the way they are recorded and measured under other GAAP.

ASC 825 applies to financial asset and liabilities defined as follows:

- *Financial asset*: Cash, evidence of an ownership interest in an entity, or a contract.
- *Financial liability*: A contract that imposes on one entity a contractual obligation to deliver cash or another financial instrument to a second entity or to exchange other financial instruments on potentially unfavorable terms with the second entity.

Examples of financial assets and liabilities to which the fair value option (FVO) applies and for which an entity has the option to use fair value accounting, include the following:

- Cash
- Investments
- Derivatives
- Receivables
- Trade payables
- Loans receivable and payable

ASC 825 applies to all financial assets and liabilities, *except*:

- Investments that would otherwise be consolidated
- Assets and liabilities covered under retirement and benefit plans
- Financial liabilities recognized under lease contracts under ASC 840 (formerly FAS 13)

- Written loan commitments not accounted for as derivatives
- Financial liabilities for demand deposit accounts

If an entity chooses to record a financial asset or liability at fair value under ASC 825, the change in the fair value is recognized in earnings as the changes occur. To date, the push to apply the fair value option to non-financial assets and liabilities has not moved forward.

¶ 1108 FASB'S PROPOSED FINANCIAL INSTRUMENTS PROJECTS

As part of its overall financial instrument classification and measurement project, in February 2013, the FASB issued an exposure draft entitled, *Financial Instruments— Overall (Subtopic 825-10) Recognition and Measurement of Financial Assets and Financial Liabilities*. The February 2013 exposure draft was accompanied by the issuance of a companion exposure draft issued in April 2013.

Collectively, these proposed statements focus on creating a comprehensive framework for the classification and measurement of financial instruments. The proposal reflects the following rules.

Scope

The proposal would apply to financial instruments. A *financial instrument* is defined as cash, evidence of an ownership interest in an entity, or a contract that both:

- Imposes on one entity a contractual obligation either to:
  - Deliver cash or another financial instrument to a second entity, or
  - Exchange other financial instruments on potentially unfavorable terms with the second entity
- Conveys to that second entity a contractual right either to:
  - Receive cash or another financial instrument from the first entity, or
  - Exchange other financial instruments on potentially favorable terms with the first entity

Balance Sheet Presentation

Depending on an entity's present rights or obligations in the instrument upon acquisition or incurrence, the proposal would require an entity to recognize a financial instrument in its statement of financial position as either of the following:

- A financial asset
- A financial liability

    NOTE: The scope would apply to financial instruments that would be an expansion of existing GAAP under ASC 820, which deals with investments in securities.

Financial Asset Rules

Upon recognition, an entity would classify each financial asset into the appropriate subsequent measurement category on the basis of both of the following:

- The contractual cash flow characteristics criterion
- The entity's business model for managing the asset

Contractual Cash Flow Characteristics Criterion

A financial asset would satisfy the contractual cash flow characteristics criterion if the contractual terms of the financial asset give rise on specified dates to cash flows that are solely payments of principal and interest on the principal amount outstanding.

Business Model for Managing the Assets

An entity that satisfies the contractual cash flow characteristics criterion (above) would classify a financial asset into one of the following three categories depending on how the asset is managed:

Proposed Treatment of Financial Instruments Financial Asset	
Manner in which asset is managed	**Financial statement measurement**
1) The asset is held and managed to collect contractual cash flows.	Amortized cost (similar to current rules for held-to-maturity securities)
2) The asset is held and managed to do both of the following: a) Hold the financial asset to collect contractual cash flows b) Sell the financial asset At recognition, the entity has not yet determined whether it will hold the individual asset to collect contractual cash flows or sell the asset.	Fair value with the changes in fair value recognized in other comprehensive income (similar to current rules for available-for-sale securities)
3) The asset fails to qualify for either (1) or (2) above.	Fair value with all changes in fair value recognized in net income (similar to current rules for trading securities)

A financial asset that does not meet the contractual cash flow characteristics criterion would be measured at fair value with all changes in fair value recognized in net income. All equity investments would be measured at fair value with the change in fair value presented in net income unless:

- The equity investment qualifies for the equity method or consolidation, or
- The equity investment does not have a readily determinable fair value.

With few exceptions, an equity investment that does not have a readily determinable fair value would be recognized at cost minus impairment, if any, plus or minus changes resulting from observable price changes in orderly transactions for the identical investment or a similar investment of the same issuer.

Financial Liability Rules

An entity would measure its financial liabilities at amortized cost. An entity would subsequently measure a liability that meets either of the following conditions at fair value with all changes in fair value recognized in net income:

- The entity's business strategy at incurrence of the liability is to subsequently transact at fair value, for example, to transfer the obligation to a third party.
- The financial liability results from a short sale.

Selected Treatment of Assets

Following is a summary of how certain financial instruments (assets and liabilities) would be measured under the proposed standard:

Financial instrument	Proposed category
Trade receivables and payables	Generally at cost
Loans and notes receivable	Generally at cost
Derivatives: Those derivatives designed as the hedging instrument in a cash flow hedge or a hedge of a net investment in a foreign operation	FV with change in other comprehensive income (OCI)
All other derivatives	FV with change in net income
Debt instruments	Cost or FV
Equity instruments (other than equity method)	FV with change in net income

Financial instrument	Proposed category
Equity investments without readily determinable fair value	FV with change in net income
	Special exception: Measured at cost, adjusted for both impairment and changes that result from observable prices changes
Long-term debt	Generally at cost

The proposal would require that an impairment loss be recognized in net income equal to the entire difference between the investment's carrying value and its fair value, if impairment exists.

Financial Statement Presentation

Balance Sheet Presentation

An entity would present financial assets and financial liabilities separately on the face of the statement of financial position, grouped by measurement category. For financial assets and liabilities measured at amortized cost, a public entity would be required to present parenthetically on the face of the balance sheet the fair value.

> **NOTE:** The parenthetical disclosure would not apply to nonpublic entities. Moreover, receivables and payables due in less than one year would not be subject to parenthetical disclosure of fair value.

All entities would be required to separately present cumulative credit losses on the face of the statement of financial position.

All entities would be required to present parenthetically (on the face of the statement of financial position) the amortized cost of an entity's own debt that is measured at fair value.

Statement of Comprehensive Income

An entity would be required to present in net income an aggregate amount for realized and unrealized gains or losses for financial assets measured at fair value with all changes in fair value included in net income.

An entity would be required to separately present the following items in net income for both financial assets measured at fair value with changes in value recognized in other comprehensive income and financial assets measured at amortized cost:

- Interest income or expense
- Changes in expected credit losses
- Realized gains or losses from sales or settlements

An entity would be required to present in net income an aggregate amount for realized and unrealized gains or losses for financial liabilities measured at fair value with all changes in fair value recognized in net income.

At a minimum, an entity would be required to present separately within net income all of the following for financial assets (and certain financial liabilities) for which qualifying changes in fair value are recognized in other comprehensive income:

- Interest income or expense for the current period, including amortization (accretion) of deferred interest
- Premium (discount) recognized upon acquisition or incurrence
- Changes in expected credit losses on financial assets for the current period
- Realized gains and losses from sales or settlements
- Foreign currency gain and loss

Other Changes

There would be changes made to the fair value option found in ASC 825 that would permit use of the fair value option on a conditional basis only, and, only for a group of financial assets or liabilities. Disclosures of financial instruments would be expanded including information on liquidity risk with financial institutions disclosing information on interest rate risk.

STUDY QUESTION

3. In accordance with the FASB exposure draft on financial instruments, how would equity investments be measured?

    a. At cost

    b. At fair value with the change presented in net income

    c. At fair value with the change presented as part of other comprehensive income

    d. At lower of cost or market

¶ 1109 FINANCIAL INSTRUMENTS—CREDIT LOSSES (SUBTOPIC 825-15)

In December 2012, the FASB issued an exposure draft entitled, *Financial Instruments—Credit Losses (Subtopic 825-15)*. The main objective of the exposure draft is to provide financial statement users with more information about the expected credit losses on financial assets and other commitments to extend credit held by a reporting entity at each reporting date.

All entities that hold financial assets that are not accounted for at fair value through net income and are exposed to potential credit risk would be affected by the proposed amendments.

Examples include:

- Loans
- Debt securities
- Trade receivables
- Lease receivables
- Loan commitments
- Reinsurance receivables
- Any other receivables that represent the contractual right to receive cash would generally be affected by the proposed amendments

The Exposure Draft would:

- Replace the current impairment model, which reflects incurred credit events, with a model that recognizes expected credit risks, and require consideration of a broader range of reasonable and supportable information to inform credit loss estimates
- Reduce complexity by replacing the numerous existing impairment models in current U.S. GAAP with a consistent measurement approach

Here are some of the proposed amendments found in the Exposure Draft:

- The proposal would require an entity to impair its existing financial assets on the basis of the current estimate of contractual cash flows not expected to be collected on financial assets held at the reporting date. The impairment would be reflected as an allowance for expected credit losses.

- The proposed amendments would remove the existing "probable" threshold in U.S. GAAP for recognizing credit losses and broaden the range of information that must be considered in measuring the allowance for expected credit losses. The estimate of expected credit losses would be based on factors that affect the expected collectibility of the assets' remaining contractual cash flows, including:

  - Relevant information about past events

  - Historical loss experience with similar assets

  - Current conditions

  - Reasonable and supportable forecasts

- An estimate of expected credit losses would always reflect both the possibility that a credit loss results and the possibility that no credit loss results. Accordingly, the proposed amendments would prohibit an entity from estimating expected credit losses solely on the basis of the most likely outcome (that is, the statistical mode).

- Financial assets carried at amortized cost less an allowance would reflect the current estimate of the cash flows expected to be collected at the reporting date, and the income statement would reflect credit deterioration (or improvement) that has taken place during the period.

- For financial assets measured at fair value with changes in fair value recognized through other comprehensive income, the balance sheet would reflect the fair value, but the income statement would reflect credit deterioration (or improvement) that has taken place during the period.

- An entity would be able to choose to not recognize expected credit losses on financial assets measured at fair value, with changes in fair value recognized through other comprehensive income, if both (1) the fair value of the financial asset is greater than (or equal to) the amortized cost basis and (2) expected credit losses on the financial asset are insignificant.

¶ 1110 HOW WOULD THE ED CHANGE CURRENT GAAP?

Current U.S. GAAP includes five different incurred loss credit impairment models for instruments within the scope of the proposed amendments. The existing models generally delay recognition of credit loss until the loss is *considered probable*. This initial recognition threshold is perceived to have interfered with the timely recognition of credit losses and overstated assets during the recent global economic crisis.

The credit loss recognition guidance in the proposed amendments would eliminate the existing probable initial recognition threshold, and instead reflect the *entity's current estimate of expected credit losses*.

When credit losses are measured under current U.S. GAAP, an entity generally only considers past events and current conditions in measuring the incurred loss. The proposed amendments *would broaden the information* that an entity is required to consider in developing its credit loss estimate.

The proposed amendments would require that an entity's estimate be based on relevant information about past events, including historical loss experience with similar assets, current conditions, and reasonable and supportable forecasts that affect the expected collectibility of the financial assets' remaining contractual cash flows. In making the estimate, an entity would consider:

- Quantitative and qualitative factors specific to the borrower, including the entity's current evaluation of the borrower's creditworthiness
- General economic conditions and an evaluation of both the current point in, and the forecasted direction of, the economic cycle (e.g., as evidenced by changes in issuer or industry-wide underwriting standards)

An estimate of expected credit losses would reflect the time value of money either explicitly or implicitly. If an entity estimates expected credit losses using a discounted cash flow model, the discount rate utilized in that model shall be the financial asset's effective interest rate.

An estimate of expected credit losses would neither be a worst-case scenario nor a best-case scenario. Rather, an estimate of expected credit losses would always reflect both the possibility that a credit loss results and the possibility that no credit loss results. However, a probability-weighted calculation that considers the likelihood of more than two outcomes would not be required. An entity would be prohibited from estimating expected credit losses based solely on the most likely outcome (that is, the statistical mode).

The Exposure Draft would also expand disclosures related to credit losses.

¶ 1111 EXAMPLE 5: ESTIMATION OF EXPECTED CREDIT LOSSES FOR TRADE RECEIVABLES USING A PROVISION MATRIX (FROM THE EXPOSURE DRAFT)

The following Example illustrates how an entity might implement the guidance for trade receivables using a provision matrix under the Exposure Draft.

Entity D manufactures and sells toys to a broad range of customers, primarily retail toy stores.

Customers typically are provided payment terms of 90 days with a two percent discount if paid within 60 days.

The entity has tracked historical loss experience for its trade receivables over the past five years and calculated the following historical loss experience:

- 0.3 percent for receivables that are current
- 8 percent for receivables that are 1-30 days past due
- 26 percent for receivables that are 31-60 days past due
- 58 percent for receivables that are 61-90 days past due
- 82 percent for receivables that are more than 90 days past due

Entity D believes that this historical loss experience is consistent with what will be experienced for financial assets held at the reporting date because the composition of the receivables at the reporting date is consistent with that used in developing the historical statistics (i.e., the shared risk characteristics of its customers has not changed significantly over time) and the economic conditions in which the historical statistics were calculated generally are consistent with the economic conditions expected over the remaining lives of the receivables.

At the reporting date, Entity D develops the following provision matrix to estimate current expected credit losses.

	Carrying value	Loss rate	Expected credit loss estimate
Current	$5,984,698	.3%	$17,954
1-30 days past due	8,272	8%	662
31-60 days past due	2,882	26%	749
61-90 days past due	842	58%	488
More than 90 days past due	1,100	82%	902
	$5,997,794		$20,755

An allowance for doubtful accounts would be recorded in the amount of $20,755 even though it is not probable that loss would be incurred.

As of early 2014, the FASB continues to redeliberate the issues in the fair value financial instrument projects and once those redeliberations are completed, the FASB will decide whether to re-expose those decisions for public comment. Regardless of the approach the FASB takes, the proposed changes to fair value accounting for financial instruments are likely to pass sometime in 2014.

CPE NOTE: When you have completed your study and review of chapters 8-11, which comprise Module 3, you may wish to take the Quizzer for this Module. Go to **CCH-Group.com/PrintCPE** to take this Quizzer online.

TOP ACCOUNTING ISSUES FOR 2015 CPE COURSE—Appendix A: Examples Illustrating Application of ASU 2014-07's Accounting Alternative

¶ 1200

EXAMPLE 1: Lessor Provides Implicit Guarantee

Facts:

- Manufacturing Entity (a private company) is a lessee of a manufacturing facility, leased from Lessor Entity. The lease starts in 20X1.
- The sole owner of Manufacturing Entity (a private company) is also the sole owner of Lessor Entity.
- Lessor Entity obtained a mortgage on the manufacturing facility in 20X1.
- Manufacturing Entity *does not* provide any guarantee or pledge of collateral for Lessor Entity's mortgage.
- The common owner of both entities has provided a guarantee of Lessor Entity's mortgage as required by the lender.
- At inception of obtaining the mortgage on the manufacturing facility, the value of the manufacturing facility leased by Manufacturing Entity was $1 million and the principal balance of the mortgage was $800,000.
- Lessor Entity owns no assets other than the manufacturing facility being leased to Manufacturing Entity. Manufacturing Entity pays property taxes on behalf of Lessor Entity and maintains the manufacturing facility. The only transaction between the two entities is the lease of the manufacturing facility.
- Effective January 1, 20X2, Manufacturing Entity elects to apply the accounting alternative so that it does not have to apply the consolidation of VIE rules to the Lessor Entity.

Example 1: Lessor Provides Implicit Guarantee

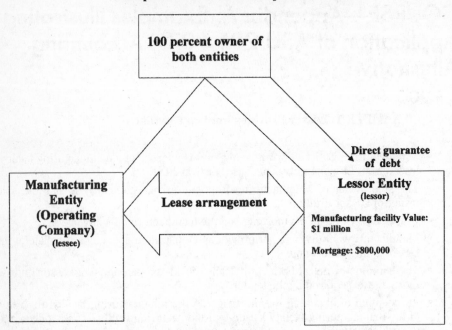

Conclusion: At January 1, 20X2 (the election date), Manufacturing Entity meets all four criteria and is permitted to elect the accounting alternative to Lessor Entity. Thus, Manufacturing Entity may elect not to apply the VIE rules to Lessor Entity and will not be required to consolidate Lessor Entity in 20X2.

The analysis of the four criteria at January 1, 20X2, follows:

Criteria	Satisfied?	Comments
Manufacturing Entity (the private company lessee) and Lessor Entity (lessor legal entity) are under common control.	Yes	Both entities have a common owner and are under common control.
Manufacturing Entity (the private company lessee) has a lease arrangement with Lessor Entity (the lessor legal entity).	Yes	The example states that there is a lease arrangement.
Substantially all activities between Manufacturing Entity (the private company lessee) and Lessor Entity (the lessor legal entity) are related to leasing activities (including supporting leasing activities) between those two entities.	Yes	The only transaction between Manufacturing Entity and Lessor Entity is the lease of the manufacturing facility.

Criteria	Satisfied?	Comments
If the Manufacturing Entity (private company lessee) explicitly guarantees or provides collateral for any obligation of the Lessor Entity (lessor legal entity) related to the asset leased by the Manufacturing Entity, then the principal amount of the obligation at inception of such guarantee or collateral arrangement *does not exceed* the value of the asset leased by the private company from the lessor legal entity.	NA	Manufacturing Entity did not provide an explicit guarantee or provide any collateral for Lessor Entity's mortgage. Criterion 4 does not apply.

Conclusion: At January 1, 20X2 (the election date), all four criteria are satisfied. Therefore, Manufacturing Entity is permitted to elect the alternative accounting by not applying the VIE rules to the Lessor Entity.

EXAMPLE 2: Lessor Pledges Assets As Collateral

Facts:

- Manufacturing Entity (a private company) is a lessee of a manufacturing facility, leased from Lessor Entity. The lease starts in 20X1.

- The sole owner of Manufacturing Entity (a private company) is also the sole owner of Lessor Entity.

- Lessor Entity obtained a mortgage on the manufacturing facility in 20X1.

- At inception of the mortgage, Manufacturing Entity *pledged its assets as collateral* for Lessor Entity's mortgage.

- The common owner of both entities has provided a guarantee of Lessor Entity's mortgage as required by the lender.

- At inception of obtaining the mortgage on the manufacturing facility, the value of the manufacturing facility leased by Manufacturing Entity was $1 million and the principal balance of the mortgage was $800,000.

- Lessor Entity owns no assets other than the manufacturing facility being leased to Manufacturing Entity. Manufacturing Entity pays property taxes on behalf of Lessor Entity and maintains the manufacturing facility. The only transaction between the two entities is the lease of the manufacturing facility.

- Effective January 1, 20X2, Manufacturing Entity has elected to apply the accounting alternative by not applying the consolidation of VIE rules to the Lessor Entity.

Example 2: Lessor Pledges Assets As Collateral

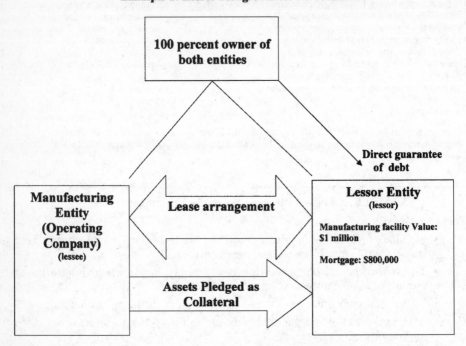

Conclusion: At January 1, 20X2 (the election date), Manufacturing Entity meets all four criteria and is permitted to elect the accounting alternative to Lessor Entity. Thus, Manufacturing Entity may elect not to apply the VIE rules to Lessor Entity and will not be required to consolidate Lessor Entity in 20X2.

The analysis of the four criteria at January 1, 20X2 follows:

Criteria	Satisfied?	Comments
Manufacturing Entity (the private company lessee) and Lessor Entity (lessor legal entity) are under common control.	Yes	Both entities have a common owner and are under common control.
Manufacturing Entity (the private company lessee) has a lease arrangement with Lessor Entity (the lessor legal entity).	Yes	The example states that there is a lease arrangement.
Substantially all activities between Manufacturing Entity (the private company lessee) and Lessor Entity (the lessor legal entity) are related to leasing activities (including supporting leasing activities) between those two entities.	Yes	The only transaction between Manufacturing Entity and Lessor Entity is the lease of the manufacturing facility.

Criteria	Satisfied?	Comments
If the Manufacturing Entity (private company lessee) explicitly guarantees or provides collateral for any obligation of the Lessor Entity (lessor legal entity) related to the asset leased by the Manufacturing Entity, then the principal amount of the obligation at inception of such guarantee or collateral arrangement *does not exceed* the value of the asset leased by the private company from the lessor legal entity.	Yes	Manufacturing Entity provided collateral for Lessor Entity's mortgage in 20X1. At the inception of providing the collateral (20X1), the principal balance of the mortgage ($800,000) did not exceed the value of the asset leased ($1 million).

Conclusion: At January 1, 20X2 (the election date), all four criteria are satisfied. Therefore, Manufacturing Entity is permitted to elect the alternative accounting by not applying the VIE rules to the Lessor Entity.

EXAMPLE 2A: Lessor Pledges Assets As Collateral (Continued)

Facts: Same facts as Example 2 except for the following:

In 20X3, two years after the Manufacturing Entity provided the collateral for Lessor Entity's mortgage, the value of the manufacturing facility and mortgage balance are as follows:

Value of manufacturing facility	$700,000
Mortgage balance	$750,000

Conclusion: In 20X3, two years after the collateral was provided for Lessor Entity's mortgage, the principal balance of the mortgage ($750,000) exceeds the value of the leased asset (manufacturing facility).

This fact is moot. Under the rules, Manufacturing Entity would continue to apply the accounting alternative (e.g., not apply the VIE rules) because the principal balance at inception ($800,000 in 20X1) did not exceed the value of the manufacturing facility ($1 million in 20X1). The fact that the value and principal balance changed subsequent to the inception of providing the collateral (20X1) is irrelevant. Criterion 4 is measured and determined at inception of providing the collateral (20X1) with subsequent changes ignored. Thus, Manufacturing Entity would still use the accounting alternative in 20X3, 20X4 and so on with no requirement to reassess Criterion 4. This is the case as long as the mortgage is not refinanced and a new guarantee or collateral is not provided by Manufacturing Entity.

EXAMPLE 2B: Lessor Pledges Assets As Collateral - Refinancing of Mortgage

Facts: Same facts as Example 2 except for the following:

In 20X3, two years after Lessor Entity provides the collateral for Lessor Entity's mortgage, Lessor Entity refinances or enters into a new obligation. The new loan requires a new collateralization or guarantee by Manufacturing Entity.

In 20X3, at the date of the refinancing or new mortgage, the value and new mortgage are as follows:

| Value of manufacturing facility | $700,000 |
| New mortgage balance | $750,000 |

Conclusion: Because there is a refinancing or new mortgage obtained by Lessor Entity, then Manufacturing Entity is required to reassess whether Criterion 4 is met in 20X3, at the inception of the new obligation.

In this example, in 20X3, the new mortgage balance of $750,000 exceeds the value of the leased asset ($700,000). Therefore, Manufacturing Entity fails Criterion 4 and is no longer permitted to elect the accounting alternative in 20X3. The result is that even though Manufacturing Entity has elected not to use the VIE rules in 20X1 and 20X2, starting in 20X3, Manufacturing Entity must apply the VIE rules to Lessor Entity. That means that in 20X3, Manufacturing Entity would test to determine whether Lessor Entity is a VIE, whether Manufacturing Entity has a variable interest in Lessor Entity, and whether Manufacturing Entity is the primary beneficiary that consolidates Lessor Entity. There is a possibility that Manufacturing Entity consolidates Lessor Entity in 20X3 solely because Lessor Entity refinanced its mortgage. Had Lessor Entity not refinanced its mortgage, the original assessment (Criterion 4) done in 20X1 would have prevailed with no reassessment done in 20X3.

EXAMPLE 3: Lessor Leases Portion of Leased Asset

Facts:

- Lessor Entity owns no assets other than a 10-floor manufacturing facility being leased:

  | Floors One to Three | Leased to Manufacturing Entity starting in 20X1 |
  | Floors Four to 10 | Leased to unrelated party |

- The only transaction between Manufacturing Entity and Lessor Entity is the lease of three floors in the manufacturing facility.

- The sole owner of Manufacturing Entity (a private company) is also the sole owner of Lessor Entity.

- Lessor Entity obtained a mortgage on the manufacturing facility in 20X1.

- At inception of the mortgage, Manufacturing Entity *pledged its assets as collateral* for Lessor Entity's mortgage on the entire manufacturing facility (all 10 floors).

- The common owner of both entities has provided a guarantee of Lessor Entity's mortgage as required by the lender.

- At inception of obtaining the mortgage on the manufacturing facility (20X1), the value of the entire manufacturing facility (all 10 floors) was $1 million and the principal balance of the mortgage on the entire 10-story facility was $800,000.

- Effective January 1, 20X2, Manufacturing Entity elects to apply the accounting alternative by not applying the consolidation of VIE rules to the Lessor Entity.

Example 3: Lessor Leases Portion of Leased Asset

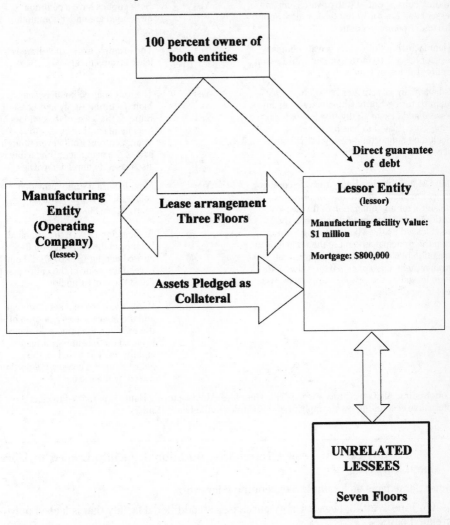

Conclusion: Manufacturing Entity meets all four criteria and is permitted to elect the accounting alternative to Lessor Entity in 20X2. Thus, Manufacturing Entity may elect not to apply the VIE rules to Lessor Entity and will not be required to consolidate Lessor Entity in 20X2.

The analysis of the four criteria follows:

Criteria	Satisfied?	Comments
Manufacturing Entity (the private company lessee) and Lessor Entity (lessor legal entity) are under common control.	Yes	Both entities have a common owner and are under common control.
Manufacturing Entity (the private company lessee) has a lease arrangement with Lessor Entity (the lessor legal entity).	Yes	The example states that there is a lease arrangement.
Substantially all activities between Manufacturing Entity (the private company lessee) and Lessor Entity (the lessor legal entity) are related to leasing activities (including supporting leasing activities) between those two entities.	Yes	The only transaction between Manufacturing Entity and Lessor Entity is the lease of three floors of the manufacturing facility to Manufacturing Entity even though part of the manufacturing facility is also leased to unrelated parties.
If the Manufacturing Entity (private company lessee) explicitly guarantees or provides collateral for any obligation of the Lessor Entity (lessor legal entity) related to the asset leased by the Manufacturing Entity, then the principal amount of the obligation at inception of such guarantee or collateral arrangement *does not exceed* the value of the asset leased by the private company from the lessor legal entity.	Yes	Manufacturing Entity provided collateral for Lessor Entity's mortgage in 20X1. At inception (20X1), the principal balance of the mortgage on the entire building ($800,000) did not exceed the value of the entire asset (10 stories) of $1 million. When there is a blanket mortgage and the lessee leases a portion of the building, the principal balance is based on the entire mortgage and the value is based on the entire property, not just the portion leased by the lessee.

Conclusion: All four criteria are satisfied. Therefore, Manufacturing Entity is permitted to elect the alternative accounting by not applying the VIE rules to the Lessor Entity.

EXAMPLE 3A: Lessor Purchases Additional Facility Leased to Unrelated Parties

Facts: Same facts as Example 3 except the following:

On June 1, 20X3, Lessor Entity purchases an additional facility that is leased only to unrelated parties.

The value of the new facility is significant to Lessor Entity, and the mortgage on the additional facility is $2 million and requires an *additional guarantee* by Manufacturing Entity. The collateral provided by Manufacturing Entity on the original Lessor Entity mortgage does not change.

Thus, in 20X3, on the date on which Manufacturing Entity provides the new guarantee, the mortgage balance and value of the lease asset is as follows:

Value of the leased manufacturing facility	$1 million
Mortgage balance	(750,000)

Conclusion: Because a new guarantee is required by Manufacturing Entity, the criteria must be reassessed in 20X3. Here is the new assessment in 20X3:

Criteria	Satisfied?	Comments
Manufacturing Entity (the private company lessee) and Lessor Entity (lessor legal entity) are under common control.	Yes	Both entities have a common owner and are under common control.
Manufacturing Entity (the private company lessee) has a lease arrangement with Lessor Entity (the lessor legal entity).	Yes	The example states that there is a lease arrangement.
Substantially all activities between Manufacturing Entity (the private company lessee) and Lessor Entity (the lessor legal entity) are related to leasing activities (including supporting leasing activities) between those two entities.	No	Manufacturing Entity fails to meet Criterion 3 when the guarantee is executed and leasing activity with unrelated parties commenced. Manufacturing Entity is engaging in significant activity outside its leasing activity with Lessor Entity by providing a guarantee on a mortgage secured by an asset that is not being leased by Manufacturing Entity. Because of the lessee's guarantee of the additional debt, substantially all activities between Manufacturing Entity (the private company lessee) and Lessor Entity (the lessor legal entity) are not related to leasing activities (including supporting leasing activities) between those two entities.
If the Manufacturing Entity (private company lessee) explicitly guarantees or provides collateral for any obligation of the Lessor Entity (lessor legal entity) related to the asset leased by the Manufacturing Entity, then the principal amount of the obligation at inception of such guarantee or collateral arrangement *does not exceed* the value of the asset leased by the private company from the lessor legal entity.	Yes.	Manufacturing Entity provides collateral for Lessor Entity's mortgage. At the inception of providing the collateral (20X1), the principal balance of the mortgage ($800,000) does not exceed the value of the asset leased ($1 million). The original Criterion 4 assessment is not updated because the debt is not refinanced. The mortgage balance and value of the additional facility are not considered.

Conclusion: Manufacturing Entity does not meet all four criteria and therefore, is not permitted to elect the alternative accounting.

Not meeting the criteria to qualify for the accounting alternative does not automatically result in consolidation of the Lessor Entity. Instead, Lessor Entity will need to be evaluated under the VIE rules for consolidation and related disclosure requirements.

What if Manufacturing Entity were not required to provide a new guarantee and, instead, simply retained the collateral given for the original Lessor Entity mortgage?

The original assessment made in 20X1 would stay in place with no reassessment made. Therefore, Manufacturing Entity would continue to elect the alternative accounting through 20X3, and not apply the VIE rules to the Lessor Entity. This is the case because there was no change in the original collateral provided by Manufacturing Entity in 20X1, and no new collateral or guarantee provided. Thus, the original assessment done in 20X1 at the inception of Manufacturing Entity providing the collateral, would not be updated.

EXAMPLE 4: Common Control Leasing Arrangement with Additional Activities Other Than Leasing or the Support of Leasing

Facts:

- Manufacturing Entity (a private company) is a lessee of a manufacturing facility, leased from Lessor Entity. The lease starts in 20X1.

- The sole owner of Manufacturing Entity (a private company) is also the sole owner of Lessor Entity.

- Lessor Entity obtained a mortgage on the manufacturing facility in 20X1.

- At inception of the mortgage (20X1), Manufacturing Entity pledged its assets as collateral for Lessor Entity's mortgage.

- The common owner of both entities has provided a guarantee of Lessor Entity's mortgage as required by the lender.

- At inception of obtaining the mortgage on the manufacturing facility (20X1), the value of the manufacturing facility leased by Manufacturing Entity was $1 million and the principal balance of the mortgage was $800,000.

- Lessor also *manufactures cosmetics products* in another facility that is unrelated to the operations of Manufacturing Entity. There is no mortgage associated with this additional facility, and Manufacturing Entity does not provide collateral or guarantee any obligations related to the cosmetics business.

- The only transaction between Manufacturing Entity and Lessor Entity is the lease of the manufacturing facility.

- On January 1, 20X2, Manufacturing Entity has elected to apply the accounting alternative by not applying the consolidation of VIE rules to the Lessor Entity.

Example 4: Common Control Leasing Arrangement with Additional Activities Other Than Leasing or the Support of Leasing

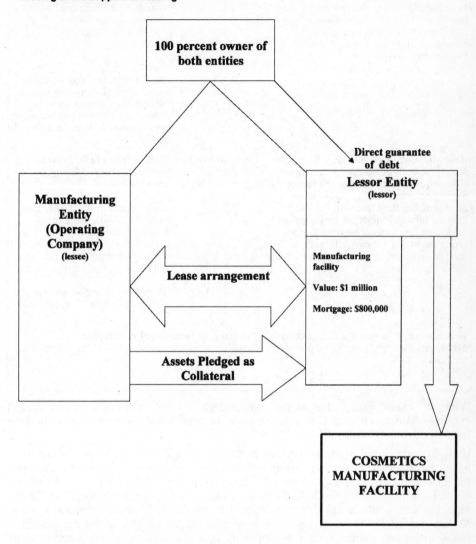

Conclusion: In this example, Manufacturing Entity meets all four criteria and, as a result of its elected accounting policy, would apply the accounting alternative to Lessor Entity based on the following analysis:

Criteria	Satisfied?	Comments
Manufacturing Entity (the private company lessee) and Lessor Entity (lessor legal entity) are under common control.	Yes	Both entities have a common owner and are under common control.
Manufacturing Entity (the private company lessee) has a lease arrangement with Lessor Entity (the lessor legal entity).	Yes	The example states that there is a lease arrangement.

Criteria	Satisfied?	Comments
Substantially all activities between Manufacturing Entity (the private company lessee) and Lessor Entity (the lessor legal entity) are related to leasing activities (including supporting leasing activities) between those two entities.	Yes	The only transaction between Manufacturing Entity and Lessor Entity is the lease of the manufacturing facility to Manufacturing Entity.
		Even though Lessor Entity has another manufacturing facility in which it manufactures cosmetics, Manufacturing Entity does not provide any guarantee or collateral for the cosmetics manufacturing facility.
If the Manufacturing Entity (private company lessee) explicitly guarantees or provides collateral for any obligation of the Lessor Entity (lessor legal entity) related to the asset leased by the Manufacturing Entity, then the principal amount of the obligation at inception of such guarantee or collateral arrangement *does not exceed* the value of the asset leased by the private company from the lessor legal entity.	Yes	Manufacturing Entity provides collateral for Lessor Entity's mortgage.
		At the inception of providing the collateral (20X1), the principal balance of the mortgage ($800,000) did not exceed the value of the asset leased ($1 million).
		There is no obligation associated with the purchase of the cosmetic facility.

Conclusion: At January 1, 20X2 (election date), all four criteria are satisfied. Therefore, Manufacturing Entity is permitted to elect the alternative accounting by not applying the VIE rules to the Lessor Entity.

What if Lessor Entity has to get a mortgage on its cosmetics facility and it requires Manufacturing Entity to provide an additional guarantee or collateral for that additional facility?

If the Manufacturing Entity is required to provide an additional guarantee or collateral for a mortgage on a second facility which is not related to leasing (the cosmetic manufacturing facility), that additional guarantee or collateral would be considered a second activity between the Manufacturing Entity and the Lessor Entity. Thus, Manufacturing Entity would fail Criterion 3, in that substantially all of activities between Manufacturing Entity and Lessor Entity would not be related to leasing activities. Instead, the two entities would be engaging in a second activity (in addition to its leasing activity) with Manufacturing Entity providing a guarantee or collateral for debt secured by property other than the leased property.

The fact that there is an additional facility would not impact Criterion 4 because the principal balance of $800,000 and the value of the leased asset ($1 million), would not be impacted by the acquisition of the additional facility. Criterion 4 is updated only if the debt is refinanced and a new guarantee and/or collateral is required.

EXAMPLE 5: Common Control Leasing Arrangement with Manufacturing Entity Engaging in Additional Activities Other Than Leasing or the Support of Leasing

Facts:

- Manufacturing Entity (a private company) is a lessee of a manufacturing facility, leased from Lessor Entity. The lease starts in 20X1.

- Manufacturing Entity also leases a second manufacturing facility from an unrelated entity.

- The sole owner of Manufacturing Entity (a private company) is also the sole owner of Lessor Entity.

- Lessor Entity obtained a mortgage on the manufacturing facility in 20X1.

- At inception of the mortgage (20X1), Manufacturing Entity pledged its assets as collateral for Lessor Entity's mortgage.

- The common owner of both entities has provided a guarantee of Lessor Entity's mortgage as required by the lender.

- At inception of obtaining the mortgage on the manufacturing facility (20X1), the value of the manufacturing facility leased by Manufacturing Entity was $1 million and the principal balance of the mortgage was $800,000.

- The only transaction between Manufacturing Entity and Lessor Entity is the lease of the manufacturing facility.

- At January 1, 20X2, Manufacturing Entity has elected to apply the accounting alternative by not applying the consolidation of VIE rules to the Lessor Entity.

Example 5: Common Control Leasing Arrangement with Manufacturing Entity Engaging in Additional Activities Other Than Leasing or the Support of Leasing

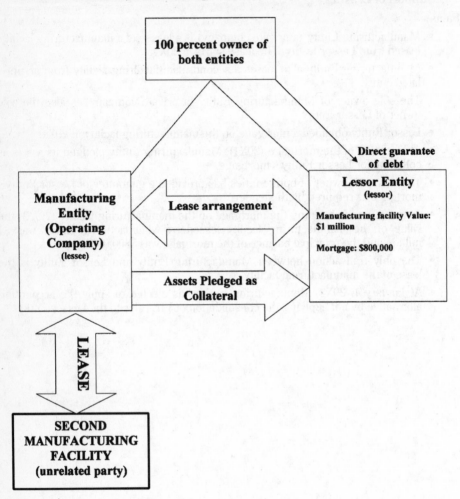

Conclusion: Here is analysis of the four criteria at January 1, 20X2.

Criteria	Satisfied?	Comments
Manufacturing Entity (the private company lessee) and Lessor Entity (lessor legal entity) are under common control.	Yes	Both entities have a common owner and are under common control.
Manufacturing Entity (the private company lessee) has a lease arrangement with Lessor Entity (the lessor legal entity).	Yes	The example states that there is a lease arrangement.
Substantially all activities between Manufacturing Entity (the private company lessee) and Lessor Entity (the lessor legal entity) are related to leasing activities (including supporting leasing activities) between those two entities.	Yes	The only transaction between Manufacturing Entity and Lessor Entity is the lease of the manufacturing facility to Manufacturing Entity. Even though Manufacturing Entity leases a second manufacturing facility, that second facility does not change the fact that the only transaction between Manufacturing Entity and Lessor Entity is the lease of the manufacturing facility.
If the Manufacturing Entity (private company lessee) explicitly guarantees or provides collateral for any obligation of the Lessor Entity (lessor legal entity) related to the asset leased by the Manufacturing Entity, then the principal amount of the obligation at inception of such guarantee or collateral arrangement *does not exceed* the value of the asset leased by the private company from the lessor legal entity.	Yes	Manufacturing Entity provides collateral for Lessor Entity's mortgage. At the inception (20X1) of providing the collateral, the principal balance of the mortgage ($800,000) does not exceed the value of the asset leased ($1 million).

Conclusion: At January 1, 20X2, all four criteria are satisfied. Therefore, Manufacturing Entity is permitted to elect the alternative accounting by not applying the VIE rules to the Lessor Entity.

TOP ACCOUNTING ISSUES FOR 2015 CPE COURSE—Appendix B: Examples Illustrating the Application of ASU 2014-07 in the Financial Statements

¶ 1300

In this appendix, the author presents several examples that demonstrate how ASU 2014-07 should be implemented.

Facts: For each of the examples, the current year financial statements are for December 31, 2014 year end, with prior year ended December 31, 2013.

The following scenarios are presented:

- **Example A:** VIE was consolidated in 2013 prior year. ASU 2014-07 election is elected in the 2014 current year. Comparative financial statements for 2014 and 2013 are presented.

- **Example B:** VIE was consolidated in 2013 prior year. ASU 2014-07 election is elected in the 2014 current year. Current year only 2014 financial statements are presented.

- **Example C:** VIE was not consolidated in 2013 prior year as VIE rules did not apply. ASU 2014-07 election is made in the 2014 current year.

- **Example D:** VIE was not consolidated in 2013 prior year as GAAP departure was made in the report. ASU 2014-07 election is made in the 2014 current year.

EXAMPLE A: Implementing the ASU

Company V (real estate lessor) and PB (operating company lessee) are under common control, with the same 100 percent owner.

Company V is a VIE that was consolidated into PB's 2013 consolidated financial statements. Effective January 1, 2014, Company PB elects the accounting alternative. PB plans to present comparative financial statements for 2013 and 2014.

Assume the following information for the following entities for 2013:

Company PB and Consolidated Subsidiary
Consolidated Statement of Income Worksheet
For the Year Ended December 31, 2013

	Company PB (Primary Beneficiary lessee) 12- months ended December 31, 2013	Company V Lessor (VIE) 12- months ended December 31, 2013	Eliminations	2013 Consolidated statement of income
Net sales	$10,000,000	$1,000,000	(3) $(1,000,000)	$10,000,000
Cost of sales	8,000,000	700,000	(3) (1,000,000)	7,700,000
Gross profit on sales	2,000,000	300,000		2,300,000
Operating expenses	1,200,000	200,000		1,400,000
Net operating income	800,000	100,000		900,000

	Company PB (Primary Beneficiary lessee) 12-months ended December 31, 2013	Company V Lessor (VIE) 12-months ended December 31, 2013	Eliminations	2013 Consolidated statement of income
Other income (expense)	100,000	0		100,000
NIBT	900,000	100,000		1,000,000
Income taxes	360,000	30,000		390,000
Net income	540,000	70,000		610,000
Retained earnings:				
Beginning of year	660,000	60,000		720,000
End of year	$1,200,000	$130,000	$ 0	$1,330,000

Company PB and Consolidated Subsidiary
Consolidated Balance Sheet Worksheet
December 31, 2013

	Company PB (primary beneficiary) Parent (At book value)	Company V (VIE) (At book value) December 31, 20X3)	Eliminations	Consolidated balance sheet December 31, 20X3
Cash	$170,000	$15,000		$185,000
Trade receivables	350,000	300,000		650,000
Inter-entity loan	400,000		(1) (400,000)	0
Fixed assets	2,000,000	830,000		2,830,000
Goodwill	140,000	0		140,000
Other prepaid assets	40,000	5,000		45,000
Total assets	$3,100,000	$1,150,000		$3,850,000
Accounts payable and accrued expenses	$500,000	$120,000		$620,000
Inter-company loan		400,000	(1) (400,000)	0
Long-term debt	1,300,000	250,000		1,550,000
Stockholders' equity:				
Common stock	100,000			100,000
Member's equity		*380,000*	*(2) (380,000)*	0
Retained earnings	1,200,000			1,200,000

	Company PB (primary beneficiary) Parent (At book value)	Company V (VIE) (At book value) December 31, 20X3)	Eliminations	Consolidated balance sheet December 31, 20X3
Noncontrolling interest in V			*(2) 380,000*	*380,000*
Total liabilities and Equity	$3,100,000	$1,150,000	$ 0	$3,850,000

		dr	cr
Elimination 1:			
Intercompany loan-V		400,000	
Intercompany loan- P			400,000
To eliminate intercompany balances			
Elimination 2:			
Member's equity		380,000	
Noncontrolling interest- V			380,000
To eliminate V's equity and reclassify it to noncontrolling interest in V			
Elimination 3:			
Net sales		1,000,000	
Cost of sales			1,000,000
To eliminate intercompany revenue and expense			

Following are the consolidated financial statements derived from the worksheets.

Company PB and Consolidated Subsidiary
Consolidated Balance Sheet
December 31, 2013

Assets:	
Cash	$185,000
Trade receivables	650,000
Total current assets	835,000
Non-current assets:	
Fixed assets	2,830,000
Goodwill	140,000
Other	45,000
Total non-current assets	3,015,000
	$3,850,000

Liabilities and stockholders' equity Current liabilities:	
Accounts payable and accrued expenses	$620,000
Long-term debt	1,550,000
Stockholders' equity:	
Common stock	100,000
Retained earnings	1,200,000
Total stockholders' equity- Company PB	1,300,000
Noncontrolling interest in variable interest entity	**380,000**
Total stockholders' equity	1,680,000
	$3,850,000

Company PB and Consolidated Subsidiary
Consolidated Statement of Income
For the Year Ended December 31, 2013

Net sales	$10,00,000
Cost of sales	7,700,000
Gross profit on sales	2,300,000
Operating expenses	1,400,000
Net operating income	900,000
Other income (expense):	100,000
NIBT	1,000,000
Income taxes	390,000
Net income including noncontrolling interest	610,000
Noncontrolling interest in Company V- variable interest entity	*(70,000)*
Net income- Company PB	540,000
Retained earnings:	
Beginning of year	660,000
End of year	$1,200,000

Company PB and Consolidated Subsidiary
Consolidated Statement of Stockholders' Equity
For the Year Ended December 31, 2013

	Common stock	Retained earnings	Noncontrolling interest in variable interest entity	Total stockholders' equity
Balance- Beginning of year	$100,000	$660,000	$310,000	$1,070,000
Net income	0	540,000	70,000	610,000
Balance- End of year	$100,000	$1,200,000	$380,000	$1,680,000

Conclusion: Because PB wants to present comparative financial statements for 2014 and 2013, PB applies the election to avoid the VIE rules retrospectively to the earliest year presented, which is 2013. That means that the four criteria must be tested as of January 1, 2013.

Assume that PB satisfies the four criteria as of January 1, 2013.

The restated financial statements for 2013 and 2014 financial statements follow. Information for 2014 is given.

Company PB
Balance Sheets
December 31, 2014 and 2013 (RESTATED) (1)

Assets	2014	2013 RESTATED PB ONLY[(1)]
Current asset:		
Cash	$200,000	$170,000
Trade receivables	700,000	350,000
Intercompany receivable	0	400,000
Total current assets	900,000	920,000
Non-current assets:		
Fixed assets	2,700,000	2,000,000
Goodwill	340,000	140,000
Other	60,000	40,000
Total non-current assets	3,100,000	2,180,000
	4,000,000	$3,100,000
Liabilities and Stockholders' Equity		
Current liabilities:		
Accounts payable and accrued expenses	600,000	$500,000
Long-term debt	1,400,000	1,300,000

Assets	2014	2013 RESTATED PB ONLY[1]
Stockholders' equity:		
Common stock	100,000	100,000
Retained earnings	1,900,000	1,200,000
Total stockholders' equity	2,000,000	1,300,000
	$4,000,000	$3,100,000

[1] The bold labels for 2013 are for information purposes only and are not required to be presented under GAAP.

Company PB
Statement of Income
For the Years Ended December 31, 2014 and 2013 (RESTATED)

	2014	2013 RESTATED PB ONLY
Net sales	$11,000,000	$10,000,000
Cost of sales	8,000,000	8,000,000
Gross profit on sales	3,000,000	2,000,000
Operating expenses	1,700,000	1,200,000
Net operating income	1,300,000	800,000
Other income (expense):	(200,000)	100,000
Net income before income taxes	1,100,000	900,000
Income taxes	400,000	360,000
Net income	$700,000	$540,000

Company PB
Statement of Stockholders' Equity
For the Years Ended December 31, 2014 and 2013 (RESTATED)

	Common stock	Retained earnings	Noncontrolling interest in variable interest entity	Total stockholders' equity
Balance- January 1, 2013				
As originally stated	$100,000	$660,000	$310,000	$1,070,000
Adjustment to deconsolidate				**(310,000)**
variable interest entity			**(310,000)**	
As restated	100,000	660,000	0	760,000

	Common stock	Retained earnings	Noncontrolling interest in variable interest entity	Total stockholders' equity
Net income- 2013	0	540,000	0	$540,000
Balance- December 31, 2013	100,000	1,200,000	0	1,300,000
Net income- 2014	0	700,000	0	700,000
Balance- December 31, 2014	$100,000	$1,900,000	$ 0	$2,000,000

Statement of Cash Flows: The author did not present the statement of cash flows in this example. That statement would also be restated in 2013 to reflect the impact of deconsolidating the variable interest entity.

NOTE 1: Summary of Significant Accounting Policies:

Consolidation of Variable Interest Entity

Effective January 1, 2014, the Company made an *accounting policy election* authorized for private companies by Accounting Standards Update (ASU) 2014-07— *Consolidation (Topic 810): Applying Variable Interest Entities Guidance to Common Control Leasing Arrangements.* Under this new accounting policy, the Company elects not to apply the accounting principles for the consolidation of variable interest entities (VIEs) to a real estate leasing company that is related to the Company through common ownership. Consequently, the 2014 financial statements do not reflect the effect, if any, of having consolidated the real estate leasing company.

For the year ended December 31, 2013, the Company had previously consolidated the real estate leasing company. Those financial statements have been *adjusted retrospectively* (When there is a change in accounting principle (policy), ASC 250 requires that the previous financial statements presented be adjusted retrospectively. The term "restated" is set aside in ASC 250 to reflect adjustments for corrections of errors and should not be used to describe a change in accounting principle (policy) such as ASU 2014-07 provides.) to deconsolidate the real estate leasing company as of January 1, 2013. The deconsolidation of the real estate leasing company resulted in an adjustment of the January 1, 2013 noncontrolling interest in the *amount of $310,000* which is reflected in the statement of stockholders' equity.

NOTE 2: Contingencies and Guarantees:

Not included in this example.

> **NOTE:** ASC 250-10-50-1(b)(2) requires that in the year of a change in an accounting principle, a required disclosure is the effect of the change on income from continued operations, net income, and other affected financial statement line items. ASU 2014-07 specifically states that this particular disclosure found in ASC 250-10-50-1(b)(2) is not required if a private-company lessee elects the accounting alternative. Thus, the only effect of the change that is disclosed is the adjustment to the beginning noncontrolling interest that is eliminated as part of the deconsolidation of the VIE.

Sample Compilation Report With Emphasis-of-Matter Paragraph
Accountant's Compilation Report

Board of Directors

Company PB

Nowhere, Massachusetts

We have compiled the accompanying balance sheets of Company PB of December 31, 2014 and 2013, and the related statements of income, stockholders' equity, and cash flows for the years then ended. We have not audited or reviewed the accompanying financial statements and, accordingly, do not express an opinion or provide any assurance about whether the financial statements are in accordance with accounting principles generally accepted in the United States of America.

Management is responsible for the preparation and fair presentation of the financial statements in accordance with accounting principles generally accepted in the United States of America and for designing, implementing, and maintaining internal control relevant to the preparation and fair presentation of the financial statements.

Our responsibility is to conduct the compilation in accordance with Statements on Standards for Accounting and Review Services issued by the American Institute of Certified Public Accountants. The objective of a compilation is to assist management in presenting financial information in the form of financial statements without undertaking to obtain or provide any assurance that there are no material modifications that should be made to the financial statements.

As disclosed in Note X to the financial statements, effective January 1, 2014, the Company made an *accounting policy election* authorized for private companies by Accounting Standards Update (ASU) 2014-07—*Consolidation (Topic 810): Applying Variable Interest Entities Guidance to Common Control Leasing Arrangements.* Under this new policy, the Company elects not to apply accounting principles for the consolidation of variable interest entities (VIEs) to a real estate leasing entity that is related to the Company through common ownership. The financial statements for 2013 have been *adjusted retrospectively* to reflect the deconsolidation of the previously consolidated real estate leasing company.

James J. Fox & Company, CPA

Date

> **NOTE:** The SSARSs do not require a report modification when an accounting principle is implemented and retrospective application is applied to the previous year. The paragraph highlighted in bold in the sample paragraph above is optional.

Independent Accountant's Review Report

Board of Directors

Company PB

Nowhere, Massachusetts

We have reviewed the accompanying balance sheets of Company PB as of December 31, 2014 and 2013, and the related statements of income, stockholders' equity, and cash flows for the years then ended. A review includes primarily applying analytical procedures to management's financial data and making inquiries of company management. A review is substantially less in scope than an audit, the objective of which is the expression of an opinion regarding the financial statements as a whole. Accordingly, we do not express such an opinion.

Management is responsible for the preparation and fair presentation of the financial statements in accordance with accounting principles generally accepted in the United States of America, and for designing, implementing, and maintaining internal control relevant to the preparation and fair presentation of the financial statements.

Our responsibility is to conduct the review in accordance with Statements on Standards for Accounting and Review Services issued by the American Institute of Certified Public Accountants. Those standards require us to perform procedures to obtain limited assurance that there are no material modifications that should be made to the financial statements. We believe that the results of our procedures provide a reasonable basis for our report.

Based on our review, we are not aware of any material modifications that should be made to the accompanying financial statements in order for them to be in conformity with accounting principles generally accepted in the United States of America.

As disclosed in Note X to the financial statements, effective January 1, 2014, the Company made an *accounting policy election* authorized for private companies by Accounting Standards Update (ASU) 2014-07—*Consolidation (Topic 810): Applying Variable Interest Entities Guidance to Common Control Leasing Arrangements.* Under this new policy, the Company elects not to apply accounting principles for the consolidation of variable interest entities (VIEs) to a real estate leasing entity that is related to the Company through common ownership. The financial statements for 2013 have been *adjusted retrospectively* to reflect the deconsolidation of the previously consolidated real estate leasing company.

James J. Fox & Company, CPA

Date

> **NOTE:** The SSARSs do not require a compilation or review report modification when an accounting principle is implemented and retrospective application is applied to the previous year. The paragraph highlighted in bold in the sample paragraph above is optional.

Independent Auditor's Report

Board of Directors

Company PB

Nowhere, Massachusetts

We have audited the accompanying financial statements of Company PB, which comprise the balance sheets as of December 31, 2014 and 2013, and the related statements of income, stockholders' equity and cash flows for the years then ended, and the related notes to the financial statements.

Management's Responsibility for the Financial Statements

Management is responsible for the preparation and fair presentation of these financial statements in accordance with accounting principles generally accepted in the United States of America; this includes the design, implementation, and maintenance of internal control relevant to the preparation and fair presentation of financial statements that are free from material misstatement, whether due to fraud or error.

Auditor's Responsibility

Our responsibility is to express an opinion on these financial statements based on our audits. We conducted our audits in accordance with auditing standards generally accepted in the United States of America. Those standards require that we plan and perform the audit to obtain reasonable assurance about whether the financial statements are free from material misstatement.

An audit involves performing procedures to obtain audit evidence about the amounts and disclosures in the financial statements. The procedures selected depend on the auditor's judgment, including the assessment of the risks of material misstatement of the financial statements, whether due to fraud or error. In making those risk assessments, the auditor considers internal control relevant to the entity's preparation and fair presentation of the financial statements in order to design audit procedures that are appropriate in the circumstances, but not for the purpose of expressing an opinion on the effectiveness of the entity's internal control. Accordingly, we express no such opinion. An audit also includes evaluating the appropriateness of accounting policies used and the reasonableness of significant accounting estimates made by management, as well as evaluating the overall presentation of the financial statements.

We believe that the audit evidence we have obtained is sufficient and appropriate to provide a basis for our audit opinion.

Opinion

In our opinion, the financial statements referred to above present fairly, in all material respects, the financial position of Company PB as of December 31, 2014 and 2013, and the results of their operations and their cash flows for the years then ended in accordance with accounting principles generally accepted in the United States of America.

Accounting Policy Election

As discussed in Note X to the financial statements, effective January 1, 2014, the Company made an *accounting policy election* authorized for private companies by Accounting Standards Update (ASU) 2014-07—*Consolidation (Topic 810): Applying Variable Interest Entities Guidance to Common Control Leasing Arrangements*. Under this new policy, the Company elects not to apply accounting principles for the consolidation of variable interest entities (VIEs) to a real estate leasing entity that is related to the Company through common ownership. The financial statements for 2013 have been *adjusted retrospectively* to reflect the deconsolidation of the previously consolidated real estate leasing company. *Our opinion is not modified with respect to that matter.*

[Auditor's signature]

[Auditor's city and state]

[Date of the auditor's report]

> **NOTE:** AU-C 708, *Consistency of Financial Statements*, requires the use of an emphasis-of-matter paragraph for a change in accounting principle from the adoption of a new accounting pronouncement. The auditor has flexibility as to the title used. For example, in lieu of the title "Accounting Policy Election," the auditor could use the generic title "Emphasis-of-Matter" or other paragraph.
>
> AU-C 708 also requires that a statement be included stating: *"Our opinion is not modified with respect to this matter."*
>
> As previously noted, it is important that the term "adjusted retrospectively" be used and not "adjusted retroactively." ASC 250, Accounting Changes and Error Corrections, saves the use of the term "retroactively" for error corrections and not changes in accounting principles (policies).
>
> AU-C 708 uses the term "as discussed" while the SSARSs use the term "as disclosed."

EXAMPLE B: Implementing the ASU

Company V (real estate lessor) and PB (operating company lessee) are under common control, with the same 100 percent owner. Company V is a VIE that was *consolidated into PB's 2013 consolidated financial statements*. Effective January 1, 2014, Company PB elects the accounting alternative. PB plans to present financial statements for 2014 only.

Conclusion: PB applies the ASU 2014-07 election to avoid the VIE rules retrospectively to the earliest year presented, which is 2014. That means that the four criteria must be tested as of January 1, 2014, and not retrospectively to 2013.

Assume that PB satisfies the four criteria as of January 1, 2014. The 2014 financial statements follow. Information for 2014 is given.

Company PB
Balance Sheet
December 31, 2014

Assets	
Current assets:	
Cash	$200,000
Trade receivables	700,000
Total current assets	900,000
Non-current assets:	
Fixed assets	2,700,000
Goodwill	340,000
Other	60,000
Total non-current assets	3,100,000
	$4,000,000
Liabilities and Stockholders' Equity	
Current liabilities:	
Accounts payable and accrued expenses	$600,000
Long-term debt	1,400,000
Stockholders' equity:	
Common stock	100,000
Retained earnings	1,900,000
Total stockholders' equity	2,000,000
	$4,000,000

Company PB
Statement of Income
For the Year Ended December 31, 2014

Net sales	$11,000,000
Cost of sales	8,000,000
Gross profit on sales	3,000,000
Operating expenses	1,700,000
Net operating income	1,300,000
Other income (expense):	(200,000)
Net income before income taxes	1,100,000
Income taxes	400,000
Net income	$700,000

Company PB
Statement of Stockholders' Equity
For the Years Ended December 31, 2014

	Common stock	Retained earnings	Noncontrolling interest in variable interest entity	Total stockholders' equity
Balance- January 1, 2014				
As originally stated	$100,000	$1,200,000	$380,000	$1,680,000
Adjustment to deconsolidate				**(380,000)**
variable interest entity			**(380,000)**	
As restated	100,000	1,200,000	0	1,300,000
Net income- 2014	0	700,000	0	700,000
Balance- December 31, 2014	$100,000	$1,900,000	$ 0	$2,000,000

Statement of Cash Flows: The author did not present the statement of cash flows in this example. Assuming 2014 is presented alone, there would be no restatement of the statement of cash flows to reflect the deconsolidation.

NOTE 1: Summary of Significant Accounting Policies:

Consolidation of Variable Interest Entity

Effective January 1, 2014, the Company made an *accounting policy election* authorized for private companies by Accounting Standards Update (ASU) 2014-07— *Consolidation (Topic 810): Applying Variable Interest Entities Guidance to Common Control Leasing Arrangements.* Under this new accounting policy, the Company elects not to apply the accounting principles for the consolidation of variable interest entities (VIEs) to a real estate leasing company that is related to the Company through common ownership. Consequently, the 2014 financial statements do not reflect the effect, if any, of having consolidated the real estate leasing company.

For the year ended December 31, 2013, the Company had consolidated the real estate leasing company. The deconsolidation of the real estate leasing company resulted in a *retrospective adjustment* of the January 1, 2014 *noncontrolling interest in the amount of $380,000* which is reflected in the statement of stockholders' equity.

NOTE 2: Contingencies and Guarantees:

Not included in this example.

Reports

Additional paragraph in compilation report (optional):

As disclosed in Note X to the financial statements, effective January 1, 2014, the Company made an *accounting policy election* authorized for private companies by Accounting Standards Update (ASU) 2014-07—*Consolidation (Topic 810): Applying Variable Interest Entities Guidance to Common Control Leasing Arrangements.* Under this new policy, the Company elects not to apply accounting principles for the consolidation of variable interest entities (VIEs) to a real estate leasing entity that is related to the Company through common ownership.

Additional paragraph in review report (optional):

As disclosed in Note X to the financial statements, effective January 1, 2014, the Company made an *accounting policy election* authorized for private companies by Accounting Standards Update (ASU) 2014-07—*Consolidation (Topic 810): Applying Variable Interest Entities Guidance to Common Control Leasing Arrangements.* Under this new policy, the Company elects not to apply accounting principles for the consolidation of variable interest entities (VIEs) to a real estate leasing entity that is related to the Company through common ownership.

Additional paragraph in audit report:

Accounting Policy Election

As discussed in Note X to the financial statements, effective January 1, 2014, the Company made an *accounting policy election* authorized for private companies by Accounting Standards Update (ASU) 2014-07—*Consolidation (Topic 810): Applying Variable Interest Entities Guidance to Common Control Leasing Arrangements.* Under this new policy, the Company elects not to apply accounting principles for the consolidation of variable interest entities (VIEs) to a real estate leasing entity that is related to the Company through common ownership.

EXAMPLE C: VIE Was Not Consolidated in Prior Year as VIE Rules Did Not Apply. ASU 2014-07 Election Is Made in the Current Year.

Company V (real estate lessor) and PB (operating company lessee) are under common control, with the same 100 percent owner. Company V was not consolidated into PB's 2013 financial statements because the VIE rules did not apply (e.g., V was not a VIE or PB was not the primary beneficiary).

Effective January 1, 2014, Company PB elects the accounting alternative. PB plans to present financial statements for 2014 only.

Conclusion: PB applies the election to avoid the VIE rules retrospectively to the earliest year presented, which is 2014. That means that the four criteria must be tested as of January 1, 2014. (Note that if PB were to present 2013 comparative financial statements, the test would have to be done as of January 1, 2013 instead of January 1, 2014.)

Assume that PB satisfies the four criteria as of January 1, 2014. The 2014 financial statements follow. Information for 2014 is given.

Company PB
Balance Sheet
December 31, 2014

Assets

Current assets:	
Cash	$200,000
Trade receivables	700,000
Total current assets	900,000
Non-current assets:	
Fixed assets	2,700,000
Goodwill	340,000
Other	60,000
Total non-current assets	3,100,000
	$4,000,000

Liabilities and Stockholders' Equity

Current liabilities:	
Accounts payable and accrued expenses	$600,000
Long-term debt	1,400,000
Stockholders' equity:	
Common stock	100,000
Retained earnings	1,900,000
Total stockholders' equity	2,000,000
	$4,000,000

Company PB
Statement of Income
For the Year Ended December 31, 2014

Net sales	$11,000,000
Cost of sales	8,000,000
Gross profit on sales	3,000,000
Operating expenses	1,700,000
Net operating income	1,300,000
Other income (expense):	(200,000)

NIBT	1,100,000
Income taxes	400,000
Net income	$700,000

Company PB
Statement of Stockholders' Equity
For the Years Ended December 31, 2014

	Common stock	Retained earnings	Noncontrolling interest in variable interest entity[1]	Total stockholders' equity
Balance- January 1, 2014	$100,000	$1,200,000	$ 0	$1,680,000
Net income 2014		700,000	0	700,000
Balance- December 31, 2014	$100,000	$1,900,000	$ 0	$2,000,000

[1] The noncontrolling interest is presented for information purposes only. Given that there would be no noncontrolling interest due to consolidation of the VIE, there would be no requirement to present it with zeroes.

Statement of Cash Flows: The author did not present the statement of cash flows in this example as the example would result in no changes to that statement.

NOTE 1: Summary of Significant Accounting Policies:

Consolidation of variable interest entity

Effective January 1, 2014, the Company made an *accounting policy election* authorized for private companies by Accounting Standards Update (ASU) 2014-07—*Consolidation (Topic 810): Applying Variable Interest Entities Guidance to Common Control Leasing Arrangements.* Under this new accounting policy, the Company elects not to apply the accounting principles for the consolidation of variable interest entities (VIEs) to a real estate leasing company that is related to the Company through common ownership. Consequently, the 2014 financial statements do not reflect the effect, if any, of having consolidated the real estate leasing company.

NOTE 2: Contingencies and Guarantees:

Not included in this example.

Reports

Additional paragraph in compilation report (optional):

As disclosed in Note X to the financial statements, effective January 1, 2014, the Company made an *accounting policy election* authorized for private companies by Accounting Standards Update (ASU) 2014-07—*Consolidation (Topic 810): Applying Variable Interest Entities Guidance to Common Control Leasing Arrangements.* Under this new policy, the Company elects not to apply accounting principles for the consolidation of variable interest entities (VIEs) to a real estate leasing entity that is related to the Company through common ownership.

Additional paragraph in review report (optional):

As disclosed in Note X to the financial statements, effective January 1, 2014, the Company made an *accounting policy election* authorized for private companies by Accounting Standards Update (ASU) 2014-07—*Consolidation (Topic 810): Applying Variable Interest Entities Guidance to Common Control Leasing Arrangements*. Under this new policy, the Company elects not to apply accounting principles for the consolidation of variable interest entities (VIEs) to a real estate leasing entity that is related to the Company through common ownership.

Additional paragraph in audit report:

Accounting Policy Election

As discussed in Note X to the financial statements, effective January 1, 2014, the Company made an *accounting policy election* authorized for private companies by Accounting Standards Update (ASU) 2014-07—*Consolidation (Topic 810): Applying Variable Interest Entities Guidance to Common Control Leasing Arrangements*. Under this new policy, the Company elects not to apply accounting principles for the consolidation of variable interest entities (VIEs) to a real estate leasing entity that is related to the Company through common ownership.

> **EXAMPLE D: VIE Was Not Consolidated in Prior Year as a GAAP Departure Was Made in Report. ASU 2014-07 Election Is Made in the Current Year.**

Company V (real estate lessor) and PB (operating company lessee) are under common control, with the same 100 percent owner. Company V was not consolidated into PB's 2013 financial statements because:

- PB chose not to test V for consolidation, and
- PB included a *GAAP departure* in its 2013 report

Effective January 1, 2014, Company PB elects the accounting alternative. PB plans to present financial statements for 2014 only.

Conclusion: PB applies the election to avoid the VIE rules retrospectively to the earliest year presented, which is 2014. That means that the four criteria must be tested as of January 1, 2014. (Note that if PB were to present 2013 comparative financial statements, the test would have to be done as of January 1, 2013 instead of January 1, 2014, even if consolidation had not been done in 2013.)

Assume that PB satisfies the four criteria as of January 1, 2014. Because the 2013 financial statements did not reflect the consolidation of V, there is no restatement of 2013 financial statements. PB would use the financial statements, notes and reports found in Example C in applying the fact pattern found in this Example D.

What would happen if in Example D, 2013 comparative financial statements are presented?

In Example D, PB had a GAAP departure because V was not tested for consolidation into PB's 2013 financial statements. The result is that the 2013 PB financial statements do not reflect the consolidation of V.

If 2013 comparative financial statements were presented comparatively with 2014, the ASU election must be tested retrospectively back to January 1, 2013. As long as the four criteria of ASU 2014-07 are met as of January 1, 2013, and there are no changes in those criteria from January 1, 2013 through December 31, 2014, the election would be reflected in both the 2013 and 2014 financial statements. From a practical point, applying the election to 2013 and 2014 means that nothing happens because the 2013 and 2014 financial statements had no consolidation of V because of the previous GAAP departure.

¶1300

What would change in the report? Previously, the 2013 year-end report had a reference to a GAAP departure in it because PB did not test (and possibly consolidate) V. In implementing the ASU retrospectively to January 1, 2013, the GAAP departure would no longer apply because testing and consolidating V would not be required going back to January 1, 2013.

For a compilation or review report, an emphasis-of-matter paragraph would be appropriate (but not required), and an other-matter paragraph would be required for the audit report, as follows:

Accountant's Compilation Report

Board of Directors

Company PB

Nowhere, Massachusetts

I (we) have compiled the accompanying balance sheets of Company PB of December 31, 2014 and 2013, and the related statements of income, stockholders' equity, and cash flows for the years then ended. I (we) have not audited or reviewed the accompanying financial statements and, accordingly, do not express an opinion or provide any assurance about whether the financial statements are in accordance with accounting principles generally accepted in the United States of America.

Management (owners) is (are) responsible for the preparation and fair presentation of the financial statements in accordance with accounting principles generally accepted in the United States of America and for designing, implementing, and maintaining internal control relevant to the preparation and fair presentation of the financial statements.

My (our) responsibility is to conduct the compilation in accordance with Statements on Standards for Accounting and Review Services issued by the American Institute of Certified Public Accountants. The objective of a compilation is to assist management in presenting financial information in the form of financial statements without undertaking to obtain or provide any assurance that there are no material modifications that should be made to the financial statements.

In our compilation report dated March 1, 2014, with respect to the 2013 financial statements, we referred to a departure from accounting principles generally accepted in the United States of America because the company did not perform the required assessment to determine whether a real estate leasing company, related by common ownership, should be consolidated into the Company's 2013 financial statements.

As disclosed in Note X to the financial statements, effective January 1, 2014, the Company made an *accounting policy election* authorized for private companies by Accounting Standards Update (ASU) 2014-07—*Consolidation (Topic 810): Applying Variable Interest Entities Guidance to Common Control Leasing Arrangements*. Under this new policy, the Company elects not to apply accounting principles for the consolidation of variable interest entities (VIEs) to a real estate leasing entity that is related to the Company through common ownership. The effect in the change in accounting principle was applied retrospectively to January 1, 2013.

James J. Fox & Company, CPA

Date

Independent Accountant's Review Report

Board of Directors

Company PB

Nowhere, Massachusetts

We have reviewed the accompanying balance sheets of Company PB as of December 31, 2014 and 2013, and the related statements of income, stockholders' equity, and cash flows for the years then ended. A review includes primarily applying analytical procedures to management's financial data and making inquiries of company management. A review is substantially less in scope than an audit, the objective of which is the expression of an opinion regarding the financial statements as a whole. Accordingly, we do not express such an opinion.

Management is responsible for the preparation and fair presentation of the financial statements in accordance with accounting principles generally accepted in the United States of America, and for designing, implementing, and maintaining internal control relevant to the preparation and fair presentation of the financial statements.

Our responsibility is to conduct the review in accordance with Statements on Standards for Accounting and Review Services issued by the American Institute of Certified Public Accountants. Those standards require me (us) to perform procedures to obtain limited assurance that there are no material modifications that should be made to the financial statements. We believe that the results of my (our) procedures provide a reasonable basis for our report.

Based on our review, we are not aware of any material modifications that should be made to the accompanying financial statements in order for them to be in conformity with accounting principles generally accepted in the United States of America.

In our review report dated March 1, 2014, with respect to the 2013 financial statements, we referred to a departure from accounting principles generally accepted in the United States of America because the company did not perform the required assessment to determine whether a real estate leasing company, related by common ownership, should be consolidated into the company's 2013 financial statements.

As disclosed in Note X to the financial statements, effective January 1, 2014, the Company made an *accounting policy election* authorized for private companies by Accounting Standards Update (ASU) 2014-07—*Consolidation (Topic 810): Applying Variable Interest Entities Guidance to Common Control Leasing Arrangements.* Under this new policy, the Company elects not to apply accounting principles for the consolidation of variable interest entities (VIEs) to a real estate leasing entity that is related to the Company through common ownership. The effect in the change in accounting principle was applied retrospectively to January 1, 2013.

Accordingly, our present statement on the 2013 financial statements, as presented herein, that we are not aware of any material modifications that should be made to the accompanying financial statements, is different from that expressed in our previous report.

James J. Fox & Company, CPA

Date

Independent Auditor's Report

Board of Directors

Company PB

Nowhere, Massachusetts

We have audited the accompanying financial statements of Company PB, which comprise the balance sheets as of December 31, 2014 and 2013, and the related statements of income, stockholders' equity and cash flows for the years then ended, and the related notes to the financial statements.

Management's Responsibility for the Financial Statements

Management is responsible for the preparation and fair presentation of these financial statements in accordance with accounting principles generally accepted in the United States of America; this includes the design, implementation, and maintenance of internal control relevant to the preparation and fair presentation of financial statements that are free from material misstatement, whether due to fraud or error.

Auditor's Responsibility

Our responsibility is to express an opinion on these financial statements based on our audits. We conducted our audits in accordance with auditing standards generally accepted in the United States of America. Those standards require that we plan and perform the audit to obtain reasonable assurance about whether the financial statements are free from material misstatement.

An audit involves performing procedures to obtain audit evidence about the amounts and disclosures in the financial statements. The procedures selected depend on the auditor's judgment, including the assessment of the risks of material misstatement of the financial statements, whether due to fraud or error. In making those risk assessments, the auditor considers internal control relevant to the entity's preparation and fair presentation of the financial statements in order to design audit procedures that are appropriate in the circumstances, but not for the purpose of expressing an opinion on the effectiveness of the entity's internal control. Accordingly, we express no such opinion. An audit also includes evaluating the appropriateness of accounting policies used and the reasonableness of significant accounting estimates made by management, as well as evaluating the overall presentation of the financial statements.

We believe that the audit evidence we have obtained is sufficient and appropriate to provide a basis for our audit opinion.

Opinion

In our opinion, the financial statements referred to above present fairly, in all material respects, the financial position of Company PB as of December 31, 2014 and 2013, and the results of their operations and their cash flows for the years then ended in accordance with accounting principles generally accepted in the United States of America.

Other Matter

In our report dated March 1, 2014, we expressed an opinion that the 2013 financial statements did not fairly present financial position, results of operations and cash flows in conformity with accounting principles generally accepted in the United State of America because the company did not perform the required assessment to determine whether a real estate leasing company, related by common ownership, should be consolidated into the company's 2013 financial statements.

As discussed in Note X to the financial statements, effective January 1, 2014, the Company made an *accounting policy election* authorized for private companies by Accounting Standards Update (ASU) 2014-07—*Consolidation (Topic 810): Applying Variable Interest Entities Guidance to Common Control Leasing Arrangements*. Under this new policy, the Company elects not to apply accounting principles for the consolidation of variable interest entities (VIEs) to a real estate leasing entity that is related to the Company through common ownership. The Company has applied the change in accounting principle retrospectively to the 2013 financial statements to conform with accounting principles generally accepted in the United States of America. Accordingly, our present opinion on the 2013 financial statements, as presented herein, is different from that expressed in our previous report.

[Auditor's signature]

[Auditor's city and state]

[Date of the auditor's report]

> **NOTE:** AU-C 706, *Emphasis-of-Matter Paragraphs and Other-Matters Paragraphs in the Independent Auditor's Report*, requires that an other-matters paragraph be included in the auditor's report when the auditor's opinion on the prior-year financial statements differs from the opinion previously issued for that year.

¶ 10,100 Answers to Study Questions

¶ 10,101 MODULE 1—CHAPTER 1

1. a. *Incorrect.* Having an investment alone is not enough to consolidate. Only if the investment elevates to more than 50 percent of the voting interest would an entity be required to consolidate another entity.

b. *Correct.* **GAAP states than an entity that has a controlling financial interest in another entity must consolidate that entity. A controlling financial interest can be achieved in different ways including a direct investment of more than 50 percent of the voting shares in another entity, and in instances in which a controlling financial interest is achieved through other than a direct financial investment.**

c. *Incorrect.* Having a loan receivable does not create a right or obligation to consolidate another entity.

d. *Incorrect.* Having a minority interest does not create a requirement to consolidate an entity. In fact, one way to consolidate is to hold more than 50 percent of the voting interest in another entity. Having a minority interest clearly does not rise to that level.

2. a. *Incorrect.* Typically, a public company, not a common-owner private company, establishes a lessor entity separate from a private company in order to structure off-balance-sheet debt arrangements.

b. *Incorrect.* Most private companies do, in fact, establish a lessor entity separate from a private company, in order to provide effective tax planning by using a pass-through entity such as an LLC.

c. *Incorrect.* Most users of private company lessee's financial statements state that consolidation of the lessor entity is not relevant to them, making the answer incorrect.

d. *Correct.* **A common owner may establish a lessor entity separate from the private company lessee is for effective legal-liability and asset protection purposes.**

3. a. *Incorrect.* Having the power to direct the VIE's most significant activities *is* one of the factors to consider. FIN 46R specifically lists the power to direct as one of the factors to consider because having the power is tantamount to acting like a de facto parent of the VIE.

b. *Incorrect.* FIN 46R lists this as one of the factors to consider because a de facto parent (primary beneficiary) would have the obligation of absorbing some of the losses of the VIE.

c. *Incorrect.* Having the right to receive the VIE's benefits that could be significant is one of the factors to consider. The reason is because if Y is a primary beneficiary, in that capacity as a de facto parent, Y would receive some of the economic benefits of VIE.

d. *Correct.* **Having at least a 50 percent investment in the VIE is *not* a factor identified by FIN 46R. There is a consolidation rule that requires consolidation if there is ownership of more than 50 percent of the voting shares of an entity. However, that rule has nothing to do with the FIN 46R rules for consolidating a VIE.**

4. a. *Correct.* **The tie-breaker rule applies when there are two related parties that are tied in terms of determining which is the primary beneficiary. The tie-breaker is used to select one of the two related parties as the primary beneficiary.**

b. *Incorrect.* The tie-breaker rule does not relate to determining which entity is a VIE.

c. *Incorrect.* The tie-breaker rule involves two related parties, not one related party and one unrelated party.

d. *Incorrect.* The tie-breaker rule does not deal with variable interests and, instead, is used to deal with a primary beneficiary.

5. a. *Incorrect.* Although husband and wife are immediate family members, each must own more than 50 percent of the respective entities. In this case, the husband owns only 25 percent of lessee even though his wife owns 100 percent of lessor.

b. *Correct.* **Father and son are immediate family members each of whom owns more than 50 percent of the voting equity of the lessee and lessor. Thus, the two entities are under common control.**

c. *Incorrect.* The same group of individuals must own more than 50 percent of the voting interest in both entities, which it does not. Thus, the two entities are not under common control.

d. *Incorrect.* Although the brother and sister are immediate family members, each must own more than 50 percent of the voting interest in the entities, which they do not.

6. a. *Incorrect.* There must be a lease between a private company lessee and a lessor under common control. A public company lessee does not qualify as a leasing activity, including supporting leasing activity, under the ASU.

b. *Incorrect.* Paying property taxes on the asset leased to the private company lessee is considered a leasing activity, including supporting leasing activity, but not the paying of taxes on an asset leased to an unrelated party.

c. *Incorrect.* A lease option related to an asset that is not leased by the private company lessee is not considered a leasing activity, including supporting leasing activity. The lease option must relate to the asset leased by the lessee in order for it to qualify as a leasing activity, including supporting leasing activity.

d. *Correct.* **The ASU states that a purchase commitment for the acquisition of the asset leased by the private company lessee is considered a supporting leasing activity. If the commitment involves the acquisition of an asset that is not leased to the private company lessee, it would not qualify.**

7. a. *Incorrect.* In most cases, the lessee's guarantee of an additional mortgage on real estate not leased by the lessee taints Criterion 3 in that the additional guarantee is an activity outside a lease between the lessee and lessor.

b. *Correct.* **The additional guarantee is considered an activity with the lessor that is not related to the lease of the underlying real estate. Thus, in most situations, the lessee fails Criterion 3 and the lessee cannot use the election under ASU 2014-07.**

c. *Incorrect.* The fact that the lessee guarantees the additional mortgage has a bearing on whether the lessee satisfies Criterion 3 because the additional guarantee on other real estate is considered an activity outside the lease between the lessee and lessor.

d. *Incorrect.* There is no 50 percent threshold found in ASU 2014-07.

8. a. *Incorrect.* Y will not consolidate X using the VIE model, but could consolidate under another consolidation model.

b. *Correct.* **Y could still consolidate X using the voting interest model under which Y would be required to consolidate X if Y owns more than 50 percent of X's voting interest.**

c. *Incorrect.* GAAP does not restrict Y from consolidating X once the election is made if Y owns more than 50 percent of the voting interest in X.

d. *Incorrect.* GAAP does address consolidation outside the ASU including use of the voting interest model.

9. a. *Incorrect.* The change is not accounted for prospectively by applying it only for future periods. The election is effective for the first annual period beginning after December 15, 2014, and interim periods within annual periods beginning after December 15, 2015. Early application is allowed for any annual or interim period before which an entity's financial statements are available to be issued.

b. *Correct.* **The ASU requires that the change be accounted for retrospectively to all periods presented, including restating all prior periods presented.**

c. *Incorrect.* The ASU follows the guidance of ASC 250 which does not permit the use of a cumulative effect of the change presented as a line item in the income statement.

d. *Incorrect.* The change made by the ASU is a change in accounting policy, not a change in accounting estimate.

¶ 10,102 MODULE 1—CHAPTER 2

1. a. *Correct.* **A private company includes a nonpublic entity. It is defined as an entity, other than a public business entity, a not-for-profit entity, or an employee benefit plan on plan accounting.**

b. *Incorrect.* The ASU excludes a not-for-profit entity from the definition of a private company. A not-for-profit entity is an entity that possesses certain characteristics, in varying degrees, that distinguish it from a business entity.

c. *Incorrect.* The ASU excludes a public business entity from its definition. A public business entity is an entity that meets certain criteria. Neither a not-for-profit entity nor an employee benefit plan is considered to be a business entity.

d. *Incorrect.* The ASU excludes an employee benefit plan that is on plan accounting under ASC 960 and 965.

2. a. *Incorrect.* The term "ready to distribute" is not used within the ASU. The process involved in creating and distributing financial statements varies depending on an entity's management and corporate governance structure and statutory and regulatory requirements.

b. *Incorrect.* Even though the financial statements are complete in form and all approvals have been obtained, that does not mean they have been issued.

c. *Correct.* **The ASU defines the term "available to be issued" as a situation in which the financial statements are complete in form and format that complies with GAAP, and all approvals, such as from management, the board of directors, and/or significant shareholders have been obtained.**

d. *Incorrect.* ASU 2014-03 does not use the term "finalized" and it is not defined in the ASU.

3. a. *Incorrect.* The ASU does not apply to foreign exchange hedges. A foreign exchange hedge is a method used by companies to eliminate their foreign exchange risk from transactions in foreign currencies by using either the cash flow hedge or the fair value method.

b. *Correct.* **The ASU's simplified method is available for a cash flow hedge of a variable-rate borrowing.**

c. *Incorrect.* Although an entity may hedge its materials costs through futures or other contracts, the ASU does not relate to material-related hedges.

d. *Incorrect.* The ASU does not apply to a hedge on inflation. An inflation hedge is an investment in assets that have inherent value such as oil, natural gas, or gold.

¶ 10,103 MODULE 1—CHAPTER 3

1. a. *Correct.* **GAAP addresses uncertainty by prescribing a basic recognition threshold for all tax positions, including state income taxes and a measurement attribute to be applied to those tax positions that meet the threshold. A tax position includes a filing position on a previously filed return and an expected filing position in a future tax return reflected in measuring current or deferred income tax assets and liabilities.**

b. *Incorrect.* Fair value is the amount at which the asset could be bought or sold in a current transaction between willing parties, or transferred to an equivalent party, other than in a liquidation sale.

c. *Incorrect.* GAAP addresses recognition and measurement of tax positions discretely.

d. *Incorrect.* Uncertainty is not addressed solely by disclosure. Complex issues may arise when applying the GAAP requirements.

2. a. *Incorrect.* The first step of the two-step process is recognition, in which the entity determines whether it is more likely than not that a tax position, based on the technical merits, will be sustained upon final resolution in the court of last resort.

b. *Incorrect.* The second step of the two-step process is measurement, in which the tax position is measured to determine the amount of the benefit to recognize in financial statements.

c. *Incorrect.* Deciding not to file a tax return is a "tax position" and the two-step process evaluates uncertainty in an entity's tax position.

d. *Correct.* **Before applying the two-step process, the entity must determine the appropriate unit of account based on the individual facts and circumstances of the tax position when considering all available evidence.**

3. a. *Incorrect.* The more-likely-than-not recognition threshold assumes the tax position will be examined by the relevant tax authority and that the tax authority has full knowledge of all relevant information.

b. *Correct.* **With the more-likely-than-not recognition threshold, the level of evidence is a matter of judgment. Although a legal tax opinion is not required to demonstrate that the threshold is met, such opinion can be external evidence supporting management's assertion.**

c. *Incorrect.* One assumption about the more-likely-than-not recognition threshold is that the tax position is assessed without considering the effect of offset or aggregation with other tax positions.

d. *Incorrect.* The more-likely-than-not recognition threshold assumes the technical merits of the tax position derive from sources of tax authority and apply to the facts and circumstances of the tax position, including certain past administrative practices and precedents.

4. a. *Incorrect.* A state taxing authority may use the income reallocation approach by using a general statute or regulatory authority to reallocate income between the two related entities.

b. *Incorrect.* A state taxing authority may use the forced combination approach to tax the combined income of two related companies.

c. *Correct.* The look-back issue occurs when the entity determines that it is not "more likely than not" that its non-filing position will be sustained under examination in a particular state.

d. *Incorrect.* A state taxing authority may use the nexus approach to assert that Company B has nexus with its state based on a statute, regulation, case law, or other applicable authority.

5. a. *Correct.* A state taxing authority may attack the transactions between the two companies in an attempt to reduce Company A expenses. A current transfer pricing study may support these expenses.

b. *Incorrect.* If Company B's tax position cannot meet the more-likely-than-not recognition threshold that it would be sustained despite a state taxing authority's attempted forced combination, Company B should not recognize the benefit of the tax position.

c. *Incorrect.* A state taxing authority may claim that Company B has nexus based on a state statute, regulation, case, or other applicable authority.

d. *Incorrect.* A state taxing authority may rely on general statutory or regulatory authority to reallocate income between the two related companies.

6. a. *Incorrect.* These amounts are required to be disclosed, as are the total amounts of interest and penalties recognized in the balance sheet.

b. *Incorrect.* This is a required disclosure and would be accompanied by other required information, including the nature of the uncertainty.

c. *Correct.* GAAP does not require an entity to disclose this detail, although it does require specific disclosure be made regarding each tax position for which it is reasonably possible that the total amount of unrecognized tax benefits will significantly increase or decrease within 12 months of the reporting date.

d. *Incorrect.* An entity has to adopt, disclose, and consistently apply an accounting policy for interest on unrecognized tax benefits, as well as one for related penalties.

¶ 10,104 MODULE 2—CHAPTER 4

1. a. *Incorrect.* Reasonably possible is a threshold used in contingencies, and not part of the liquidation basis of accounting.

b. *Incorrect.* The probable threshold is not used in the liquidation basis of accounting. Instead, it is used in the contingency rules.

c. *Incorrect.* The ASU does not use the more likely than not threshold. It is used in FASB Interpretation (FIN) 48, *Accounting for Uncertainty in Income Taxes.*

d. *Correct.* The ASU requires use of the liquidation basis of accounting when liquidation is imminent. Liquidation is imminent when one of two specific types of events occurs.

2. a. *Incorrect.* Using the liquidation basis of accounting, unrecognized assets, such as those that are fully depreciated, should not be recorded at their original cost.

b. *Incorrect.* The asset is unrecognized on the GAAP balance sheet as it is fully depreciated. Using the liquidation basis of accounting, those assets are not retained at their GAAP net book value.

c. *Correct.* **ASU 2013-07 states that an entity shall recognize items previously not recognized, but that it expects to sell in liquidation. In such a case, the equipment is fully depreciated and thus, unrecognized. When it is recorded under the liquidation basis of accounting, it is recorded at the amount of cash that Company X expects to receive from sale of the equipment, which is $20,000.**

d. *Incorrect.* Fair value is not used in the liquidation basis of accounting, although in many instances, the liquidation value can be the same or similar to the fair value.

3. a. *Incorrect.* Y should not use the liquidation basis of accounting throughout the 10-year period. Such a basis would only be used if Y does not following the original plan found within the governing documents.

b. *Incorrect.* Because Y is a limited-life entity, Y should not use the liquidation basis of accounting if it follows the 10-year plan of liquidation.

c. *Correct.* **A limited life entity does not follow the liquidation basis as long as it follows the plan found in the governing document, which in this case is 10 years. However, if the entity deviates from the original plan in a forced liquidation at less than fair value, it should use the liquidation basis. In this case, because Y has to liquidate assets in a forced liquidation in year six, not the plan of year 10, Y should use the liquidation basis of accounting starting in year six.**

d. *Incorrect.* Y should use the liquidation basis of accounting if it deviates from the original 10-year plan.

4. a. *Incorrect.* Although traditional GAAP uses the matching principle, the liquidation basis of accounting does not match revenue and expense so that the accrual is not limited to current year costs only.

b. *Incorrect.* There is no rule that limits the accrual to those costs incurred up to two years.

c. *Correct.* **The liquidation basis of accounting requires that costs be accrued through the end of the liquidation period.**

d. *Incorrect.* The accrual is required if there is a reasonable basis for estimation, but it is not required if there is not a reasonable basis for estimation.

¶ 10,105 MODULE 2—CHAPTER 5

1. a. *Incorrect.* Transactions involving trading securities are not part of other comprehensive income. However, certain foreign exchange transactions under ASC 830 are other comprehensive income items.

b. *Correct.* **Transactions involving available-for-sale securities go through stockholders' equity and are part of other comprehensive income.**

c. *Incorrect.* Transactions involving debt securities held to maturity are not part of other comprehensive income. One example of an other comprehensive income item is certain pension transactions under ASC 715.

d. *Incorrect.* Transactions involving non-security investments are not part of other comprehensive income. One example of an other comprehensive income item is certain derivative transactions under ASC 815.

2. a. *Incorrect.* Change in equity is not part of the comprehensive income.

b. *Correct.* **The formula for comprehensive income is: net income +- other comprehensive income. Comprehensive income consists of changes in equity that are from non-owner sources.**

c. *Incorrect.* Non-cash transactions have nothing to do with the comprehensive

d. *Incorrect.* The change in working capital has nothing to do with comprehensive income.

3. a. *Incorrect.* One example is unrealized gains and losses from transfers of securities from the held-to-maturity category to available-for-sale, not the other way around.

b. *Incorrect.* One example is a subsequent increase in the fair value of available-for sale securities previously written down as an impairment, but not as an other-than-temporary impairment.

c. *Incorrect.* One example is amounts recognized in other comprehensive income for debt securities classified as available-for-sale and held-to-maturity related to an other-than-temporary impairment recognized if a portion of the impairment was not recognized in earnings.

d. *Correct.* **Unrealized gains and losses on securities available for sale is an example of a transaction involving available-for-sale securities that would be part of other comprehensive income.**

4. a. *Incorrect.* GAAP requires a financial statement format and not just a disclosure of comprehensive income.

b. *Correct.* **One of the two format options is to present one single continuous statement of income and comprehensive income.**

c. *Incorrect.* Presenting comprehensive income as a section within the statement of stockholders' equity was one of the options previously available but was eliminated.

d. *Incorrect.* This is not an option. One of the options is to combine the statement of income and comprehensive income.

5. a. *Correct.* **One presentation is to present each component net of its individual tax effect. Alternatively, this requirement can be satisfied by presenting the total tax expense as one line item assigned to other comprehensive income, with a separate note provided that discloses the breakout of income tax expense assigned to each other comprehensive income component.**

b. *Incorrect.* Although one presentation is to show the total other comprehensive income with one total allocation of income taxes, there is a requirement to present the tax effect of each component in the notes.

c. *Incorrect.* The tax effects are required to be allocated to other comprehensive income.

d. *Incorrect.* The tax effect must be presented in the financial statements.

6. a. *Incorrect.* The presentation must be made regardless of whether a single or two-statement format is used.

b. *Correct.* The changes may be reflected in either the statement of stockholders' equity or the notes to the financial statements.

c. *Incorrect.* The changes may be shown in the notes to the financial statements but they may also be reflected elsewhere instead.

d. *Incorrect.* Accumulated other comprehensive income must be presented as a separate component in the equity section of the balance sheet. The individual components need not be presented as long as they are presented elsewhere, such as in the statement of stockholders' equity or in the notes to the financial statements.

7. a. *Incorrect.* Such adjustments do not affect multiple financial statements.

b. *Correct.* Reclassification adjustments avoid double counting of comprehensive income items that are presented as part of net income in one period, and as part of other comprehensive income in that period or prior periods.

c. *Incorrect.* Reclassification adjustments have nothing to do with disclosures.

d. *Incorrect.* Reclassification adjustments do not deal with the particular line item in the statement of comprehensive income.

8. a. *Incorrect.* Once the investment is sold, the translation adjustment is not retained in equity and is reported in net income.

b. *Correct.* ASU 2013-05 clarifies that upon sale, the component is removed from equity and reported in net income.

c. *Incorrect.* ASC 805 does not provide for removing a portion of the component and retaining the remainder in equity, when it relates to the sale of a foreign investment. The sale of an investment in a foreign entity includes two types of events, including events that result in an acquirer obtaining control of an acquiree in which it held an equity interest immediately before the acquisition date.

d. *Incorrect.* Upon sale, the component is not reclassified to a separate section of equity. The sale of an investment in a foreign entity includes two types of events, including events that result in the loss of a controlling financial interest in an investment in a foreign entity.

9. a. *Incorrect.* The pro rata portion rule does not apply to a partial sale of a non-foreign entity.

b. *Incorrect.* The entire cumulative transaction adjustment is released into income only if the sale represents a complete or substantially complete liquidation, which in this example, it does not.

c. *Correct.* Because the sale is that of a non-foreign entity and the sale does not represent a complete or substantially complete liquidation, the adjustment should not be released into income.

d. *Incorrect.* There is no rule under which the adjustment should be reclassified into a separate section of equity, regardless of whether the entity is foreign or non-foreign.

¶ 10,106 MODULE 2—CHAPTER 6

1. a. *Incorrect.* SSARS No. 19 does include the regulatory basis as an example of an OCBOA. The regulatory basis of accounting is used to comply with the requirements or financial reporting provisions of a governmental regulatory agency.

b. *Incorrect.* The definition of OCBOA includes the income tax basis of accounting, which is a basis of accounting that the reporting entity uses or expects to use to file its income tax return.

c. *Correct.* **OCBOA is a basis** *other than* **GAAP so that the GAAP basis is not included within the scope of OBCOA.**

d. *Incorrect.* The cash or modified cash basis is one example of OCBOA.

2. a. *Incorrect.* Because the entity is a C corporation for tax purposes, a tax provision should be reflected if there is one.

b. *Incorrect.* The entity would be presented as a sole proprietorship only if no tax return were to be filed, which is not the case in the example given. Because the entity is a C corporation, it will be required to file a tax return.

c. *Correct.* **Because the entity is taxed as a C corporation, the financial statements should reflect the type of entity (LLC) along with the tax provision that results from the entity being taxed as a C corporation.**

d. *Incorrect.* Because the entity is not taxed as a partnership for tax purposes, the financial statements should not present the entity as a partnership.

3. a. *Incorrect.* Such income is nontaxable income and is a permanent difference that is presented in the statement of income even though excluded from taxable income.

b. *Incorrect.* COD income is presented on the statement of income, and not disclosed only.

c. *Correct.* **COD income, as a permanent difference, is presented as income on the statement of income**

d. *Incorrect.* Income tax basis financial statements do not present comprehensive income.

¶ 10,107 MODULE 2—CHAPTER 7

1. a. *Incorrect.* Predictability is *not* a requirement under ASC 405-40. The total amount of the obligation may change subsequent to the reporting date.

b. *Incorrect.* The ASC does not use the term "calculable."

c. *Correct.* **The total amount must be fixed in order for ASC 405-40 to apply. However, the total amount may change subsequent to the reporting date because of factors unrelated to measurement uncertainty.**

d. *Incorrect.* The total amount should not be variable because the amount of the obligation must be determined. If the amount is variable, that obligation amount cannot be measured on the obligor's balance sheet.

2. a. *Correct.* **The ASC does not apply to guarantors who must follow the guidance of ASC 460, Guarantees.**

b. *Incorrect.* Whether the guarantor follows ASC 460 has no effect on whether ASC 405-40 applies. ASC 460-25-3 states that the issuance of a guarantee imposes a noncontingent obligation to stand ready to perform in the event that the specified triggering events or conditions occur.

c. *Incorrect.* Whether the guarantor is the primary obligor is not a factor in determining whether ASC 405-40 applies. The provisions of Section 450-20-25 regarding a guarantor's contingent obligation under a guarantee should not be interpreted as prohibiting a guarantor from initially recognizing a liability for a guarantee even though it is not probable that payments will be required under that guarantee.

d. *Incorrect.* ASC 405-40-15-1 does address whether it applies to guarantors as opposed to borrowers.

3. a. *Incorrect.* Because the transaction is a debit, it cannot be a loss contingency.

b. *Correct.* Where there is no contractual arrangement for recovery of the funded amounts, the entity should consider whether the receivable is a gain contingency.

c. *Incorrect.* There is no reason why the debit would ever be considered a deferred credit. A deferred credit in most cases results from money received in advance of it being earned, such as customer prepayments.

d. *Incorrect.* There is no reason why the debit would be treated as an operating expense. Operating expenses are costs which a business incurs during the normal course of doing business.

¶ 10,108 MODULE 3—CHAPTER 8

1. a. *Incorrect.* GAAP provides that an intangible asset with an indefinite life should not be amortized, but should be tested annually for impairment.

b. *Correct.* Because the useful life is indefinite, it should not be amortized until its life is determined to be no longer indefinite.

c. *Incorrect.* There is no "may" in GAAP in that there is no discretion on amortizing or not amortizing the intangible asset. The intangible asset is not amortized while the life is indefinite. Once no longer indefinite, it should not be amortized.

d. *Incorrect.* The 15-year period is a tax life, not related to GAAP.

2. a. *Incorrect.* One example is deteriorating, not strong, general economic conditions. If there were strong general economic conditions, it would be unlikely that the goodwill asset value would be declining. Instead, goodwill would likely be increasing.

b. *Incorrect.* One example is an increase, not decrease, in the competitive environment. If there is a decrease in the competitive environment, business would be expected to be better and asset values, including goodwill, would increase, and not be impaired.

c. *Correct.* If there is a negative or declining cash flow trend, there could be deteriorating asset values resulting in a decline in goodwill.

d. *Incorrect.* One example is if there is an increase, not reduction, in the cost of key raw materials. If there is a reduction in costs, one would think that profitability would improve so that the likelihood of goodwill impairment would be low.

3. a. *Correct.* The ASU eliminates the tabular reconciliation of goodwill during the period. The tabular format requires that the following be reflected: gross amount and accumulated impairment losses at beginning of period, additional goodwill recognized during the period, and adjustments resulting from subsequent recognition of deferred tax assets during the period.

b. *Incorrect.* The ASU adds, rather than eliminates, the requirement to disclose the aggregate amortization expense for the period.

c. *Incorrect.* The ASU carries over the disclosure of the gross carrying amounts of goodwill at the end of the period, thereby not eliminating it.

d. *Incorrect.* The ASU adds, rather than eliminates, the amount of accumulated amortization at the end of the period.

¶ 10,109 MODULE 3—CHAPTER 9

1. a. *Incorrect.* Under existing GAAP, in order for a lease to qualify as a capital lease, the present value of the minimum lease payments must be equal to or exceed 90% or more (and not 10%) of the fair value of the asset.

b. *Incorrect.* Under existing GAAP, in order for a lease to qualify as a capital lease, the lease term must be *at least 75 percent* of the remaining useful life of the leased asset.

c. **Correct. Under current GAAP, ASC 840, *Leases* divides leases into two categories: operating and capital leases. Under existing GAAP, if there is a bargain purchase at the end of the lease, this is one of the criteria which would define the lease as a capital lease.**

d. *Incorrect.* Under existing GAAP, if there is a transfer of ownership, the lease qualifies as a capital lease.

2. a. **Correct. The proposal uses the right-of-use model under which a lease obligation is recorded at the present value of cash flows with the recording of a corresponding right-of-use asset.**

b. *Incorrect.* Operating leases are part of existing GAAP and have nothing to do with the proposed lease standard.

c. *Incorrect.* The term "capital lease" is part of existing GAAP and is not used in the proposed model even though the new model does capitalize assets and liabilities.

d. *Incorrect.* The concept of "true lease" is found in taxation and not in GAAP.

3. a. *Incorrect.* The proposed standard would not require the company to record a lease asset and liability for a short-term lease of 12 months or less. This would be required for lease terms of more than 12 months.

b. *Incorrect.* The proposed standard would permit, but not require, that the company record a short-term lease as an operating lease.

c. **Correct. If the lease is 12 months or less, a lessee would be able to elect to record the lease as an operating lease, or would also be allowed to record the lease asset and liability, similar to other leases. In accordance with the right-of-use model, a lessee would recognize assets and liabilities for any leases that have a maximum possible lease term of more than 12 months.**

d. *Incorrect.* The proposed standard does address these leases, and gives options as to how to deal with them.

4. a. *Incorrect.* Total expense (interest and amortization) on the lessee's income statement would be higher, not lower, in the earlier years of new leases.

b. *Incorrect.* There would be a positive (not negative) shift to cash from operations from cash from financing activities in the statement of cash flows.

c. *Incorrect.* In most cases, total expense for GAAP will differ from total expense for income tax purposes resulting in deferred income taxes being recorded.

d. **Correct. The lessee's EBITDA may increase as there is a shift from rent expense to interest and amortization expense. Interest and amortization are not deducted in arriving at EBITDA while rent expense under existing operating leases is deducted.**

5. a. *Incorrect.* The proposed standard is not likely to expand leases because those leases will have lease obligations that have to be recorded on the lessee's balance sheet.

b. *Incorrect.* Shorter, not longer, leases will be the trend so that smaller liabilities are recorded on the lessee's balance sheet.

c. *Correct.* **Tenants in single-tenant buildings with long-term leases may choose to buy because they already have to record lease obligations that are similar to the debt they will have to record in a purchase.**

d. *Incorrect.* The status quo is not likely to be the case given the enormity of the impact of the proposed standard on company balance sheets.

6. a. *Incorrect.* GAAP depreciation under a purchase may be lower, not higher, because the useful life used to depreciate the purchased asset is usually longer than the lease term used to amortize the lease.

b. *Correct.* **The useful life used to depreciate an asset under a purchase is likely to be longer than the lease term used to amortize a lease thereby resulting in lower depreciation with a purchase than amortization with a Type A lease.**

c. *Incorrect.* There is no indication that the amounts would be the same, as the terms used for depreciation would differ than those for amortization.

d. *Incorrect.* Even if the option periods are included in the lease term, that term will be lower than the useful life of the purchase. Thus, depreciation will always be lower than amortization.

¶ 10,110 MODULE 3—CHAPTER 10

1. a. *Incorrect.* This is not an example of a public-sector entity. A governmental body would be an example.

b. *Incorrect.* The entity is not a governmental body and also does not meet the criterion for the other example.

c. *Correct.* **Even though the entity is non-governmental, responsibility to provide public service has been delegated to it, thereby meeting the definition of a public-sector entity.**

d. *Incorrect.* One example is an entity, to which responsibility is delegated to provide a public, not a private for-profit service.

2. a. *Incorrect.* The ASU applies to collateralized loans, not unsecured loans.

b. *Incorrect.* Although the EITF did consider whether the scope of the ASU should be expanded to include commercial real estate loans, it decided against it.

c. *Correct.* **The ASU applies specifically to mortgage loans collateralized by residential real estate properties. The EITF did not to extend the scope of the ASU to commercial real estate loans because the foreclosure processes and applicable laws for those assets are much different from residential real estate.**

d. *Incorrect.* The ASU does not provide for loans that are collateralized by securities. Instead, it applies to loans that are collateralized by certain real estate properties only.

3. a. *Correct.* **A public business entity is a business entity that meets certain criteria. One such criterion is that the entity is a conduit bond obligor for securities that are traded.**

b. *Incorrect.* X is a business entity, not a nonbusiness entity, due to the fact that it is a conduit obligor for securities.

c. *Incorrect.* There is no indication that X is a not-for-profit entity.

d. *Incorrect.* Because X is involved with securities, it comes under the authority of the SEC. Therefore, X is a public, not private, business entity.

4. a. *Incorrect.* The ASU does not provide an option to show the benefit as a deferred tax credit.

b. *Incorrect.* Although there are exceptions to the general rule that could result in a credit to a liability, this is not general rule.

c. *Correct.* **The ASU is quite clear that an unrecognized tax benefit, or a portion of an unrecognized tax benefit, shall be presented as a reduction to a deferred tax asset for a net operating loss carryforward, a similar tax loss, or a tax credit carryforward.**

d. *Incorrect.* There is no situation in which the credit should be presented as part of other comprehensive income in stockholders' equity. Neither the general rule nor the exceptions to the general rule allow this.

5. a. *Incorrect.* Once the investment is sold, the translation adjustment is not retained in equity and is reported in net income.

b. *Correct.* **ASU 2013-05 clarifies that upon sale, the component is removed from equity and reported in net income.**

c. *Incorrect.* ASU 2013-05 does not provide for removing a portion of the component and retaining the remainder in equity, when it relates to the sale of a foreign investment. The sale of an investment in a foreign entity includes two types of events, including events that result in an acquirer obtaining control of an acquiree in which it held an equity interest immediately before the acquisition date.

d. *Incorrect.* Upon sale, the component is not reclassified to a separate section of equity. The sale of an investment in a foreign entity includes two types of events, including events that result in the loss of a controlling financial interest in an investment in a foreign entity.

¶ 10,111 MODULE 3—CHAPTER 11

1. a. *Incorrect.* Investors stated that the FASB *should* move toward a fair value model and should make that a priority.

b. *Correct.* **In *A Comprehensive Business Reporting Model*, investors stated, "Fair value information is the only information relevant for financial decision making." Financial statements based on outdated historical costs are less useful for making such assessments.**

c. *Incorrect.* Investors stated that the fair value model is more useful for making decisions, and not the historical cost model.

d. *Incorrect.* Investors stated that the historical cost model, and not the fair value model, is inconsistent with the way in which investors measure an entity.

2. a. *Incorrect.* Inputs used to measure fair value that result principally from or are substantiated with observable market data by correlation are an example of Level 2 inputs.

b. *Incorrect.* Observable inputs used to measure fair value that are other than quoted prices included in Level 1 are classified as Level 2 inputs.

c. *Incorrect.* Observable, unadjusted, quoted market prices in active markets for identical assets or liabilities that are accessible are classified as Level 1 inputs.

d. *Correct.* **ASC 820 requires that in the absence of quoted prices for identical or similar assets or liabilities, fair value should be estimated using multiple-valuation techniques consistent with the market approach, income approach, and cost approach whenever the information necessary to apply those techniques is available without undue cost and effort.**

3. a. *Incorrect.* Loans and notes receivable are generally measured at cost, but not equity investments.

b. *Correct.* **All equity investments would be measured at fair value with the change in fair value presented in net income. If an entity chooses to record a financial asset or liability at fair value under ASC 825, the change in the fair value is recognized in earnings as the changes occur.**

c. *Incorrect.* Some derivatives are presented at fair value with the change in other comprehensive income, but this is not entirely true of equity investments.

d. *Incorrect.* Lower of cost or market (LCM) is not a measurement that would be used for financial instruments under the proposed standard. LCM is an inventory issue.

Index

References are to paragraph (¶) numbers.

¶ 10,200 CPE Quizzer Instructions

This CPE Quizzer is divided into three Modules. To obtain CPE Credit, go to **CCH-Group.com/PrintCPE** to complete your Quizzers online for immediate results and no Express Grading Fee. There is a grading fee for each Quizzer submission.

Processing Fee:	Recommended CPE:
$70.00 for Module 1	5 hours for Module 1
$70.00 for Module 2	5 hours for Module 2
$42.00 for Module 3	3 hours for Module 3
$182.00 for all Modules	13 hours for all Modules

Instructions for purchasing your CPE Tests and accessing them after purchase are provided on the **CCHGroup.com/PrintCPE** website.

To mail or fax your Quizzer, send your completed Answer Sheet for each Quizzer Module to **CCH Continuing Education Department, 4025 W. Peterson Ave., Chicago, IL 60646**, or fax it to (773) 866-3084. Each Quizzer Answer Sheet will be graded and a CPE Certificate of Completion awarded for achieving a grade of 70 percent or greater. The Quizzer Answer Sheets are located at the back of this book.

Express Grading: Processing time for your mailed or faxed Answer Sheet is generally 8-12 business days. To use our Express Grading Service, at an additional $19 per Module, please check the "Express Grading" box on your Answer Sheet and provide your CCH account or credit card number **and your fax number**. CCH will fax your results and a Certificate of Completion (upon achieving a passing grade) to you by 5:00 p.m. the business day following our receipt of your Answer Sheet. **If you mail your Answer Sheet for Express Grading, please write "ATTN: CPE OVERNIGHT" on the envelope.** NOTE: CCH will not Federal Express Quizzer results under any circumstances.

Recommended CPE credit is based on a 50-minute hour. Participants earning credits for states that require self-study to be based on a 100-minute hour will receive 1/2 the CPE credits for successful completion of this course. Because CPE requirements vary from state to state and among different licensing agencies, please contact your CPE governing body for information on your CPE requirements and the applicability of a particular course for your requirements.

Date of Completion: If you mail or fax your Quizzer to CCH, the date of completion on your Certificate will be the date that you put on your Answer Sheet. However, you must submit your Answer Sheet to CCH for grading within two weeks of completing it.

Expiration Date: December 31, 2015

Evaluation: To help us provide you with the best possible products, please take a moment to fill out the course Evaluation located after your Quizzer. A copy is also provided at the back of this course if you choose to mail or fax your Quizzer Answer Sheets.

One **complimentary copy** of this course is provided with certain copies of CCH publications. Additional copies of this course may be downloaded from **CCH-Group.com/PrintCPE** or ordered by calling 1-800-248-3248 (ask for product 10024493-0002).

¶ 10,301 Quizzer Questions: Module 1

1. Under the VIE model for consolidations, a reporting entity has a controlling financial interest in a VIE when it has which one of the following?

    a. It has the power to direct the VIEs activities that are most significant.

    b. It manages the overall operations of the VIE.

    c. It represents more than 80 percent of the VIE's revenue.

    d. The reporting entity has a significant loan due from the VIE.

2. Which of the following is a reason why a common owner might establish a lessor entity separate from a private company lessee?

    a. For estate planning purposes

    b. To simplify accounting and reduce accounting fees

    c. To strip the asset out of the primary entity

    d. To satisfy the lender

3. A private company lessee may elect an alternative not to apply the VIE guidance to a lessor entity if certain criteria are met, one of which is that the private company lessee and the lessor entity:

    a. Have a formal written lease agreement

    b. Have an inter-entity loan agreement

    c. Are under common control

    d. Are about to go public

4. FIN 46R states that an entity's equity is sufficient if the entity has demonstrated that it can obtain:

    a. Recourse financing of at least AA grade

    b. Non-recourse investment-grade financing

    c. An unsecured loan sufficient to fund its operations for at least 12 months

    d. A secured loan with or without a personal guarantee

5. Which of the following is *not* generally considered a variable interest that an operating company lessee might have in a real estate lessor (VIE)?

    a. A guarantee of lessor's debt

    b. Collateral for the lessor's bank loan

    c. A direct loan from the lessee to the lessor

    d. A market-value lease

6. Which of the following is a type of guarantee of the lessor's debt, made by the owner, that is treated as a guarantee made by the operating company lessee?

    a. An indirect guarantee

    b. An explicit guarantee

    c. An implicit guarantee

    d. A completed guarantee

7. Which of the following entities can elect the accounting alternative under ASU 2014-07?

    a. A public company

    b. A private company

    c. A non-profit company

    d. A pension plan

8. Facts: A grandfather owns 100 percent of the voting interest in a lessor and his grandson owns 100 percent of the voting interest in a lessee. The lessor and lessee _____ being under common control.

    a. May qualify as

    b. Do not qualify as

    c. Do qualify as

    d. Are not permitted to qualify as

9. Per ASU 2014-07, which of the following is *not* a leasing activity (including supporting leasing activities), assuming it relates to an asset leased by a private company lessee?

    a. An explicit guarantee

    b. Collateral provided

    c. An implicit guarantee

    d. A lease option

10. In applying Criterion 2 of ASU 2014-07, the lease arrangement:

    a. Is limited to real estate

    b. Is not limited to real estate

    c. Is limited to personal property

    d. Is limited to intangible property

11. In applying the Criterion 4 assessment of ASU 2014-07, which of the following is true once the assessment is made?

    a. Criterion 4 is reassessed annually.

    b. The assessment is updated based on a series of triggering events that are identified within the ASU.

    c. Criterion 4 is reassessed only if the lessor entity subsequently refinances or enters into any new obligation(s) that requires collateralization and/or a guarantee by the private company lessee.

    d. The assessment must be updated continuously.

12. In order for an entity to elect the accounting alternative under ASU 2014-07, there must be a(an):

    a. Lease arrangement

    b. Written contract

    c. Service contract

    d. Derivative contract

13. ASU 2014-07 states that if the VIE accounting alternative is elected, it should be applied by a private company lessee to which one of the following?

    a. All future lessor entities under common control, but not to any current or past entities

    b. All current and future lessor entities under common control

    c. All current and past (but not future) lessor entities under common control

    d. All lessor entities under common control that existed at the date of the election

14. The election to adopt ASU 2014-07's accounting alternative is a (an):

    a. Change in accounting estimate

    b. Accounting policy election

    c. Correction of an error

    d. Special one-time election authorized by ASC 250

15. Company Y, a private company lessee, elects the accounting alternative under ASU 2014-07 effective January 1, 2014. Y is presenting comparative financial statements for 2013. On which date should Y perform the four-criteria test?

    a. January 1, 2015

    b. January 1, 2014

    c. December 31, 2014

    d. January 1, 2013

16. In order to qualify for cash flow hedge accounting, ASC 815-20-25, Derivatives and Hedging, states that all of the following criteria must be met *except:*

    a. There must be an informal designation and documentation throughout hedge period.

    b. There must be eligibility of hedged items and transactions.

    c. There must be eligibility of hedging instruments.

    d. There must be hedging effectiveness.

17. Which one of the following entities is an eligible entity that can use the simplified hedge accounting approach?

    a. Public business entity

    b. Not-for-profit entity

    c. Employee benefit plan

    d. Private company

18. ASU 2014-03 states that a receive-variable, pay-fixed interest rate swap for which the simplified hedge accounting approach is applied may be measured subsequently at _____ instead of fair value.

    a. Settlement value

    b. Present value

    c. Liquidation value

    d. Original cost

19. Which of the following is true concerning the effective date and transition of ASU 2014-03?

    a. Early application of the ASU is not permitted.

    b. The disclosures in ASC 250, Accounting Changes and Error Corrections, paragraphs 250-10-50-1 through 50-3 must be applied in the period that the entity adopts ASU 2014-03.

    c. ASU 2014-03 rules related to the simplified hedge accounting approach shall be applied in one of three ways.

    d. It is effective for annual periods beginning after December 15, 2015, and interim periods within annual periods beginning after December 15, 2016.

20. Under ASC 825-10-50-3, certain entities are exempt from fair value disclosures only if all of the following conditions are met *except:*

    a. The entity is a nonpublic entity.

    b. The entity's total assets at the financial statement date are less than $100 million.

    c. The entity's total liabilities at the financial statement date are less than $50 million.

    d. The entity has no instrument that is accounted for as a derivative instrument under Topic 815 other than commitments related to the origination of mortgage loans that will be held for sale during the reporting period.

21. Which of the following is *not* a tax position as defined by GAAP?

    a. Decision not to file a tax return

    b. Shift of income between jurisdictions

    c. Decision to file a tax return

    d. Characterization of income

22. What is the first step of the two-step process?

    a. Audit

    b. Recognition

    c. Derecognition

    d. Measurement

23. Which of the following is one of the criteria that should be used when assessing the more-likely-than-not recognition threshold?

    a. The tax position is evaluated by considering the possibility of offset or aggregation with other positions.

    b. Assuming that the tax position will be examined by the applicable taxing authority, which has complete knowledge of all relevant information.

    c. The technical merits of the tax position are developed from sources of tax law authority without consideration of administrative practices and precedents of the taxing authority.

    d. A tax opinion must be obtained as external evidence supporting management's assertions.

24. The unit of account for analyzing a tax position will differ from state to state based partially on the approach the taxpayer expects the taxing authority to take during an examination. Which of the following is an approach to be considered?

    a. Nexus approach

    b. Impairment approach

    c. Expense-reallocation approach

    d. Fair-value-option approach

25. Which of the following is *not* a required disclosure for unrecognized tax benefits?

    a. The accounting policy for the classification of interest and penalties

    b. Tax years that are still subject to examination by major tax jurisdictions

    c. The total amount of interest and penalties recognized in the statement of financial position

    d. The nature of the uncertainty for which it is reasonably possible that unrecognized tax benefits will significantly decrease within 24 months of the reporting date

¶ 10,302 Quizzer Questions: Module 2

26. Which of the following is correct as to which costs should be accrued by an entity using the liquidation basis of accounting?

    a. Costs should be accrued for the current year only using the matching principle.

    b. An entity shall accrue costs it expects to incur through the end of the liquidation, not to exceed two years.

    c. Costs should be accrued through the end of the liquidation.

    d. An entity must accrue all costs using its best estimate even if there is no reasonable basis for the estimation.

27. Once the liquidation basis of accounting is implemented, how should assets be measured at each reporting date?

    a. The assets should remain on the statement at the liquidation basis that existed at inception with no subsequent remeasurement.

    b. The assets should be remeasured.

    c. The assets should be converted back to original GAAP carrying value.

    d. GAAP provides no guidance on this issue.

28. ASU 2013-07 requires that which of the following statements be prepared for an entity using the liquidation basis of accounting?

    a. Statement of income

    b. Balance sheet - liquidation basis

    c. Statement of net assets in liquidation

    d. Statement of changes in cash flow

29. If liquidation is imminent, which of the following is true?

    a. There is an assumption that the entity will continue to operate as a going concern for at least one year from the balance sheet date.

    b. There is no longer an assumption that the entity will continue to operate as a going concern.

    c. The entity should convert to fair value accounting for all significant assets and liabilities at the balance sheet date.

    d. The concept of going concern is not considered if liquidation is imminent because the concepts of going concern and liquidation are mutually exclusive and can co-exist.

30. If the liquidation basis of accounting is used, fair value disclosures_____.

    a. Are required

    b. Are not permitted

    c. Are encouraged but not required

    d. Must be blended with the liquidation basis of accounting to provide hybrid disclosures

31. Which of the following is an example of an other comprehensive income item that previously bypassed the income statement and was recorded directly to stockholders' equity?

    a. Certain foreign exchange transactions

    b. Certain purchases of long-lived assets

    c. Certain transactions involving intangible assets

    d. Certain transactions involving long-term debt

32. The definition of comprehensive income is a change in equity from _____.

    a. Non-owner sources

    b. Investor sources

    c. Lender sources

    d. Equity holder sources

33. Which of the following accurately describes differences between how U.S. GAAP and IFRS present comprehensive income?

    a. IFRS allows three alternatives for presenting comprehensive income, whereas GAAP only allows two.

    b. U.S. GAAP requires a consecutive presentation of the statement of income and comprehensive income but IFRS does not.

    c. IFRS allows three alternatives for presenting comprehensive income, whereas GAAP only allows one.

    d. IFRS requires that reclassification adjustments from other comprehensive income to net income be presented on the face of the financial statements. U.S. GAAP allows the option to present those adjustments in the notes to financial statements.

34. There are essentially ___categories of other comprehensive income items.

    a. Two

    b. Three

    c. Four

    d. Five

35. Which of the following would *not* be included in other comprehensive income?

    a. Gains associated with postretirement benefits that are not recognized immediately as a component of net periodic benefit cost

    b. Realized losses on available-for-sale securities

    c. Gains on derivative instruments that are designated as cash flow hedges

    d. Foreign exchange translation adjustments

36. If a company's financial statements are being compiled and management has elected to omit substantially all disclosures and the statement of cash flows, then:

    a. The company is exempt from complying with ASC 220 because it is not presenting a full set of financial statements.

    b. The company must present comprehensive income in a financial statement only if it has other comprehensive income items.

    c. Even if the company has other comprehensive income items, it is not required to present comprehensive income in a financial statement or modify the compilation report.

    d. The company must follow the provisions under ASC 958-205 for Not-for-profit organizations.

37. If statements are prepared on an OCBOA (income tax basis), a statement of comprehensive income _____.

    a. Is required

    b. Is not required

    c. May be required because other comprehensive income items may be present

    d. May be added if a special election is made in the report

38. Which of the following is an example of the caption that should be presented for the total of other comprehensive income on the balance sheet?

    a. Accumulated other comprehensive income

    b. Total other comprehensive income

    c. Aggregate other comprehensive income

    d. Cumulative other comprehensive income

39. The sale of an investment in a foreign entity includes which of the following?

    a. Events that result in the loss of a controlling financial interest in an investment in the foreign entity

    b. Events that result in an acquirer losing control of an acquire

    c. The sale of a domestic, non-foreign entity

    d. A transaction in which an entity gains control of another entity

40. Which of the following are exempt from ASC 220?

    a. Investment companies, because they are exempt from providing a statement of cash flows

    b. Defined benefit pension plans, because they are exempt from providing a statement of cash flows

    c. Entities that only have items of other comprehensive income in one of two periods presented.

    d. Not-for-profit organizations that must follow the provisions of ASC Subtopic 958-205

41. Which of the following is ***not*** true regarding the tax effects of other comprehensive income items?

    a. An entity may present components of other comprehensive income in the statement in which other comprehensive income is reported net of tax effects.

    b. An entity may present components of other comprehensive income in the statement in which other comprehensive income is reported before the tax effects with one amount shown for the total income tax expense allocated to total other comprehensive income.

    c. An entity must present the amount of income tax expense allocated to each component of other comprehensive income in the notes to financial statements.

    d. The income tax expense allocated to each component of other comprehensive income may be presented parenthetically for each component of other comprehensive income in the statement in which other comprehensive income is presented.

42. Under ASC 830-30-40, if a reporting entity sells a part of its ownership in a foreign entity, how should the cumulative translation adjustment component be treated?

    a. A pro rata portion should be released into income

    b. All of the adjustment should be released into income

    c. None of the adjustment should be released into income

    d. All of the adjustment should be reclassified into a separate section of equity

43. ASC 220 provides that an entity that discloses the effect of reclassifications on the line items in the statement in which net income is presented, should do so:

    a. On either a before-tax basis or a net-of-tax basis

    b. Only on a before-tax basis

    c. Only on a net-of-tax basis

    d. Without any allocation of taxes to the transaction

44. Company X has current period reclassifications out of accumulated other comprehensive income. How should X present the current period reclassification?

    a. Only on the face of the income statement

    b. Only as a separate disclosure in the notes

    c. Either a. or b.

    d. Either a separate disclosure in the notes, on the face of the income statement, or in supplementary information clearly marked as such

45. If an entity has a non-controlling interest in another entity, how should comprehensive income be presented?

    a. Before the non-controlling interest, but not after it

    b. After the non-controlling interest, but not before it

    c. Before and after the non-controlling interest

    d. Comprehensive income is ignored in this situation

46. SSARS No. 19's definition of _____ is a basis of accounting that the reporting entity uses or expects to use to file its income tax return for the period covered by the financial statements.

    a. Regulatory basis

    b. Cash basis

    c. Income tax basis

    d. Compliance basis

47. If a grantor trust files a Form 1041 Grantor Trust information return, how should the accountant report on the trust?

    a. As a trust

    b. As a sole proprietorship

    c. As a partnership

    d. As an S corporation

48. With respect to income tax basis financial statements, nontaxable revenues and non-deductible expenses are:

    a. Included in income tax basis statements and included as part of taxable income

    b. Included in income tax basis statements yet not included as part of taxable income

    c. Excluded from income tax basis statements altogether

    d. Partially included in income tax basis statements depending on the amount

49. With respect to income tax basis financial statements, how must an entity deal with the GAAP disclosure of management's evaluation of subsequent events?

    a. Such a disclosure is required.

    b. Such a disclosure is not required.

    c. The date for subsequent events is different for income tax basis financial statements.

    d. Such a disclosure is not permitted under income tax basis financial statements.

50. A company issues income tax basis financial statements. Which of the following is correct with respect to the consolidation of variable interest entity (VIE) rules as they relate to the income tax basis financial statements?

    a. The rules in FIN 46R apply to the income tax basis financial statements.

    b. The rules apply if there is more than 50 percent ownership in a VIE.

    c. The rules in FIN 46R do not apply because the Internal Revenue Code does not recognize variable interest entities.

    d. The company has the option of applying the FIN 46R rules to the financial statements.

51. In ASC 405-40, a reporting entity measures an obligation that is sum of two parts. One part consists of any additional amount the reporting entity _____ on behalf of its co-obligors.

    a. Expects to pay

    b. Plans to incur

    c. Would prefer to record

    d. Is permitted to fund

52. Company X is a co-borrower and has a range of the additional amount that X expects to pay with no better estimate within that range. Which amount should X use as the additional amount?

    a. The maximum amount within the range

    b. The minimum amount within the range

    c. The average amount within the range

    d. No amount should be used if there is a range of amounts

53. Under ASC 460, at the inception of a guarantee, the guarantor shall recognize a liability for that guarantee, measured at _____.

    a. Net realizable value

    b. Carrying value

    c. Fair value

    d. The face value of the guarantee

54. Company X guarantees the debt of its subsidiary, Company Y, to a third party. Which of the following is correct?

    a. ASC 460, Guarantees, applies to all guarantees

    b. ASC 460, Guarantees, does not apply to X's guarantee

    c. ASC 460, Guarantees, applies to joint and several obligations, not guarantees

    d. X may, but is not required to, use the ASC 460 guidance to deal with its guarantee, or has the choice to use the contingency rules.

55. Under ASC 405-40, if two related parties are co-obligors, how should the transaction be accounted for?

    a. No liability should be booked as related parties are exempt from ASC 405-40.

    b. The entities should still follow ASC 405-40.

    c. The parties should follow the contingency rules.

    d. The parties should follow the special guarantee rules in ASC 460.

¶ 10,303 Quizzer Questions: Module 3

---

56. An intangible asset with a finite life should be _____.

   a. Amortized

   b. Tested annually for impairment

   c. Combined with intangibles with indefinite lives and not amortized

   d. Expensed as there is no future benefit

57. Company Y is a nonpublic (private) company with goodwill and wishes to elect ASU 2014-02's accounting alternative. Over what life may Y amortize its goodwill using the accounting alternative?

   a. 10 years straight line

   b. Goodwill may not be amortized

   c. 15 years straight line

   d. 40 years straight line or accelerated

58. ASU 2014-02's accounting alternative applies to which one of the following goodwill transactions?

   a. Goodwill that an entity recognizes in a business combination

   b. Internally generated goodwill

   c. Goodwill from investments recorded at cost

   d. Goodwill that has been fully amortized

59. The threshold used in the qualitative approach for goodwill impairment is _____.

   a. Probable

   b. More likely than not

   c. Reasonably possible

   d. Remote

60. Which of the following is the formula used for the new, single-step quantitative test for goodwill impairment loss authorized under ASU 2014-02 for private companies?

   a. Carrying amount less fair value of an entity's stockholder's equity

   b. Market value less fair value of the entity's goodwill

   c. Fair value of total assets less fair value of goodwill

   d. Discount cash flows less carrying amount of goodwill

61. One key change under the proposed lease standard is:

   a. A very small portion of operating leases, but not capital leases, would be brought onto the balance sheet.

   b. Capital leases, but not operating leases, would be brought onto the balance sheet.

   c. No leases would be capitalized.

   d. Most existing operating leases would be brought onto the balance sheet.

62. Under the proposed lease standard, which of the following is true as it relates to the lessee?

   a. An asset is recognized representing the sum of the lease payments over the lease term.

   b. An asset is not recognized.

   c. An asset is recognized representing the lessee's right to use the leased asset for the lease term.

   d. An asset is recognized only if four criteria are met.

63. Under the proposed lease standard, the lessee would recognize a liability at the present value of the lease payments discounted at which of the following permitted rates if the lessor's imputed rate cannot be readily determined?

   a. The lessor's borrowing rate

   b. The lessee's incremental borrowing rate

   c. The interest rate for similar obligations in the market

   d. 110% of the applicable federal rate

64. How would a lessee account for initial direct costs incurred in connection with a lease, under the proposed lease standard?

   a. Initial direct costs are included in the lease asset that is recorded at the commencement date.

   b. Initial direct costs are not part of the lease asset.

   c. Initial direct costs are expensed as period costs.

   d. The proposed lease standard is silent as to how to account for initial direct costs.

65. What happens to existing leases on the date of adoption of the proposed lease standard?

   a. Existing operating leases are grandfathered but capital leases are not.

   b. Existing capital leases are grandfathered but operating leases are not.

   c. The proposed standard does not grandfather any existing leases.

   d. Existing leases are phased into the new standard over a four-year period.

66. Under the proposed lease standard, which of the following is true?

   a. Lease terms are likely to shorten to decrease the amount of the lease obligation.

   b. Lease terms are likely to get longer to reduce the amount of the lease obligation.

   c. Lease terms are likely to shorten to increase the amount of the lease asset recorded.

   d. Lease terms are likely to get longer to reduce the amount of the lease asset recorded.

67. The proposed lease standard would likely result in which of the following occurring for existing operating leases?

    a. Total lease expense for tax purposes would be greater than total GAAP expense.

    b. Total GAAP expense would be greater than lease expense for tax purposes.

    c. GAAP and tax expense would be identical.

    d. There would be no change in the total expense for GAAP or tax purposes from current practice.

68. Under the proposed lease standard _____.

    a. Deferred tax assets would likely be created.

    b. Deferred tax assets would likely be reduced.

    c. Deferred tax liabilities would likely be created.

    d. Deferred tax liabilities would likely be reduced.

69. One potential impact from the proposed lease standard would be that the debt-equity ratio would be _____.

    a. Higher

    b. Lower

    c. The same

    d. Either higher or lower depending on several factors

70. How would options to extend a lease be accounted for in determining the lease term under the proposed lease standard?

    a. The lease term should take into account the effect of any options to extend the lease in certain cases.

    b. Lease options are only considered once they are exercised.

    c. The proposed standard states that options are too vague and should not be considered in determining the lease term.

    d. Only certain options to extend within a short-term period are considered because it is difficult to estimate the likelihood of the options being exercised.

71. In accordance with ASU 2014-05, service concession arrangements are not within the scope of _____.

    a. ASC 840, *Leases*

    b. Revenue and costs related to operation services under ASC Topic 605, *Revenue Recognition*

    c. Revenue and costs related to construction under ASC Topic 605, *Revenue Recognition*

    d. ASC 853, *Service Concession Arrangements*

72. In accordance with ASU 2014-04, which of the following is a situation in which an in-substance repossession or foreclosure occurs?

    a. The creditor receives physical possession of the debtor's assets.

    b. The creditor is promised that he or she will receive possession of the debtor's assets in the future upon a triggering event, such as the debtor's death.

    c. The creditor believes he or she will ultimately prevail in obtaining the debtor's assets once a future foreclosure is completed.

    d. The creditor estimates that the fair value of the underlying collateral exceeds the carrying amount of the debt.

73. Which of the following is a public business entity?

    a. A not-for-profit entity

    b. An employee benefit plan

    c. An entity that files financial statements with the SEC

    d. A private company that files financial statements

74. Under ASC 830-30-40, if a reporting entity sells a part of its ownership in a foreign entity, how should the cumulative translation adjustment component be treated?

    a. A pro rata portion should be released into income.

    b. All of the adjustment should be released into income.

    c. None of the adjustment should be released into income.

    d. All of the adjustment should be reclassified into a separate section of equity.

75. ASU 2013-11 provides an exception to the general rule under which an unrecognized tax benefit shall be presented _____ and not combined with deferred tax assets, to the extent a net operating loss carryforward, a similar tax loss, or a tax credit carryforward is not available at the reporting date under the tax law.

    a. As a liability

    b. As a deferred tax credit

    c. As a reduction to the deferred tax asset

    d. As a credit to other comprehensive income

76. Which of the following is a current challenge to a fair value model noted by its critics?

    a. The historical cost model is more relevant.

    b. Fair value accounting introduces a degree of volatility to the model.

    c. Fair value accounting is too objectives-based.

    d. Fair value accounting will reveal an entity's true value from period to period.

77. Under the fair value hierarchy, which of the following is a description of a Level 1 input?

    a. Quoted prices for identical assets or liabilities in active markets

    b. Other than quoted prices for identical assets or liabilities

    c. Quoted prices for similar assets and liabilities in active markets

    d. Quoted prices for identical or similar assets and liabilities in markets that are not active

78. The FASB's The Fair Value Option for Financial Asset and Financial Liabilities _____.

   a. Creates the option of recording certain financial assets and liabilities at fair value for initial and subsequent measurement

   b. Defines the exchange price

   c. Requires a fair value election to be made on an annual basis

   d. Applies to investments that would otherwise be consolidated

79. Which of the following does ASC 820, *Fair Value Measurements*, do?

   a. Clarifies that book value is the price that would be received for an asset

   b. Develops a five-level hierarchy for valuation

   c. Requires expanded disclosures about the use of fair value to remeasure assets and liabilities

   d. Requires that fair value should always be estimated, even when quoted prices are available

80. In accordance with the FASB's proposed financial instruments project, an entity would classify each financial asset into a category on the basis of two criteria, one of which is the:

   a. Entity's business model for managing the asset

   b. Duration of holding the underlying asset

   c. Extent to which the asset is a "critical component"

   d. Entity's intent and historical actions taken in connection with similar assets

¶ 10,400 Answer Sheets

¶ 10,401 Top Accounting Issues for 2015 CPE Course: MODULE 1

(10014576-0003)

Go to **CCHGroup.com/PrintCPE** to complete your Quizzer online for instant results and no Express Grading Fee.

A $70.00 processing fee will be charged for each user submitting Module 1 for grading. If you prefer to mail or fax your Quizzer, remove both pages of the Answer Sheet from this book and return them with your completed Evaluation Form to: CCH Continuing Education Department, 4025 W. Peterson Ave., Chicago, IL 60646-6085 or fax your Answer Sheet to CCH at 773-866-3084. You must also select a method of payment below.

NAME _____

COMPANY NAME _____

STREET _____

CITY, STATE, & ZIP CODE _____

BUSINESS PHONE NUMBER _____

E-MAIL ADDRESS _____

DATE OF COMPLETION _____

METHOD OF PAYMENT:

☐ Check Enclosed ☐ Visa ☐ Master Card ☐ AmEx

☐ Discover ☐ CCH Account* _____

Card No. _____ Exp. Date _____

Signature _____

EXPRESS GRADING: Please fax my Course results to me by 5:00 p.m. the business day following your receipt of this Answer Sheet. By checking this box I authorize CCH to charge $19.00 for this service.

☐ Express Grading $19.00 Fax No. _____

* Must provide CCH account number for this payment option

Wolters Kluwer

CCH

Module 1: Answer Sheet

(10014576-0003)

Please answer the questions by indicating the appropriate letter next to the corresponding number.

1. _____	8. _____	15. _____	22. _____
2. _____	9. _____	16. _____	23. _____
3. _____	10. _____	17. _____	24. _____
4. _____	11. _____	18. _____	24. _____
5. _____	12. _____	19. _____	25. _____
6. _____	13. _____	20. _____	
7. _____	14. _____	21. _____	

Please complete the Evaluation Form (located after the Module 3 Answer Sheet) and return it with this Quizzer Answer Sheet to CCH at the address on the previous page. Thank you.

¶ 10,402 Top Accounting Issues for 2015 CPE Course: MODULE 2

(10014577-0003)

Go to **CCHGroup.com/PrintCPE** to complete your Quizzer online for instant results and no Express Grading Fee.

A $70.00 processing fee will be charged for each user submitting Module 2 for grading. If you prefer to mail or fax your Quizzer, remove both pages of the Answer Sheet from this book and return them with your completed Evaluation Form to: CCH Continuing Education Department, 4025 W. Peterson Ave., Chicago, IL 60646-6085 or fax your Answer Sheet to CCH at 773-866-3084. You must also select a method of payment below.

NAME _____

COMPANY NAME _____

STREET _____

CITY, STATE, & ZIP CODE _____

BUSINESS PHONE NUMBER _____

E-MAIL ADDRESS _____

DATE OF COMPLETION _____

METHOD OF PAYMENT:

☐ Check Enclosed ☐ Visa ☐ Master Card ☐ AmEx

☐ Discover ☐ CCH Account* _____

Card No. _____ Exp. Date _____

Signature _____

EXPRESS GRADING: Please fax my Course results to me by 5:00 p.m. the business day following your receipt of this Answer Sheet. By checking this box I authorize CCH to charge $19.00 for this service.

☐ Express Grading $19.00 Fax No. _____

* Must provide CCH account number for this payment option

Wolters Kluwer
CCH

Module 2: Answer Sheet

(10014577-0003)

Please answer the questions by indicating the appropriate letter next to the corresponding number.

26. _____	34. _____	42. _____	50. _____
27. _____	35. _____	43. _____	51. _____
28. _____	36. _____	44. _____	52. _____
29. _____	37. _____	45. _____	53. _____
30. _____	38. _____	46. _____	54. _____
31. _____	39. _____	47. _____	55. _____
32. _____	40. _____	48. _____	
33. _____	41. _____	49. _____	

Please complete the Evaluation Form (located after the Module 3 Answer Sheet) and return it with this Quizzer Answer Sheet to CCH at the address on the previous page. Thank you.

¶ 10,403 Top Accounting Issues for 2015 CPE Course: MODULE 3

(10014578-0003)

Go to **CCHGroup.com/PrintCPE** to complete your Quizzer online for instant results and no Express Grading Fee.

A $42.00 processing fee will be charged for each user submitting Module 3 for grading. If you prefer to mail or fax your Quizzer, remove both pages of the Answer Sheet from this book and return them with your completed Evaluation Form to: CCH Continuing Education Department, 4025 W. Peterson Ave., Chicago, IL 60646-6085 or fax your Answer Sheet to CCH at 773-866-3084. You must also select a method of payment below.

NAME _____

COMPANY NAME _____

STREET _____

CITY, STATE, & ZIP CODE _____

BUSINESS PHONE NUMBER _____

E-MAIL ADDRESS _____

DATE OF COMPLETION _____

METHOD OF PAYMENT:

☐ Check Enclosed   ☐ Visa   ☐ Master Card   ☐ AmEx

☐ Discover   ☐ CCH Account* _____

Card No. _____   Exp. Date _____

Signature _____

EXPRESS GRADING: Please fax my Course results to me by 5:00 p.m. the business day following your receipt of this Answer Sheet. By checking this box I authorize CCH to charge $19.00 for this service.

☐ Express Grading $19.00   Fax No. _____

* Must provide CCH account number for this payment option

Wolters Kluwer

CCH

Module 3: Answer Sheet

(10014578-0003)

Please answer the questions by indicating the appropriate letter next to the corresponding number.

56. _____	63. _____	70. _____	77. _____
57. _____	64. _____	71. _____	78. _____
58. _____	65. _____	72. _____	79. _____
59. _____	66. _____	73. _____	80. _____
60. _____	67. _____	74. _____	
61. _____	68. _____	75. _____	
62. _____	69. _____	76. _____	

Please complete the Evaluation Form (located after the Module 3 Answer Sheet) and return it with this Quizzer Answer Sheet to CCH at the address on the previous page. Thank you.

¶ 10,500 Top Accounting Issues for 2015 CPE Course: Evaluation Form

(10024493-0002)

Please take a few moments to fill out and mail or fax this evaluation to CCH so that we can better provide you with the type of self-study programs you want and need. Thank you.

About This Program

1. Please circle the number that best reflects the extent of your agreement with the following statements:

		Strongly Agree				Strongly Disagree
a.	The Course objectives were met.	5	4	3	2	1
b.	This Course was comprehensive and organized.	5	4	3	2	1
c.	The content was current and technically accurate.	5	4	3	2	1
d.	This Course was timely and relevant.	5	4	3	2	1
e.	The prerequisite requirements were appropriate.	5	4	3	2	1
f.	This Course was a valuable learning experience.	5	4	3	2	1
g.	The Course completion time was appropriate.	5	4	3	2	1

2. This Course was most valuable to me because of:

_____ Continuing Education credit   _____ Convenience of format

_____ Relevance to my practice/employment   _____ Timeliness of subject matter

_____ Price   _____Reputation of author

_____ Other (please specify) _____

3. How long did it take to complete this Course? (Please include the total time spent reading or studying reference materials and completing CPE Quizzer).

Module 1_____   Module 2_____   Module 3_____

4. What do you consider to be the strong points of this Course?

5. What improvements can we make to this Course?

General Interests

(10024493-0002)

1. Preferred method of self-study instruction:

_____ Text   _____ Audio   _____ Computer-based/Multimedia   _____ Video

2. What specific topics would you like CCH to develop as self-study CPE programs?

_____

_____

_____

3. Please list other topics of interest to you _____

_____

_____

About You

1. Your profession:

_____ Accountant   _____ Auditor

_____ Controller   _____ CPA

_____ Enrolled Agent   _____ Risk Manager

_____ Other (please specify)

_____

2. Your employment:

_____ Self-employed   _____ Public Accounting Firm

_____ Service Industry   _____ Non-Service Industry

_____ Banking/Finance   _____ Government

_____ Education   _____ Other _____

3. Size of firm/corporation:

_____ 1   _____ 2-5   _____ 6-10   _____ 11-20   _____ 21-50   _____ 51+

4. Your Name _____

Firm/Company Name _____

Address _____

City, State, Zip Code _____

E-mail Address _____

THANK YOU FOR TAKING THE TIME TO COMPLETE THIS SURVEY!

¶ 10,600 CCH Learning Center

At Wolters Kluwer, CCH we recognize the value of Continuing Professional Education—to educate and train your workforce, bring added value to your clients or organization, and gain a competitive edge in the marketplace. But keeping up with legislative and regulatory changes and industry developments can be a full-time job. Let CCH and the CCH Learning Center serve as your gateway to compelling self-study CPE courses and research resources. With the CCH Learning Center you get:

- **More Than 300 Up-To-Date Courses:** The CCH Learning Center offers more than 300 informative courses covering tax, financial and estate planning, and accounting/auditing issues, with new courses being added all the time. Go to the Course Catalog at CCHGroup.com/CPE to see descriptions of all the courses you can take.

- **Expert Authors And Superior Content:** Our team of professional analysts, editors, and contributing authors has more experience and more expertise than any other tax publisher in the country, which ensures you get current, reliable, real-world insights to help you handle the toughest topics and issues.

- **Approved CPE:** CCH is an approved QAS (Quality Assurance Service) provider with NASBA—one of the first CPE sponsors to be approved under the rigorous new CPE requirements.

- **24/7 Access:** CCH Learning Center courses are available online 24 hours a day, seven days a week and you get immediate Quizzer results and certification, so you can make sure you hit your CPE deadlines.

- **Opportunities To Apply Knowledge:** CCH Learning Center courses provide integrated learning activities, study questions, client letters, checklists, and other resources that let you apply what you learn.

- **Convenient Print Formats:** CCH Learning Center lets you print out hard copies of the courses, giving you a quick and easy way to take the course whenever you want—away from the computer at home, on the plane, wherever!

- **Links to CCH® INTELLICONNECT™ and Accounting Research Manager™:** For additional research, guidance, and access to late breaking developments, CCH Learning Center's tax courses include links to sources of additional explanation and authority within Intelliconnect™ and the accounting and auditing courses include links to authoritative and proposed literature within Accounting Research Manager™.

To purchase a subscription or learn more about the CCH Learning Center, contact your CCH Representative at 1-888-CCH-REPS or visit the Online Store at **www.CCHGroup.com**.

Customer Support: If you have any questions about or need assistance with the CCH Learning Center or have any account related issues, CCH Customer Support is readily available at 1-800-248-3248.

Wolters Kluwer

CCH

4025 W. Peterson Ave.
Chicago, IL 60646-6085
800 248 3248
CCHGroup.com